Buddhism in Southeast Asia

Buddhism in Southeast Asia

Dr Arvind Kumar Singh

MD Publications Pvt Ltd
New Delhi
www.mdppl.com

Published by :

MD Publications Pvt Ltd
'MD House', 11, Darya Ganj
New Delhi - 110 002
Phone : +91-11-41563325 (Customer Service)
+91-11-41562846 (Editorial)
E-mail (orders): contact@mdppl.com
Website: www.mdppl.com

ISBN : 978-81-7533-166-2

Published and Printed by Mrs. Rajni Gupta on behalf of **MD Publications Pvt Ltd** at Times Press, New Delhi.

CONTENTS

PREFACE

Buddhism is one of the oldest religions in the world. It is a path of practice and spiritual development leading to insight into the true nature of life. Buddhist practices such as meditation are means of changing oneself in order to develop the qualities of awareness, kindness, and wisdom. The experience developed within the Buddhist tradition over thousands of years has created an incomparable resource for all those who wish to follow a path — a path which ultimately culminates in Enlightenment.

The basic tenets of Buddhist teaching are straightforward and practical: nothing is fixed or permanent; actions have consequences; change is possible. Thus Buddhism addresses itself to all people irrespective of race, nationality, or gender. It teaches practical methods (such as meditation) which enable people to realize and utilize its teachings in order to transform their experience, to be fully responsible for their lives and to develop the qualities of Wisdom and Compassion. There are millions of Buddhists in the world today and their numbers are growing with every passing day. Different people follow different paths, but all traditions are characterized by non-violence, lack of dogma, tolerance of differences, and, usually, by the practice of meditation.

Buddhism is the main religion in Southeast Asia. Thailand, Vietnam, Cambodia, Laos, Myanmar are Buddhist countries. Apart from these countries, a sizable Buddhist population resides in other Southeast Asian countries like Malaysia, Indonesia, Philippines and Singapore. This book touches various aspects of Buddhism in Southeast Asia in a different way. We hope that readers will like this endeavour.

I am very grateful to Mr. Pranav Gupta, Director, MD Publications Pvt Ltd, New Delhi who readily expressed acceptance and supported me fully for completing this book.

Dr Arvind Kumar Singh

Chapter - 1

SOUTHEAST ASIA
AN INTRODUCTION

Southeast Asia or Southeastern Asia, sometimes abbreviated to SEA, is a sub region of Asia, consisting of the countries that are geographically south of China, east of India and north of Australia. The region lies on the intersection of geological plates, with heavy seismic and volcanic activity.

Southeast Asia consists of two geographic regions: the Asian mainland, and island arcs and archipelagoes to the east and southeast. The mainland section consists of Cambodia, Laos, Myanmar, Thailand and Vietnam; the population of which is primarily, Tibeto-Burman, Tai peoples and Austro-Asiatic peoples; the dominant religion is Buddhism followed by Islam, and Christianity. The maritime section consists of Brunei, East Timor, Indonesia, Malaysia, the Philippines, and Singapore. Some definitions include Taiwan at the north. Austronesian peoples predominate in this region; the dominant religion is Islam, followed by Christianity.

Definitions of "Southeast Asia" vary, but most definitions include the area represented by the countries:

- Brunei
- Cambodia
- Indonesia
- Laos
- Malaysia
- Myanmar
- The Philippines

- Singapore
- Thailand
- Vietnam
- East Timor

All of the above are members of the ASEAN, except East Timor (also known as Timor Leste), which is an ASEAN candidate state. The area, together with part of South Asia, was widely known as the East Indies or simply the Indies until the twentieth century. Christmas Island and the Cocos (Keeling) Islands are considered part of Southeast Asia though they are governed by Australia. Taiwan is sometimes considered part of Southeast Asia as well as East Asia but it is not a member of ASEAN. Sovereignty issues exist over some islands in the South China Sea. Papua is politically part of Southeast Asia through Indonesia, although geographically it is often considered as part of Oceania.

GEOGRAPHY

Southeast Asia is geographically divided into two regions, namely Mainland Southeast Asia (or Indochina) and the Maritime Southeast Asia (or the Malay Archipelago) (Indonesian language: *Nusantara).* Mainland Southeast Asia includes:

- Cambodia
- Laos
- Myanmar
- Thailand
- Vietnam

Maritime Southeast Asia includes:

- Brunei
- East Timor
- Indonesia
- Malaysia
- Philippines
- Singapore

The eastern parts of Indonesia and East Timor (east of Wallace Line) are considered to be geographically parts of Oceania.

The Andaman and Nicobar Islands of India are geographically considered part of Southeast Asia. North-East India is culturally Southeast Asia and sometimes considered both South Asian and Southeast Asian. Hainan Island and several other southern Chinese regions such as Yunnan, Guizhou and Guangxi are considered both East Asian and

Southeast Asian. Taiwan, which sits on the Tropic of Cancer and borders the South China Sea, is likewise often included in definitions of Southeast Asia as well as East Asia.

HISTORY

Solheim and others have shown evidence for a *Nusantao* (*Nusantara*) maritime trading network ranging from Vietnam to the rest of the archipelago as early as 5000 BCE to 1 CE. The peoples of Southeast Asia, especially those of Austronesian descent, have been seafarers for thousands of years, some reaching the island of Madagascar. Their vessels, such as the vinta, were ocean-worthy. Magellan's voyage records how much more maneuverable their vessels were, as compared to the European ships. Passage through the Indian Ocean aided the colonization of Madagascar by the Austronesian people as well as commerce between West Asia and Southeast Asia. Gold from Sumatra is thought to have reached as far west as Rome.

Originally most people were animist. This was later replaced by Brahmanic Hinduism. Theravada Buddhism soon followed in 525. In 1400s, Islamic influences began to enter. This forced the last Hindu court in Indonesia to retreat to Bali.

In Mainland Southeast Asia, Myanmar, Cambodia and Thailand retained the Theravada form of Buddhism, brought to them from Sri Lanka. This type of Buddhism was fused with the Hindu-influenced Khmer culture.

The history of Southeast Asia has been characterized as interaction between regional players and foreign powers. Though 11 countries currently make up the region, the history of each country is intertwined with all the others. For instance, the Malay empires of Srivijaya and Malacca covered modern day Indonesia, Malaysia, and Singapore while the Burmese, Thai, and Khmer peoples governed much of Indochina. At the same time, opportunities and threats from the east and the west shaped the direction of Southeast Asia. The history of the countries within the region only started to develop independently of each other after European colonialization was at full steam between the 17th and the 20th century.

Evidences suggest that the earliest non-aboriginal Southeast Asians came from southern China and were Austronesian speakers. Contemporary research by anthropologists, linguists (Blust, Reid, Ross, Pawley), and archaeologists (Bellwood) suggests that the inhabitants of the Malay Archipelago migrated from southern China to islands of the Philippines around 2,500 BCE and later spread to modern day Malaysia and Indonesia.

The earliest population of Southeast Asia was animist before Hinduism and Buddhism were exported from the Indian subcontinent. Islam arrived mostly through Indian Muslims and later dominated much of the archipelago around the 13th century while Christianity came along when European colonization started around the 16th century.

During the classical age, the existence of Southeast Asia had been known to the Greeks. The Greek astronomer Ptolemy in his *Geographia* named the Malay Peninsula as *Aurea Chersonesus* (Golden Peninsula) while Java was called *Labadius*. Labadius was probably a corruption of Sanskrit *Yavadvipa* which refers to the same island. An ancient Hindu text may have earlier referred to Southeast Asia as *Suvarnabhumi* which means land of gold.

The region has been an important source of spices and this was one of the reasons European explorers were attracted to the Far East. During the colonization period, states of the region became important assets to the British, the Dutch and the French. British Malaya for instance was the world's largest producer of tin and rubber while the Dutch East Indies was the source of Dutch's wealth.

During the 1990s, Southeast Asia emerged as the fastest growing economy in the world. Its successes have made some to call Southeast Asia as an economic miracle and "Four Asian Tigers". Though the Asian Financial Crisis struck in the late 1990s and left many crippled, the economy of the region has started to pick up again at a more sustainable rate as demand from the United States and People's Republic of China soar.

ANCIENT AND CLASSICAL KINGDOMS

Southeast Asia has been inhabited since prehistoric times. The communities in the region evolved to form complex cultures with varying degrees of influence from India and China.

The ancient kingdoms can be grouped into two distinct categories. The first is agrarian kingdoms. Agrarian kingdoms had agriculture as the main economic activity. Most agrarian states were located in mainland Southeast Asia. Examples are the Ayutthaya Kingdom, based on the Chao Phraya River delta and the Khmer Empire on the Tonle Sap. The second type is maritime states. Maritime states were dependent on sea trade. Malacca and Srivijaya were maritime states.

A succession of trading systems dominated the trade between China and India. First, goods were shipped through Funan to the Isthmus of Kra, portaged across the narrow, and then transshipped for India and points west. Around the sixth century, CE merchants began sailing to Srivijaya where goods were transshipped directly. The limits of technology and contrary winds during parts of the year made it difficult for the ships of the time to proceed directly from the Indian Ocean to the South China Sea. The third system involved direct trade between the Indian and Chinese coasts.

The first dominant power to arise in the archipelago was Srivijaya in Sumatra. From the fifth century CE, the capital, Palembang, became a major seaport and functioned as an entrepot on the Spice Route between India and China. Srivijaya was also a notable center of Vajrayana Buddhist learning and influence. Srivijaya's wealth and influence faded when changes in nautical technology in the tenth century CE enabled Chinese and Indian merchants to ship cargo directly between their countries and also enabled the Chola state in southern India to carry out a series of destructive attacks on Srivijaya's possessions, ending Palembang's entrepot function.

In the Philippines, the Laguna Copperplate Inscription dating from 900 CE relates a granted debt from a *Maharlika* caste nobleman named *Namwaran* who lived in the Manila area. This document shows strong Srivijayan influence, and mentions a leader of Medan, Sumatra.Java was dominated by a kaleidoscope of competing agrarian kingdoms including the Sailendras, Mataram, Singosari, and finally Majapahit.

INDIANIZED KINGDOM

The concept of the Indianized kingdom, first described by George Coedès, is based upon the Hindu and Buddhist cultural and economic influences in Southeast Asia. Despite being culturally akin to Hindu cultures to western historians these kingdoms were truly indigenous and independent of India. States such as Srivijaya, Majapahit and Khmer empire developed territories and economies that rivaled those in India itself. Borobudur, for example, is the largest Buddhist monument ever built. Coedes has been criticized for understating the Southeast Asian element of these kingdoms, in an unconscious echo of the European "civilising mission." More recent scholars tend to emphasize the contribution of Southeast Asian societies and rulers to the formation of these states. In particular, where Coedès saw Indian merchants as the founders of these states, contemporary scholars see Southeast Asian rulers as founding them and then importing Indian ritual specialists as advisers on *rajadharma*, or the practices of Indian kingship. The modern view is supported by the argument that merchants would not have possessed the ritual knowledge so prominent in these kingdoms.

Very little is known about Southeast Asian religious beliefs and practices before the advent of Indian merchants and religious influences from the second century BCE onwards. Prior to the 13th century, Buddhism and Hinduism were the main religions in Southeast Asia.

In Jawa Dwipa Hindu kingdom of Java and Sumatra exists around 200 BCE. The history of the Malay-speaking world begins with the advent of Indian influence, which dates back to at least the 3rd century BC. Indian traders came to the archipelago both for its abundant forest and maritime products and to trade with merchants from China, who also discovered the Malay world at an early date. Both Hinduism and Buddhism were well established in the Malay Peninsula by the beginning of the 1st century CE, and from there spread across the archipelago.

Cambodia was first influenced by Hinduism during the beginning of the Funan kingdom. Hinduism was one of the Khmer Empire's official religions. Cambodia is the home to one of the only two temples dedicated to Brahma in the world. Angkor Wat is also a famous Hindu temple of Cambodia.

The Majapahit Empire was an Indianized kingdom based in eastern Java from 1293 to around 1500. Its greatest ruler was Hayam Wuruk, whose reign from 1350 to 1389 marked the empire's peak when it dominated other kingdoms in the southern Malay Peninsula, Borneo, Sumatra, Bali and the Philippines. The rest of the Philippines also provided tributes to the empire.

The Cholas excelled in maritime activity in both military and the mercantile fields. Their raids of Kedah and the Srivijaya, and their continued commercial contacts with the Chinese Empire, enabled them to influence the local cultures. Many of the surviving examples of the Hindu cultural influence found today throughout the Southeast Asia are the result of the Chola expeditions.

The Indianized kingdoms developed a close affinity and internalised Indian religious, cultural and economic practices without significant direct input from Indian rulers themselves. While the issue remains controversial, it is thought that Indianization was the work of Indian traders and merchants, although later the travels of Buddhist monks such as Atisha became important. Also a significant part of the current population in South East Asia has a trace of Indian ancestry from distant antiquity although the knowledge of the ancestry is mostly lost. Most Indianized kingdoms combined both Hindu and Buddhist beliefs and practices in a syncretic manner. Kertanagara, the last king of Singhasari, described himself as Sivabuddha, a simultaneous incarnation of the Hindu god and the Buddha. Southeast Asian rulers enthusiastically adopted elements of *rajadharma*, (Hindu and Buddhist beliefs, codes and court practices) to legitimate their own rule and constructed cities, such as Angkor, to affirm royal power by reproducing a map of sacred space derived from the *Ramayana* and *Mahabharat*. Southeast Asian rulers frequently adopted lengthy Sanskrit titles and founded cities, such as Ayutthaya in Thailand, named after those in the Indian epics.

These kingdoms prospered from the Spice Route, trade among themselves and the Indian kingdoms. The influence of Indian culture is visible in the script, grammar, religious observances, festivities, architecture and artistic idioms even today. The influence of Indian and Chinese cultures blended with native cultures, created a new synthesis. The Southeast Asian region was previously called by the name Indochina. The influence of Indian and Chinese cultures is both strongly visible in this region even today, with the majority of the region being Indianized and Vietnam Sinocized. The reception of Hinduism and Buddhism aided the civilizational maturity of these kingdoms but also subjected them to aggression by Indian and Chinese rulers. The Chinese ruled Vietnam for a millennium, while the Chola dynasty of South India ruled over Srivijaya briefly. And though Southeast Asia is an economic powerhouse in its own right, the need to balance Chinese economic and political influence with that of India remains an important factor for the region.

Cultural and trading relations between the powerful Chola kingdom of South India and the South East Asian Hindu kingdoms led the Bay of Bengal to be called "The Chola Lake" and the Chola attacks on Srivijaya in the tenth century CE are the sole example of military attacks by Indian rulers against Southeast Asia. The Pala dynasty of Bengal which controlled the heartland of Buddhist India maintained close economic, cultural and religious ties, particularly with Srivijaya.

The subsequent advent of Islam, carried by Arab traders, and Christianity carried by Portuguese, Spanish and Dutch colonial rulers significantly weakened the connection with India. Hinduism and Buddhism had found acceptance because of the cultural preferences of Southeast Asian societies rulers. In contrast, Islam and Catholicism became predominant by proselytization and military force.

Chinese influence grew with the gradual migration of Chinese traders and merchants who introduced a strong Confucian strain to the syncretic culture. Chinese influence dominated in Vietnam, although other states such as the Khmer empire and Malacca were drawn into China's diplomatic orbit. While Buddhism remains the dominant religion in mainland Southeast Asia, Hinduism survives in Bali and Christianity is the dominant religion in the Philippines and eastern Indonesia. Cultural practices like the performances of the Hindu epic, the Ramayana across all of Southeast Asia. Traces of Hindu culture are visible also in the Sanskrit etymology of words in Bahasa Malaysia, Indonesian and other regional languages as well as personal names.

CULTURAL COMMONALITIES

A defining characteristic of the cultural link between South East Asia and Indian subcontinent is the spread of ancient Indian Vedic/Hindu and Buddhist culture and philosophy into Myanmar, Thailand, Malaya, Laos and Cambodia. Indian scripts are also found in South East Asian islands ranging from Sumatra, Java, Bali, south Sulawesi and most of the Philippines. The impact of Indian culture is visible in the following notable examples:

- Hinduism is practiced by majority of Bali's population.
- Hindu mythological figure Garuda features in the coat of arms of Indonesia, Thailand and Ulán Bator.
- Hindu temple architecture-style features prominently on several ancient temples in South East Asia including Angkor Wat, which was dedicated to Hindu God Vishnu and features on the flag of Cambodia.
- Batu Caves in Malaysia is the most popular Hindu shrine outside India.
- Erawan Shrine, dedicated to Hindu god Brahma, in Thailand is one of the most popular religious shrines in the country.

- Kaharingan, an indigenous religion followed by Dayak people of Borneo, is categorized as a form of Hinduism in Indonesia.

GREATER INDIA

Only Since World War II has the term Southeast Asia been used to describe the area to the east of India and to the south of China, which includes the Indo-Chinese Peninsula, the Malay Archipelago and the Philippines, roughly forming a circle from Burma through Indonesia to Vietnam. Before the term Southeast Asia became common usage, the region was often described as *Further or Greater India,* and it was common to describe the Indonesian region or Malay Archipelago as the East Indies. The reason may be found in the fact that, prior to Western dominance, Southeast Asia was closely allied to India culturally and commercially. The history of Indian expansion covers a period of more than fifteen hundred years.

This region was broadly referred to by ancient Indians as Suvarnabhumi (the Land of Gold) or Suvarnadvipa (the Island of Gold), although scholars dispute its exact definition. Sometimes the term is interpreted to mean only Indonesia or Sumatra. Arab writers such as Al Biruni testify that Indians called the whole Southeast region Suwarndib (Suvarnadvipa). Hellenistic geographers knew the area as the Golden Ghersonese. The Chinese called it Kin-Lin; Kin means gold. During the last two thousand years, this region has come under the influence of practically all the major civilizations of the world: Indian, Chinese, Islamic, and Western. Of these, Indian culture appears to have blended best with the indigenous culture.

The name Java comes from the Sanskrit Jawadwip, which means a (dvip) island (yawa) shaped like a barley corn. The Vedic Indians must have charted Java, Yawadvip, thousands of years ago because Yawadvip is mentioned in India's earliest epic, the Ramayana. The Ramayana reveals some knowledge of the eastern regions beyond seas; for instance Sugriva dispatched his men to Yavadvipa, the island of Java, in search of Sita. It speaks of Burma as the land of silver mines. The *Agni Purana*, along with many other Puranas, calls India proper as Jambudvipa as distinguished from Dvipantara or India of the islands or overseas India. Towards the end of the fifth century, Aryabhatta, the Indian astronomer, wrote that when the sun rose in Ceylon it was midday in Yavakoti (Java) and midnight in the Roman land. In the Surya Siddhanta reference is also made to the Nagari Yavakoti with golden walls and gates.

The term Greater India has several related meanings:

- In medieval literature and geography: the term "Greater India" (P. *Indyos mayores*) was used at least from the mid 15th century. The term, which seems to have been used with variable precision, sometimes meant only the Indian subcontinent; however, at other times, in some accounts of European nautical voyages, "Greater India" (or "India Major") extended from the Malabar (present-day northern Kerala) to *India extra Gangem* (lit. "India, beyond the Ganges," but usually the East Indies, *i.e.* present-day Malay Archipelago) and "India Minor," from Malabar to Sind.

- In late 19th-century geography: The term "Greater India" included: "(a) Himalaya, (b) Punjab, (c) Hindustan, (d) Burma, (e) Indo-China, (f) Sunda Islands, (g) Borneo, (h) Celebes, and (i) Philippines." (Similarly "Greater Australia" included "(a) West Australia, (b) East Australia, (c) New Zealand, (d) Melanesia, (e) Micronesia, (f) Polynesia."
- In 20th-century history, art history, linguistics, and allied fields: The term "Greater India," now largely out of favor, consists of "all the Asian lands including Burma, Java, Cambodia, Bali, and the former Champa and Funan polities of present-day Vietnam," in which pre-Islamic Indian culture left an "imprint in the form of monuments, inscriptions and other traces of the historic 'Indianising' process." In some accounts, many Pacific societies and "most of the Buddhist world including Ceylon, Tibet, central Asia, and even Japan were held to fall within this web of Indianising 'culture colonies'" This particular usage—implying cultural "sphere of influence" of India—was spurred by the formation of *The Greater India Society* by a group of Bengali men of letters and does not go back to before the 1920s (lasting well into the 1970s in history and later in other fields).
- In late 20th- and 21st-century geology: The term "Greater India," still current, is used to mean "the Indian sub-continent plus a postulated northern extension," in plate tectonic models of the India–Asia collision. Although its usage in geology pre-dates plate tectonic theory, the term has seen increased usage since the 1970s.

INDIAN CULTURAL SPHERE

The meaning of "Greater India" as Indian cultural sphere was popularized by a network of Bengali scholars in the 1920s who were all members of the Calcutta-based *Greater India Society*. The movement's early leaders included the historian R. C. Majumdar (1888–1980); the philologists Suniti Kumar Chatterji (1890–1977) and P.C. Bagchi (1898–1956), the historians Phanindranath Bose and Kalidas Nag (1891–1966). Some of their formulations were inspired by the then ongoing excavations in Angkor by French archaeologists and by the writings of French Indologist Sylvain Lévi. The *Greater India Society* scholars postulated a benevolent ancient Indian cultural colonization of South-east Asia, in stark contrast—in their view—to the colonialism of the early 20th century.

"The ancient Hindus of yore were not simply a spiritual people, always busy with mystical problems and never troubling themselves with the questions of 'this world' . . . India also has its Napoleons and Charlemagnes, its Bismarcks and Machiavellis. But the real charm of Indian history does not consist in these aspirants after universal power, but in its peaceful and benevolent Imperialism—a unique thing in the history of mankind. The colonizers of India did not go with sword and fire in their hands; they used . . . the weapons of their superior culture and religion [to bring] the world under their sway. Wherever they went, they conquered the world through their culture . . . . This fascinating and forgotten chapter of Indian history is being gradually reconstructed by the constant efforts of Indologists . . . .The Buddhist age has attracted special attention, and the French savants have taken much pains [sic] to investigate the splendid monuments of the Indian cultural empire in the Far East."

The term was used in historical writing in India well into the 1970s. For example, the fifteenth chapter of the *An Advanced History of India* titled, "Colonial and Cultural Expansion (of Ancient India)", and written by R. C. Majumdar, concluded with:

"We may conclude with a broad survey of the Indian colonies in the Far East. For nearly fifteen hundred years, and down to a period when the Hindus had lost their independence in their own home, Hindu kings were ruling over Indo-China and the numerous islands of the Indian Archipelago, from Sumatra to New Guinea. Indian religion, Indian culture, Indian laws and Indian government molded the lives of the primitive races all over this wide region, and they imbibed a more elevated moral spirit and a higher intellectual taste through the religion, art, and literature of India. In short, the people were lifted to a higher plane of civilization. A greater India was established by a gentle fusion of races, which richly endowed the original inhabitants with the spiritual heritage of India.... The colonial and cultural expansion of India is one of the most brilliant, but forgotten, episodes of Indian history, of which any Indian may justly feel proud."

The term "Greater India" as well as the notion of an explicit Hindu colonization of ancient Southeast Asia have been linked to both Indian nationalism and Hindu nationalism, however, many Indian nationalists, like Nehru and Tagore, although receptive to "an idealisation of India as a benign and uncoercive world civiliser and font of global enlightenment," stayed away from explicit "Greater India" formulations. In addition, some scholars have seen the Hindu/Buddhist acculturation in ancient Southeast Asia as "a single cultural process in which Southeast Asia was the matrix and South Asia the mediatrix."

In the field of Art History, especially in American writings on the Indian Art History, the term survived longer due to the influence of art theorist Ananda Coomaraswamy. Coomaraswamy's view of pan-Indian art history was influenced by the "Calcutta cultural nationalists."

TRADE AND COLONIZATION

European colonization

Europeans first came to Southeast Asia in the sixteenth century. It was the lure of trade that brought Europeans to Southeast Asia while missionaries also tagged along the ships as they hoped to spread Christianity into the region.

Portugal was the first European power to establish a bridgehead into the lucrative Southeast Asia trade route with the conquest of the Sultanate of Malacca in 1511. The

Netherlands and Spain followed and soon superseded Portugal as the main European powers in the region. The Dutch took over Malacca from the Portuguese in 1641 while Spain began to colonize the Philippines (named after Phillip II of Spain) from 1560s. Acting through the Dutch East India Company, the Dutch established the city of Batavia (now Jakarta) as a base for trading and expansion into the other parts of Java and the surrounding territory.

Britain, in the form of the British East India Company, came relatively late onto the scene. Starting with Penang, the British began to expand their Southeast Asian empire. They also temporarily possessed Dutch territories during the Napoleonic Wars, In 1819 Stamford Raffles established Singapore as a key trading post for Britain in their rivalry with the Dutch. However, their rivalry cooled in 1824 when an Anglo-Dutch treaty demarcated their respective interests in Southeast Asia. From the 1850s onwards, the pace of colonization shifted to a significantly higher gear.

This phenomenon, denoted New Imperialism, saw the conquest of nearly all Southeast Asian territories by the colonial powers. The Dutch East India Company and British East India Company were dissolved by their respective governments, who took over the direct administration of the colonies. Only Thailand was spared the experience of foreign rule, although, Thailand itself was also greatly affected by the power politics of the Western powers.

By 1913, the British occupied Burma, Malaya and the Borneo territories, the French controlled Indochina, the Dutch ruled the Netherlands East Indies while Portugal managed to hold on to Portuguese Timor. In the Philippines, Filipino revolutionaries declared independence from Spain in 1898 but was handed over to the United States despite protests as a result of the Spanish-American War.

Colonial rule had a profound effect on Southeast Asia. While the colonial powers profited much from the region's vast resources and large market, colonial rule did develop the region to a varying extent. Commercial agriculture, mining and an export based economy developed rapidly during this period. Increased labor demand resulted in mass immigration, especially from British India and China, which brought about massive demographic change. The institutions for a modern nation state like a state bureaucracy, courts of law, and print media and to a smaller extent, modern education, sowed the seeds of the fledgling nationalist movements in the colonial territories.

Decolonization

In the inter-war years, these nationalist movements grew and often clashed with the colonial authorities when they demanded self-determination. With the rejuvenated nationalist movements in wait, the Europeans returned to a very different Southeast Asia after World War II. Indonesia declared independence in 17 August 1945 and subsequently fought a bitter war against the returning Dutch; the Philippines were granted independence in 1946 after a bloody war with the United States; Burma secured their independence from Britain in 1948, and the French were driven from Indochina in 1954 after a bitterly fought war against the Vietnamese nationalists. The newly-established United Nations provided a forum both for nationalist demands and for the newly demanded independent nations.

During the Cold War, countering the threat of communism was a major theme in the decolonization process. After suppressing the communist insurrection during the Malayan Emergency from 1948 to 1960, Britain granted independence to Malaya and later, Singapore, Sabah and Sarawak in 1957 and 1963 respectively within the framework of the Federation of Malaysia. In one of the most bloody single incidents of violence in Cold War Southeast Asia, General Suharto seized power in Indonesia in 1965 and initiated a massacre of approximately 500,000 alleged members of the Indonesian Communist Party (PKI). Recent evidence from the US National Security Archive published by George Washington University suggests this massacre was carried out with the support of the United States embassy in Jakarta, which supplied lists of names of suspected PKI members to Suharto.

The United States intervention against communist forces in Indochina during a conflict commonly referred to in the United States as the Vietnam War meant that Vietnam, Laos and Cambodia had to go through a prolonged and protracted war in their route to independence.

In 1975, Portuguese rule ended in East Timor. However, independence was short-lived as Indonesia annexed the territory soon after. Finally, Britain ended its protectorate of the Sultanate of Brunei in 1984, marking the end of European rule in Southeast Asia.

CONTEMPORARY SOUTHEAST ASIA

A region of Asia bounded roughly by the Indian subcontinent on the west, China on the north, and the Pacific Ocean on the east. It includes Indochina, the Malay Peninsula, and the Malay Archipelago.

Vast region of Asia (1990 est. pop. 442,500,000), c.1, 740,000 sq mi (4,506,600 sq km), bounded roughly by the Indian subcontinent on the west, China on the north, and the Pacific Ocean on the east. The name "Southeast Asia" came into popular use after World War II and has replaced such phrases as "Further India," "the East Indies," "Indo-China," and "the Malay Peninsula," which formerly designated all or part of the region. Southeast Asia includes the Indochina Peninsula, which juts into the South China Sea, the Malay Peninsula, and the Indonesian and Philippine Archipelagos. The region has 10 independent countries: Brunei, Cambodia, Indonesia, Laos, Malaysia, Myanmar, the Philippines, Singapore, Thailand, and Vietnam.

Peninsular Southeast Asia is a rugged region traversed by many mountains and drained by great rivers such as the Thanlwin, Ayeyarwady, Chao Phraya, and Mekong. Insular Southeast Asia is made up of numerous volcanic and coral islands. Southeast Asia has a generally tropical rainy climate, with the exception of the northwestern part, which has a humid subtropical climate. The wet monsoon winds are vital for the economic well-being of the region. Tropical forests cover most of the area. Rice is the chief crop of the region; rubber, tea, spices, and coconuts are also important. The region has a great variety of minerals and produces most of the world's tin.

People

Population is unevenly distributed, with the highest density in lowland areas. Most of the people live in small agrarian villages; the largest cities are Jakarta, Indonesia; Bangkok, Thailand; Singapore; Manila, Philippines; and Ho Chi Minh City, Vietnam. There is a great diversity in culture, history, religion, and ethnic composition. Many different languages are spoken, such as those of the Tibeto-Burman, Mon-Khmer, and Malayo-Polynesian families. Religions include Buddhism, Hinduism, Islam, Roman Catholicism, and Confucianism. Animism is still practiced among many more isolated peoples of the region.

History

Most of the influences that molded the societies of Southeast Asia predate European colonization, coming from early Chinese and Indian sources. Several great civilizations, including those of the Khmers and Malays, have flourished there. In the late 15th cent., Islamic influences grew strong but were overshadowed by the arrival of Europeans, who established their power throughout Southeast Asia; only Thailand remained free of colonial occupation. Because of Southeast Asia's strategic location between Japan and India, and the importance of shipping routes that traverse it, the region became the scene of battles between Allied and Japanese forces during World War II.

After the war the countries of Southeast Asia have reemerged as independent nations. They have been plagued by political turmoil, weak economies, ethnic strife, and social inequities, although the situation for most Southeast Asian nations improved in the 1980s and 90s. Throughout the 1960s and early 1970s, however, there were open conflicts between Communist and non-Communist factions throughout most of the region, especially in Vietnam, Laos, and Cambodia (see Vietnam War). In 1967 Indonesia, Malaysia, the Philippines, Singapore, and Thailand created the Association of Southeast Asian Nations (ASEAN), the objectives of which are to promote regional economic growth, political stability, social progress, and cultural developments. Since then, Brunei (1984), Vietnam (1995), Laos (1997), and Myanmar and Cambodia (1999) have joined ASEAN. In 1997 a monetary collapse in Thailand sparked a general economic crisis in several nations in the region; the results were most severe in Indonesia, which underwent economic, political, and social turmoil in the late 1990s.sss

Modern Southeast Asia has been characterized by high economic growth by most countries and closer regional integration. Indonesia, Malaysia, the Philippines, Singapore and Thailand have traditionally experienced high growth and are commonly recognized as the more developed countries of the region. As of late, Vietnam too had been experiencing an economic boom. However, Myanmar, Cambodia, Laos and the newly independent East Timor are still lagging economically.

On August 8, 1967, Association of Southeast Asian Nations (ASEAN) was founded by Thailand, Indonesia, Malaysia, Singapore, and the Philippines. Since Cambodian admission into the union in 1999, East Timor is the only Southeast Asian country that is not part of ASEAN, although plans are under way for eventual membership. The association aims to enhance cooperation among Southeast Asian community. ASEAN Free Trade Area has been established to encourage greater trade among ASEAN members. ASEAN has also been a front runner in greater integration of Asia-Pacific region through East Asia Summits.

Geography

Geologically, the Indonesian archipelago is one of the most active vulcanological regions in the world. Geological uplifts in the region have also produced some impressive mountains, culminating in Mount Kinabalu in Sabah, Malaysia on the island of Borneo with a height of 4,101 meters (13,455 ft) and also Puncak Jaya in Papua, Indonesia at 4,884 meters (16,024 ft), on the island of New Guinea.

The Golden Triangle is one of Asia's two main illicit opium-producing areas. It is an area of around 350,000 square kilometres that overlaps the mountains of four countries of Southeast Asia: Myanmar (Burma), Laos, Vietnam, and Thailand. (Other interpretations of the Golden Triangle also include a section of Yunnan Province, China.) Along with Afghanistan in the Golden Crescent and Pakistan, it has been one of the most extensive opium-producing areas of Asia and of the world since the 1950s. The Golden Triangle also designates the confluence of the Ruak River and the Mekong River, since the term has been appropriated by the Thai tourist industry to describe the nearby junction of Thailand, Laos, and Burma.

Opium and morphine base produced in northeastern Burma are transported by horse and donkey caravans to refineries along the Thailand–Burma border for conversion to heroin and heroin base. Most of the finished products are shipped across the border into various towns in North Thailand and down to Bangkok for further distribution to international markets. In the past major Thai Chinese and Burmese Chinese traffickers in Bangkok have controlled much of the foreign sales and movement of Southeast Asian heroin from Thailand, but a combination of law enforcement pressure, publicity and a regional drought has significantly reduced their role. As a consequence, many less-predominant traffickers in Bangkok and other parts of Thailand now control smaller quantities of the heroin going to international markets.

Heroin from Southeast Asia is most frequently brought to the United States by couriers, typically Thai and U.S. nationals and Hong Kong Chinese, traveling on commercial airlines. California and Hawaii are the primary U.S. entry points for Golden Triangle heroin, but small percentages of the drug are trafficked into New York City and Washington, D.C. While Southeast Asian groups have had success in trafficking heroin to the United States, they initially had difficulty arranging street level distribution. However, with the incarceration of Asian traffickers in American prisons during the 1970s, contacts between Asian and American prisoners developed. These contacts have allowed Southeast Asian traffickers' access to individuals and organizations distributing heroin at the retail level.

Boundaries

The Australasian continental plate defines a region adjacent to Southeast Asia, which is also politically separated from the countries of Southeast Asia. But a cultural touch point lies between Papua New Guinea and the Indonesian region of Papua and West Papua, which shares the island of New Guinea with Papua New Guinea.

Climate

The climate in Southeast Asia is mainly tropical – hot and humid all year round. There is a lot of rainfall. Southeast Asia has a wet and dry season caused by seasonal shift in winds or monsoon. The tropical rain belt causes additional rainfall during the monsoon season. The rain forest is the second largest on earth (with the Amazon being the largest). Exception to this type of climate and vegetation is the mountain areas in the northern region, where high altitudes lead to milder temperatures and drier landscape. Other parts fall out of this climate because they are desert like.

The animals of Southeast Asia are diverse; on the islands of Borneo and Sumatra, the Orangutan (man of the forest), the Asian Elephant, the Malayan tapir, the Sumatran Rhinoceros and the Bornean Clouded Leopard can be also found. Six subspecies of the Binturong or *bearcat* exist in the region, though the one endemic to the island of Palawan is now classed as vulnerable.

The Wild Asian Water Buffalo, and on various islands related dwarf species of Bubalus such as Anoa were once widespread in Southeast Asia, nowadays the Domestic Asian Water buffalo is common across the region, but its remaining relatives are rare and endangered.

The mouse deer, a small tusked deer as large as a toy dog or cat, can be found on Sumatra, Borneo and Palawan Islands. The gaur, a gigantic wild ox larger than even wild Water buffalo, is found mainly in Indochina.

Birds such as the peafowl and drongo live in this sub region as far east as Indonesia. The babirusa, a four-tusked pig, can be found in Indonesia as well. The hornbill was prized for its beak and used in trade with China. The horn of the rhinoceros, not part of its skull, was prized in China as well.

The Indonesian Archipelago is split by the Wallace Line. This line runs along what is now known to be a tectonic plate boundary, and separates Asian (Western) species from Australasian (Eastern) species. The islands between Java/Borneo and Papua form a mixed zone, where both types occur, known as Wallacea.

The shallow waters of the Southeast Asian coral reefs have the highest levels of biodiversity for the world's marine ecosystems, where coral, fish and mollusks abound. The whale shark can be found in the South China Sea.

The trees and other plants of the region are tropical; in some countries where the mountains are tall enough, temperate-climate vegetation can be found. These rainforest areas are currently being logged-over, especially in Borneo.

While Southeast Asia is rich in flora and fauna, Southeast Asia is facing severe deforestation which causes habitat loss for various endangered species such as orangutan and the Sumatran tiger. At the same time, haze has been a regular occurrence. The worst regional haze occurred in 1998 in which multiple countries were covered with thick haze. In reaction, several countries in Southeast Asia signed the ASEAN Agreement on Transboundary Haze Pollution in order to combat haze pollution.

Economy

The region is also one of the most productive in manufacturing microprocessors. Reserves of oil are also present in the region.

Seventeen telecommunications companies have contracted to build a new submarine cable to connect Southeast Asia to the U.S. This is to avoid disruption of the kind recently caused by the cutting of the undersea cable from Taiwan to the U.S. in a recent earthquake.

Demographics

Southeast Asia has an area of approx. 4,000,000 km² (1.6 million square miles). As of 2004, more than 593 million people lived in the region, more than a fifth of them (125 million) on the Indonesian island of Java, the most densely populated large island in the world. The distribution of the religions and people is diverse in Southeast Asia and varies by country. Some 30 million overseas Chinese also live in Southeast Asia, most prominently in Christmas Island, Malaysia, the Philippines, Singapore, Indonesia and Thailand, and also, as the Hoa, in Vietnam.

Religions

Countries in Southeast Asia practice many different religions. Mainland SEA countries, which are, Thailand, Cambodia, Laos, Myanmar, and Vietnam practice predominantly Buddhism. Singapore is also predominantly Buddhist. Ancestor worship and Confucianism is also widely practiced in Vietnam and Singapore. In the Malay Archipelago, people living in Malaysia, western Indonesia and Brunei practice mainly Islam. Christianity is predominant in the Philippines, eastern Indonesia and East Timor. The Philippines has the largest Roman Catholic population followed very distantly by Vietnam. East Timor is also predominantly Roman Catholic due to a history of Portuguese rule.

Religions and peoples are diverse in Southeast Asia and not one country is homogeneous. In the world's most populous Muslim nation, Indonesia, Hinduism is dominant on islands such as Bali. Christianity also predominates in Philippines, New Guinea and Timor. Pockets of Hindu population can also be found around Southeast Asia in Singapore, Malaysia etc. Garuda, the phoenix who is the mount (*vahanam*) of Vishnu, is a national symbol in both Thailand and Indonesia; in the Philippines, gold images of Garuda have been found on Palawan; gold images of other Hindu gods and goddesses have also been found on Mindanao. Balinese Hinduism is somewhat different from Hinduism practiced elsewhere, as Animism and local culture is incorporated into it. Christians can also be found throughout Southeast Asia; they are in the majority in East Timor and the Philippines, Asia's largest Christian nation. In addition, there are also older tribal religious practices in remote areas of Sarawak in East Malaysia and Papua in eastern Indonesia. In Myanmar, Sakka (Indra) is revered as a *nat*. In Vietnam, Mahayana Buddhism is practiced, which is influenced by native animism but with strong emphasis on Ancestor Worship.

Languages

Each of the languages has been influenced by cultural pressures due to trade and historical colonization as well. Thus, for example, a Filipino, educated in English and Filipino, as well as in his native tongue (e.g., Visayan), might well speak another language, such as Spanish for historical reasons, or even Chinese for economic reasons; a Malaysian might well speak Malay, Chinese as well as English, again for economic reasons.

CULTURES

Cinema

Southeast Asian cinema refers to the film industry and films produced in, and/or by natives of, Southeast Asia. By definition, it describes any films produced in Brunei, Burma, Cambodia, East Timor, Indonesia, Laos, Malaysia, the Philippines, Singapore, Thailand and Vietnam. Southeast Asian cinema is a sub-section of continental Asian cinema, which in turn comes under the umbrella term of World cinema, a term used in some Anglophone countries to describe any foreign language films.

Games

The Southeast Asian Games (also known as the SEA Games), is a biennial multi-sport event involving participants from the current 11 countries of Southeast Asia. The games are under regulation of the Southeast Asian Games Federation with supervision by the International Olympic Committee (IOC) and the Olympic Council of Asia.

The Southeast Asian Games owes its origins to the Southeast Asian Peninsular Games or SEAP Games. On May 22, 1958, delegates from the countries in Southeast Asian peninsula attending the 3rd Asian Games in Tokyo, Japan had a meeting and agreed to establish a sport organization. The SEAP Games was conceptualized by Laung

Sukhumnaipradit, then Vice-President of the Thailand Olympic Committee. The proposed rationale was that a regional sports event will help promote cooperation, understanding and relations among countries in the Southeast Asian region.

Thailand, Burma (now Myanmar), Malaya (now Malaysia), Laos, South Vietnam and Cambodia (with Singapore included thereafter) were the founding members. These countries agreed to hold the Games biannually. The SEAP Games Federation Committee was formed.

The first SEAP Games were held in Bangkok from 12-17 December, 1959 comprising more than 527 athletes and officials from Thailand, Burma, Malaysia, Singapore, South Vietnam and Laos participating in 12 sports.

At the 8th SEAP Games in 1975, the SEAP Federation considered the inclusion of Indonesia and the Philippines. The two countries were formally admitted in 1977, the same year when SEAP Federation changed their name to Southeast Asian Games Federation (SEAGF), and the games were known as the Southeast Asian Games. Brunei was admitted at the 10th SEA Games in Jakarta, Indonesia, and East Timor at the 22nd SEA Games in Hanoi, Vietnam.

In December 2005, the Philippines hosted the Games for the third time, after 1981 and 1991 editions. With its 113 gold medals, it copped the over-all championship for the first time since it joined in 1977. The 2007 Southeast Asian Games held in the Thailand, which started from 6 December and ended on 15 December 2007, hosting the biennial event for the sixth time and it was also the most protested SEAG ever. The next host for the SEA Games is Laos. It is Laos' first time as the host for the biannual games.

Dance and Music

Dance in much of Southeast Asia also includes movement of the hands, as well as the feet. Puppetry and shadow plays were also a favored form of entertainment in past centuries. The Arts and Literature in some of Southeast Asia is quite influenced by Hinduism brought to them centuries ago.

In Indonesia, though they converted to Islam, they retained many forms of Hindu influenced practices, cultures, arts and literatures. An example will be the Wayang Kulit (Shadow Puppet) and literatures like the Ramayana. This is also true for mainland Southeast Asia (excluding Vietnam). Dance movements, Hindu gods, Arts were also fused into Thai, Khmer, Lao and Burmese cultures. In Vietnam, the Vietnamese share many cultural similarities with the Chinese.

Southeast Asian music includes the musical traditions of this sub region of Asia. This sub region consists of eleven countries, namely, Brunei, Cambodia, East Timor, Indonesia, Laos, Malaysia, Myanmar, Philippines, Singapore, Thailand, and Vietnam.

Traditional music in Southeast Asia is as varied as its many ethnic and cultural divisions. Main styles of traditional music can be seen: Court music, folk music, music styles of smaller ethnic groups, and music influenced by genres outside the geographic region.

Of the court and folk genres, Gong-chime ensembles and orchestras make up the majority (the exception being lowland areas of Vietnam). *Gamelan* orchestras from Indonesia, *Piphat/Pinpeat* ensembles of Thailand & Cambodia and the *Kulintanzg* ensembles of the southern Philippines, Borneo, Sulawesi and Timor are the three main distinct styles of musical genres that have influenced other traditional musical styles in the region. String instruments also are popular in the region.

Writing

The history of Southeast Asia has led to a wealth of different authors, from both within and without writing about the region.

Originally, Indians were the ones who taught the native inhabitants about writing. This is shown through Brahmic forms of writing present in the region such as the Balinese script shown on split palm leaf called *lontar*, right:

The antiquity of this form of writing extends before the invention of paper around the year 100 in China. Note each palm leaf section was only several lines, written longitudinally across the leaf, and bound by twine to the other sections. The outer portion was decorated. The alphabets of Southeast Asia tended to be abugidas, until the arrival of the Europeans, who used words that also ended in consonants, not just vowels. Other forms of official documents, which did not use paper, included Javanese copperplate scrolls. This would have been more durable in the tropical climate of Southeast Asia.

Baybayin or Alibata (known in Unicode as the *Tagalog script*) is a pre-Spanish Philippine writing system that originated from the Javanese script Old Kawi. The writing system is a member of the Brahmic family (and an offshoot of the Vatteluttu alphabet) and is believed to have been in use as early as the 14th century. It continued in use during the Spanish colonization of the Philippines up until the late 19th Century. The term *baybayin* literally means *syllables*. Closely related scripts are Hanunóo, Buhid, and Tagbanwa.

The Philippine Baybayin is one of a dozen or so individual alphabets from such Southeast Asian islands as Sumatra, Java, and Sulawesi which are derived from ancient India and share the Sanskrit characteristic that any consonant is pronounced with the vowel *a* following it— diacritical marks being used to express other vowels (this vowel occurs with greatest frequency in Sanskrit, and also probably in all Philippine languages.None of these other scripts, however, enjoys the wealth of documentary testimony spread across four centuries which exists for Philippine Baybayin.

The Thai alphabet is used to write the Thai language and other minority languages in Thailand. It has forty-four consonants, fifteen vowel symbols that combine into at least twenty-eight vowel forms, and four tone marks.

The character set is an abugida, a writing system in which consonants include an inherent vowel sound. The inherent vowel is described as an implied 'a' or 'o', below. Consonants are written horizontally from left to right, with vowels symbols arranged above, below, to the left or to the right of the corresponding consonant or in a combination of those positions.

Jawi is an adapted Arabic alphabet for writing the Malay language. Jawi is one of the two official scripts in Brunei and Malaysia as the script for the Malay language. Usage wise, it was the standard script for the Malay language but has since been replaced by the Roman script, and Jawi has since been relegated to a script used for religious and cultural purposes. Day-to-day usage of Jawi is maintained in more conservative Malay-populated areas such as Pattani in Thailand and Kelantan in Malaysia.

The Jawi alphabet has existed for many centuries in Nusantara (the Malay world). Its development is linked with the arrival of Islam. It consists of mostly Arabic characters along with some extra characters unique to Jawi. The Jawi alphabet is one of the earliest scripts used for writing Malay. Jawi has been in use since the era of the kingdom of Pasai, to the era of the Sultanate of Malacca, Sultanate of Johor and also Acheh and Sultanate of Patani in the 17th century. Evidence of this is found in the Terengganu Inscription Stone (Batu Bersurat Terengganu), dated 1303 A.D. (702H by the Islamic calendar), whereas the earliest use of the Roman alphabet is found near the end of the 19th century. The Jawi script was the official script for Unfederated Malay States during British protectorate.

Thai has its own set of Thai numerals which are based on the Hindu Arabic numeral system, but the standard western Hindu-Arabic numerals, *tua lek hindu arabik*) are also commonly used.

Chapter - 2

BUDDHISM IN SOUTHEAST ASIA

The history of Buddhism spans the 6th century BCE to the present, starting with the birth of the Buddha Siddhartha Gautama. This makes it one of the oldest religions practiced today. Starting in India, the religion evolved as it spread through Central Asia, East Asia, and Southeast Asia. At one time or another it affected most of the Asian continent. The history of Buddhism is also characterized by the development of numerous movements and schisms, foremost among them where the Theravada, Mahâyâna and Vajrayana traditions, with contrasting periods of expansion and retreat.

Buddhism is both a world religion and a philosophy with between 230 and 500 million adherents worldwide. It is based on the teachings of Buddha Shakyamuni, sometimes known simply as "the Buddha", (Siddhârtha Gautama) who lived c. 5th century BCE in ancient India, in parts of what is now Nepal and the Indian states of Uttar Pradesh and Bihar.

Buddhism has spread through two main traditions; Theravada which extended south and east and now has widespread following in Southeast Asia, and Mahayana, which diffused first west, then north and later east throughout East Asia. Both traditions have since spread throughout the world. There are considerable differences between the various existing traditions regarding their canon of authentic scriptures, their emphasis on specific parts of what they respectively consider the Buddha's teachings and their subsequent interpretations as well as in the practices they consider most beneficial.

THE GREAT DEPARTURE

According to the Buddhist tradition, the historical Buddha Siddhartha Gautama was born to the Shakya clan, at the beginning of the Magadha period (546–324 BCE), in the plains of Lumbini in Ancient India. He is also known as the *Shakyamuni* (literally "The sage of the Shakya clan"). After an early life of luxury under the protection of his father, Suddhodana, the ruler of Kapilavastu (later to be incorporated into the state of

Magadha), Siddhartha entered into contact with the realities of the world and concluded that life was inescapably bound up with suffering and sorrow. Siddhartha renounced his meaningless life of luxury to become an ascetic. He ultimately decided that asceticism couldn't end suffering, and instead chose a middle way, a path of moderation away from the extremes of self-indulgence and self-mortification.

At the age of 29, Siddhartha left his palace in order to meet his subjects. Despite his father's effort to remove the sick, aged and suffering from the public view, Siddhartha was said to have seen an old man. Disturbed by this, when told that all people would eventually grow old by his charioteer Channa, the prince went on further trips where he encountered, variously, a diseased man, a decaying corpse, and an ascetic. Deeply depressed by these sights, he sought to overcome old age, illness, and death by living the life of an ascetic.

He became a wandering ascetic, practiced yogic disciplines and meditation, studied with various teachers, and attained high states of consciousness; but still he did not find the answer to his question. He practiced severe forms of asceticism, almost to the point of death by starvation, all without gain. Finally he sat under a bodhi tree, determined not to rise from meditation until he had gained the insight he sought. Not long after, he attained enlightenment; he became the Buddha — the Awakened One. He had ascended through various stages of meditative awareness, he had seen all of his past lives, and he had seen directly into reality, into the nature of existence and the causes of suffering and rebirth. He pondered whether to try to teach these insights, so subtle and difficult to grasp to others; perhaps it would be futile. But finally he decided that at least some of the people would be able to understand; perhaps more importantly, they could be shown the path to arrive at these insights themselves. He gave his first sermon to a few disciples in the Deer park at Benares, and then continued to wander and teach for the next forty-five years, until his death at the age of eighty.

He was born in the 6th century BCE, a time of great turmoil and political change in India; many were unsatisfied with the Vedic religion, and new teachings had emerged, among them the Upanishads. The Buddha stood largely outside the Vedic tradition, criticizing many of its central teachings. Nevertheless, he had been influenced by that tradition and his teachings in turn would have a profound effect on later teachers in the Hindu tradition, such as Shankara; even in such Hindu classics as the Bhagavad Gita, some reaction can be seen to Buddhist teachings. But later centuries would see the Buddha's influence wane in India and instead spread to other Asian countries. Today Buddhism has spread throughout the world. Various sects have arisen as later teachers have reinterpreted and expounded upon the Buddha's basic teachings. Buddhism may be considered a religion, a philosophy, a way of life, or all three; here we will deal mainly with Buddhism as a philosophical system.

For the remaining 45 years of his life, the Buddha is said to have traveled in the Gangetic Plain, in what is now Uttar Pradesh, Bihar and southern Nepal, teaching his doctrine and discipline to an extremely diverse range of people— from nobles to outcaste street sweepers, mass murderers such as Angulimala and cannibals such as Alavaka. This extended to many adherents of rival philosophies and religions. The Buddha founded the community of Buddhist monks and nuns (the *Sangha*) to continue the dispensation after his Parinirvâna (Pâli: Parinibbâna) or "complete Nirvâna", and made thousands of converts. His religion was open to all races and classes and had no caste structure. He was also subject to attack from opposition religious groups, including attempted murders and framings.

The Buddha intended his philosophy to be a practical one, aimed at the happiness of all creatures. While he outlined his metaphysics, he did not expect anyone to accept this on faith but rather to verify the insights for themselves; his emphasis was always on seeing clearly and understanding. To achieve this, however, requires a disciplined life and a clear commitment to liberation; the Buddha laid out a clear path to the goal and also observations on how to live life wisely. The core of this teaching is contained in the Noble Eightfold Path, which covers the three essential areas of Buddhist practice: ethical conduct, mental discipline ('concentration; or 'meditation'), and wisdom. The goals are to cultivate both wisdom and compassion; then these qualities together will enable one ultimately to attain enlightenment.

The following points are the fundamentals of Buddha's teachings:

- The Four Noble Truths: that suffering is an inherent part of existence; that the origin of suffering is ignorance and the main symptoms of that ignorance are attachment and craving; that attachment and craving can be ceased; and that following the Noble Eightfold Path will lead to the cessation of attachment and craving and therefore suffering.

  The Noble Eightfold Path: right understanding, right thought, right speech, right action, right livelihood, right effort, right mindfulness, and right concentration.
- Dependent origination: that any phenomenon 'exists' only because of the 'existence' of other phenomena in a complex web of cause and effect covering time past, present and future. Because all things are thus conditioned and transient (anicca), they have no real independent identity (anatta).
- Rejection of the infallibility of accepted scripture: Teachings should not be accepted unless they are borne out by our experience and are praised by the wise.
- **Anicca** (Sanskrit: **anitya**): That all things are impermanent.
- **Anatta** (Sanskrit: **anâtman**): That the perception of a constant "self" is an illusion.
- **Dukkha** (Sanskrit: **dukkha**): That all beings suffer from all situations due to unclear mind.

However, in some Mahayana schools, these points have come to be regarded as more or less subsidiary. There is some disagreement amongst various schools of Buddhism over more esoteric aspects of Buddha's teachings, and also over some of the disciplinary rules for monks.

The Buddha's reluctance to name a successor or to formalise his doctrine led to the emergence of many movements during the next 400 years: first the schools of Nikaya Buddhism, of which only Theravada remains today, and then the formation of Mahayana and Vajrayana, pan-Buddhist sects based on the acceptance of new scriptures and the revision of older techniques.

Despite of the support and patronage by Harshavardhana and by Pala kings, who came later, by the end of twelfth century A.D, Buddhism declined as a major religious force in the sub-continent . The growing influence of Bhakti movement and the religious bigotry of the Muslim invaders sealed what ever opportunities it had for revival and renewal. However Buddhism continued to flourish in other parts of the world, especially in China, Korea, Japan, Cambodia, Thailand and other far eastern countries.

Today Buddhism is practised in various parts of the world. In India it has the dubious distinction of a separate religion as well as a movement with in Hinduism. The Hindus consider the Buddha as an incarnation of Lord Vishnu. But the Buddhists disagree. As a religion, except in certain parts like Sikkim, Ladakh, Buddhism is a minority religion in India.

But in neighboring Nepal, Bhutan and Ceylon it is still very popular religion. Though it greatly disappeared in main land China, it still survives in many far eastern countries and Japan. The west was introduced to Buddhism mainly in the last century. It is presently attracting many new followers from the western world. As a religion and as a way of life, Buddhism has a great religions appeal to the educated and liberal minded people of the west. It has an inherent strength, a certain dignified charm . It will continue to attract many new followers.

Southeast Asia

During the 1st century CE, the trade on the overland Silk Road tended to be restricted by the rise in the Middle-East of the Parthian empire, an unvanquished enemy of Rome, just as Romans were becoming extremely wealthy and their demand for Asian luxury was rising. This demand revived the sea connections between the Mediterranean and China, with India as the intermediary of choice. From that time, through trade connection, commercial settlements, and even political interventions, India started to strongly influence Southeast Asian countries. Trade routes linked India with southern Burma, central and southern Siam, lower Cambodia and southern Vietnam, and numerous urbanized coastal settlements were established there.

For more than a thousand years, Indian influence was therefore the major factor that brought a certain level of cultural unity to the various countries of the region. The Pali and Sanskrit languages and the Indian script, together with Theravada and Mahayana Buddhism, Brahmanism, and Hinduism, were transmitted from direct contact and through sacred texts and Indian literature such as the Ramayana and the Mahabharata.

From the 5th to the 13th century, South-East Asia had very powerful empires and became extremely active in Buddhist architectural and artistic creation. The main Buddhist influence now came directly by sea from the Indian subcontinent, so that these empires essentially followed the Mahayana faith. The Sri Vijaya Empire to the south and the Khmer Empire to the north competed for influence, and their art expressed the rich Mahayana pantheon of the Bodhisattvas.

The Buddha's teachings on ethics and living a good life also extended to the realm of the social and political. He was ahead of his time in many ways; considering all people as equal, he rejected the caste system and openly encouraged women to become students and teachers. He taught that governments had a responsibility to lead by example, to teach people ethics and to eliminate poverty by providing opportunities for the people to become prosperous. He was clearly opposed to all forms of war, and taught that violence can never create security. In keeping with these teachings, Buddhism is rare among world religions in that its followers never attempted to spread their beliefs through the use of force. Unique among victorious leaders, the Buddhist emperor Asoka in the third century BCE renounced violence and war, and put Buddhist ethical virtues at the center of his government.

Regarding the Buddhist path as a philosophy, one may consider its epistemology: certain claims of knowledge have been made, but how can they be known to be true? As stated above, the Buddha himself never asked anyone to accept unproven claims on faith, and in fact discouraged them from doing so. He maintained that his teachings could be verified by direct insight and reasoning, by anyone willing to consider them and to follow the necessary path of self-discipline. Starting from a few basic assumptions, such as impermanence and dependent origination, he derived a complex and consistent system of philosophy which has stood for centuries. Later teachers have validated his claim that others could reach the same insights, and they have expanded upon his basic teachings with impressive intuitive depth and intellectual rigor.

In this way the Buddhist teaching has itself become a kind of interactive and self-evolving process, much like its idea of pratityasamutpada. However, the end goal is still Nirvana, which is an experience ultimately beyond all concepts and language, even beyond the Buddhist teachings. In the end even the attachment to the Dharma, the Buddhist teaching, must be dropped like all other attachments. The tradition compares the teaching to a raft upon which one crosses a swift river to get to the other side; once one is on the far shore, there is no longer any need to carry the raft. The far shore is Nirvana, and it is also said that when one arrives, one can see quite clearly that there was never any river at all.

BUDDHISM IN SOUTHEAST ASIA

Charles F. Keyes describes mainland Southeast Asia (Burma, Thailand, Laos, Cambodia, and Vietnam) as the "crossroad of religions" whereby "a large diversity of autochthonous tribal religions are intermingled with Hinduism, Theravada and

Mahayana Buddhism, Taoism, Confucianism, Islam, and Christianity, as well as the modern secular faith of Marxist-Leninism". The complex blending of early primitive religious practices and those influenced by China over several centuries were reshaped by political change in the twentieth century. Because of the Han conquest between 124 B.C.E. and 43 C.E., Vietnam looked to China for religious guidance with the influx of Confucianism, Daoism, and Buddhism. This influence remained long after Vietnam's independence from China in the eleventh century. Vietnam, Cambodia, and Thailand were shaped by Indian Hinduism and Buddhism up to the fifteenth century. Traditional tribal societies that relied on archaic rituals and Sino-Indian religions were slowly changed by Christian missionaries. As new agricultural systems emerged, adherence to folk culture began to wane.

According to James J. Fox, island cultures of Southeast Asia (Malaysia, the Philippines, and Java) were similarly influenced by Chinese and Indian traditions alongside Islam. In the late twentieth century, about 90 percent of Indonesia's population was Muslim, while the Philippines still were predominantly Catholic. Even in the early 2000s, the eclectic blend of religions focuses on a type of animism with the predominance of life force in every creature. In collectively describing the spirit of Southeast Asia, Fox writes:

Equally, the same spiritual premises may promote notions of achievement. A recurrent image of life involves the metaphor of the "journey of achievement." Myths recount the founding journeys of the ancestors, folk tales extol the attainments of heroic journeys, and dreams and séances can take the form of a spiritual journey. Furthermore, many societies encourage a period of journeying in early adulthood as a means of gaining knowledge, wealth, fame, and experience.

In the twentieth century, various religious movements emerged in the island cultures of Southeast Asia to address the effects of globalization on ancient cultures. James J. Peacock categorizes these movements into three groups: Hindu-Buddhism, Muslim, and Christian movements. For example, Budi Utomo (high endeavor) in Java and Bali sought to reestablish religious beliefs against a growing Western technology and value system that replaced traditional beliefs of Javanist-Hindu-Buddhists. As Peacock relates: "Looking to India's Rabindranath Tagore and Mohandas Gandhi as inspirations in the revival of these traditions, Budi Utomo was controlled by the aristocracy and intelligentsia and never gained a broad popular following, although it had amassed some ten thousand members within a year of its founding". Much more widespread, the Muslim movements ranged from Indonesia to Singapore, Malaysia, and the Philippines.

Because of the completion of the Suez Canal in 1870, many Asian Muslims were able to travel easily to Mecca in the Middle East. The reciprocal influence of modern interpretations of Islam led to the founding of the Kaum Muda (new faction). With emphasis on textual exegesis, this movement spread from Singapore to Indonesia. With this entrenchment, Christianity gained a strong foothold in the Philippines. Summarizing the complex political interconnections of religious groups, Peacock writes of the early 2000s: "In Indonesia, the Muslims have generally acted as an oppositional force complementing the government, while the Hindu-Buddhist streams have either fed into the Javanist-oriented national culture and government or provided personal fulfillment outside the governmental arena".

The ancient indigenous religion of both mainland and island SE Asia is Animism. Its exact temporal beginnings are unknown and probably simply developed naturally with the development of the early Bronze Age communities. It continues to exert a strong influence on the modern cultures both Buddhist and Islamic of SE Asia. Together with aspects of Confucianism from China, Animism underpins all the adopted religions of the region. It may go back as early as the earliest known human communities such as that of Ban Chiang in North East Thailand which is thought to date from 3,000 BC. Buddhism and Hinduism, according to the archaeological finds of the Malayan peninsula, Indonesia and the southern delta regions of Thailand, Burma, Cambodia, made their appearance about the first to third centuries of the Christian millennium. They seem to have come with Indian traders and missionaries from Indian and Ceylon. Knowledge of their philosophies, art work, and administrative approaches accompanied the rise of the first commercial states in these regions such as Funan, Chen-la, Sating Pra, Nakhon Sri Thammarat, Takua Pa. Whilst Hinduism took root most strongly in Cambodia from eight to thirteenth centuries and in Indonesia in about the same time frame, it remained a superficial influence in Thailand, Burma, Laos where Buddhism took hold most strongly.

In Indonesia, Hinduism saw the rise of the great empires of Sri Vijaya, Malayu, Mataram, and Majapahit. In Cambodia, it was the basis of the ancient Angkorian civilisation. However, archaeological finds in Thailand and southern Burma show that Theravada Buddhism was most dominant in the ancient kingdom of Dvaravati up to about the eleventh century when it was overtaken by the Khmer and the Thai. Theravada Buddhism however conquered its conquerors and spread throughout Pagan Burma (11th century), the first great classical Thai kingdom at Sukhothai (13th-14th centuries) and post Angkor Cambodia as well as Laos.

In the early centuries of the Common Era, the people in various parts of Southeast Asia came to know of Buddhism as a result of increased contact with the Indian merchants who had come to the region to trade. These merchants not only established trading stations in Southeast Asia, but also brought their religions and cultures with them. Under their influence, the local people began to practice a mixture of Buddhism and Hinduism, while retaining at the same time many of their old beliefs and customs.

The first clear evidence of the spread of Buddhism outside India dates from the reign of King Asoka (3rd century BCE), whose inscriptions show that he sent Buddhist missionaries too many different regions of the subcontinent as well as into certain border areas. Asokan emissaries were sent to Sri Lanka and to an area called Suvarnabhumi, which many modern scholars have identified with the Mon country in southern Myanmar (Burma) and central Thailand.

According to Sinhalese tradition, Buddhism took root in Sri Lanka soon after the arrival of Asoka's son, the monk Mahinda and six companions. These monks converted King Devanampiya Tissa and much of the nobility. King Tissa built the Mahavihara monastery, which became the main centre of the version of Theravada Buddhism that was ultimately dominant in Sri Lanka. After Tissa's death (*c.* 207 BCE), Sri Lanka was ruled by kings from South India until the time of Dutthagamani (101–77 BCE), a descendant of Tissa, who overthrew King Elara. Dutthagamani's association with Buddhism clearly strengthened the religion's ties with Sri Lankan political institutions.

During the 1st millennium CE, the Theravada tradition in Sri Lanka coexisted with various forms of Hinduism, Mahayana Buddhism, and Esoteric Buddhism. As Buddhism declined in India, it underwent a major revival and reform in Sri Lanka, where the Theravada traditions of the Mahavihara became especially prominent. Sri Lanka became a Theravada kingdom with a *Sangha* that was unified under Mahavihara leadership and ruled by a monarch who legitimated his rule in Theravada terms. This newly constituted Theravada tradition subsequently spread from Sri Lanka into Southeast Asia, where it exerted a powerful influence.

The peoples of Southeast Asia have not been mere satellites of the more powerful Indian and Chinese civilizations. On the contrary, the cultures that arose in these three vast areas might better be thought of as alternative developments that occurred within a greater Austro-Asiatic civilization, sometimes called the Asia of the monsoons. The transmission of Buddhism and Hinduism to Southeast Asia can thus be regarded as the spread of the religious symbols of the more advanced Austro-Asiatic peoples to other Austro-Asiatic groups sharing some of the same basic religious presuppositions and traditions.

In Southeast Asia the impact of Buddhism was felt in very different ways in three separate regions. In two of these (the region of Malaysia/Indonesia and the region on the mainland extending from Myanmar to southern Vietnam), the main connections have been with India and Sri Lanka via trade routes. In Vietnam, the third region, the main connections have been with China.

BUDDHISM IN BURMA

As early as the time of King Ashoka of India, monks were sent to Thaton to spread the Buddha's teachings. Thaton was a trading centre of southern Burma. However, from the first century C.E. onwards, trade between India and Burma expanded and there was increased contact with the Indian traders and their religious beliefs. Buddhism was widely accepted by the people in Thaton as more Buddhist missionaries arrived from Indian Buddhist centres. Thaton soon became an important centre for Theravada Buddhism.

In later centuries, Vajrayana Buddhism was introduced to the people in northern Burma. They practiced it together with Hinduism and local folk beliefs. In the middle of the eleventh century, a powerful king, Anawratha, brought northern and southern Burma under his rule. As he was a strong supporter of Theravada Buddhism he made it the national religion. He had Buddhist texts and relics brought from Sri Lanka. He also began the construction of monasteries and stupas in the capital city of Pagan, and this was continued by his successors. Pagan soon developed into a centre of Buddhist culture.

In the succeeding centuries, Burma underwent several periods of wars and political unrest, but Buddhism continued to prosper under the patronage of various kings and became part of the life of the common people. In every village, schools were set up in the monasteries. Here monks taught the children basic Buddhist teachings as well as reading and writing. The traditional structure of the Buddhist community suffered when Burma came under British colonial rule in the nineteenth century. However, Buddhism has regained its traditional place of importance in the life of the Burmese people since Burma became independent in the middle of the twentieth century.

BUDDHISM IN THAILAND

Before the thirteenth century, the region now called Thailand was composed of many small independent kingdoms. Buddhist influence had already been felt in this region as a result of contact with neighbouring countries. At the end of the thirteenth century, Theravada Buddhism gained the support of the Thai king, Ramkham-haeng. He invited Buddhist monks to teach in his capital city of Sukothai. He also established relations with Sri Lanka by sending monks there to study. Furthermore, he began the tradition of appointing a Sangha chief to oversee the administration of the monastic community. Under his patronage, all the people in his kingdom were said to have become Buddhists.

About half a century later, there was another devout and learned king called Luthai who was a strong supporter of Buddhism. He joined the Order for a period of time and is said to have initiated the Thai tradition of Buddhists becoming monks for a limited period of time, usually about three months.

In spite of the wars in the centuries following, Buddhism continued to grow in importance and enjoyed uninterrupted state support. The Thai Order is as influential today as it was in the past. However, some reforms have been introduced since the turn of the present century. There is greater emphasis on Buddhist education and the monks are actively involved not only in teaching the religion, but also in providing secular education for the lay people. Many monks still teach in the primary and secondary schools that have been set up in the Buddhist monasteries throughout the country. Many others also pursue higher studies at Buddhist colleges and universities. Over the past few decades, some monks have been sent overseas to spread the teachings of the Buddha.

BUDDHISM IN CAMBODIA

By the end of the fourth century, Indian influence had spread throughout the kingdom of the Cambodians. In the following two centuries, the rulers practiced Hinduism but gave some support to the Buddhist communities, which practiced mainly Mahayana Buddhism.

The Buddhist monks of the region were learned, and in the fifth century some were said to have been invited to China to translate Buddhist texts from Indian languages to Chinese. In the seventh century, Cambodia had a succession of rulers who patronized Hinduism and suppressed Buddhism. It was not until the ninth century that Buddhism began to receive some royal patronage from the rulers.

King Jayavarman VII, who ruled from the end of the twelfth century to the early years of the thirteenth century, was a devout Buddhist. Under him Mahayana Buddhism became for a time the dominant religion of the kingdom. He built the new city of Angkor (called Angkor Thom), in the centre of which was a temple called the Bayon. At the centre of the temple was a huge tower with four human faces carved on it. Surrounding the central tower were other smaller towers also carved with human faces. These faces portray the king as the "Buddha-king".

It was also during the reign of Jayavarman VII that Burmese monks began to teach Theravada Buddhism among the common people. The Thais who invaded Cambodia in the fourteenth century also contributed to the spread of Theravada Buddhism. By the middle of the century, Theravada Buddhism had become widely accepted by the Cambodian people.

In the centuries that followed, Buddhism continued to be practiced by the people of Cambodia. Even when the country came under French colonial rule in the mid-nineteenth century, Buddhism was still being patronized by the kings, though on a reduced scale. After Cambodia had gained independence, some progress was made in Buddhist education and the publication of texts. At present, however, owing to political unrest, the future of Buddhism in Cambodia is uncertain.

BUDDHISM IN LAOS

There lived in the middle of the fourteenth century, Fa Ngoun, a descendant of a royal family of Laos. He spent his earlier years in exile in Cambodia with his father. Fa Ngoun was looked after by a Cambodian monk who later took him to the court of the Cambodian king. There he married a princess who was a devout Buddhist. With the help of the king of Cambodia, he later returned to Laos to rule over it. At his wife's request, Fa Ngoun invited Buddhist monks from Cambodia to teach in his kingdom. Thus Buddhism was brought to the people in Laos.

In a later period, the Thai Buddhist tradition also influenced Buddhism in Laos. The structure of the Sangha in Laos followed closely that of Thailand. Many monks were also said to have gone to Thailand to study.

BUDDHISM IN VIETNAM

In the early centuries, there were a number of small states in the territory of present Vietnam. Buddhism from China influenced the northern state, being for several centuries under the domination of the Chinese empire. The earliest monks were said to have come from China at the end of the second century CE Later, monks from India and Central Asia also arrived by land and sea. The people who also worshipped the native deities practiced the Pure Land school of Buddhism. The Chan school of Buddhism, on the other hand, flourished in the monasteries and among Buddhist scholars. Both the rulers and the common people for their literacy respected its monks. Some of them became famous scholars, poets, writers and even royal advisors.

The southern states were exposed to Indian influence from the beginning of the Common Era. Both Mahayana Buddhism and Hinduism were practiced then. From the fifteenth century onwards, these southern states were gradually assimilated by the powerful northern state, and as a result the Chinese form of Buddhism also came to influence the south. Finally when Vietnam became unified as a nation, it was the Chinese form of Buddhism that was commonly practiced.

At the beginning of the present century, Buddhism in Vietnam underwent some modernization. Buddhist national organizations were set up and education was emphasized. However, this process was hindered by a continuous period of wars, and came to a virtual stop when the country came under Communist rule.

BUDDHISM IN INDONESIA AND THE MALAY PENINSULA

It is said that late in the fifth century, a Buddhist monk from India landed in a kingdom in central Java and converted its queen to Buddhism. She in turn converted her son and made Mahayana Buddhism the official religion of the kingdom.

At the end of the seventh century, Yi-jing, a Buddhist pilgrim from China, visited Sumatra, which was part of the Srivijaya kingdom. He found that Buddhism was widely accepted by the people and Palembang, the capital of Srivijaya, was an important centre for Buddhist learning. Yi-jing studied there for some time before continuing on his journey to India.

In the middle of the eighth century, central Java was under the rule of the Sailendra kings who were Buddhists. They built various Buddhist monuments in Java, the most famous of which is the Borobudur. This monument was completed in the early part of the ninth century. It consists of a series of six square terraces above which are three circular platforms. Right at the top is a central stupa. The walls of the monument are carved with reliefs depicting scenes from the Buddha's life, the stories of His past lives and Mahayana Buddhist sutras. It is said that the ascent of the Borobudur symbolizes man's progress out of Samsara to Nirvana.

In the middle of the ninth century, a Sailendra prince became king of Srivijaya. Under the Sailendra kings, Srivijaya grew in wealth and power. By that time, the kingdom already included Sumatra, Java and the Malay Peninsula. During this period of prosperity, which lasted till the end of the twelfth century, Vajrayana Buddhism gained wide acceptance alongside Hindu practices, throughout the empire.

Chapter - 3

Buddhism in Myanmar

Myanmar, or Burma as the nation has been known throughout history, is one of the major countries following Theravada Buddhism. In recent years Myanmar has attained special eminence as the host for the Sixth Buddhist Council, held in Yangon (Rangoon) between 1954 and 1956, and as the source from which two of the major systems of Vipassana meditation have emanated out into the greater world: the tradition springing from the Venerable Mahasi Sayadaw of Thathana Yeiktha and that springing from Sayagyi U Ba Khin of the International Meditation Centre.

EARLIEST CONTACTS WITH BUDDHISM

MYANMAR AND ITS PEOPLES

There are four dominant ethnic groups in the recorded history of Myanmar: the Mon, the Pyu, the Myanmar, and the Shan. Uncertainty surrounds the origins of the Mon; but it is clear that, at least linguistically, they are related to the Khmer. What is known is that they settled in the south of Myanmar and Thailand while the Khmer made northern Thailand, Laos, and Cambodia their home. These two peoples were probably the first migrants to the region, apart from Indian merchants who established trading colonies along the coast. The Mon with their distinct language and culture competed for centuries with the Myanmar. However, today their influence and language is limited to remote areas of the south.

The Pyu, like the Myanmar, are a people of Tibeto-Burman origin with a distinct culture and language. They lived in the area around Prome long before the Myanmar pushed into the plains of Myanmar from the north. Their language was closely related to the language of the Myanmar and was later absorbed by it. Their script was in use until about the fourteenth century, but was then lost.

The Myanmar people began to colonise the plains of Myanmar only towards the middle of the first millennium AD. They came from the mountainous northern regions and may well have originated in the Central Asian plains.

After the Myanmar, the Shan flooded in from the North, finally conquering the entire region of Myanmar and Thailand. The Thai people are descended from Shan tribes. The northeast region of modern Myanmar is still inhabited predominantly by Shan tribes.

THE REGION

In the sixth century BC, most of what we now know as Myanmar, Thailand, Laos, and Cambodia was sparsely populated. While migrants from the east coast of India had formed trading colonies along the coast of the Gulf of Martaban, these coastal areas of Myanmar and Thailand were also home to the Mon. By this time, the Khmer probably controlled Laos, Cambodia, and northern Thailand, while Upper Myanmar may already have been occupied to some extent by Myanmar tribes.

As these early settlers did not use lasting materials for construction, our knowledge of their civilization remains scant. We do know, however, that their way of life was very simple — as it remains today in rural areas — probably requiring only wooden huts with palm-leaf roofs for habitation. We can assume that they were not organised into units larger than village communities and that they did not possess a written language. Their religion must have been some form of nature worship or animism, still found today among the more remote tribes of the region.

There were also more highly developed communities of Indian origin, in the form of trading settlements located along the entire coast from Bengal to Borneo. In Myanmar, they were located in Thaton (Suddhammapura), Pegu (Ussa), Yangon (Ukkala, then still on the coast), and Mrauk-U (Dhannavati) in Arakan; also probably along the Tenasserim and Arakan coasts. These settlers had mainly migrated from Orissa on the northeastern coast of the Indian subcontinent, and also from the Deccan in the southeast. In migrating to these areas, they had also brought their own culture and religion with them. Initially, the contact between the Hindu traders and the Mon peasants must have been limited. However, the Indian settlements, their culture and traditions, were eventually absorbed into the Mon culture.

G.E. Harvey, in his *History of Burma,* relates a Mon legend which refers to the Mon fighting Hindu strangers who had come back to re-conquer the country that had formerly belonged to them. This Mon tale confirms the theory that Indian people had formed the first communities in the region but that these were eventually replaced by the Mon with the development of their own civilization. As well as the Indian trading settlements, there were also some Pyu settlements, particularly in the area of Prome where a flourishing civilization later developed.

Also, it is assumed that some degree of migration from India to the region of Tagaung and Mogok in Upper Myanmar had taken place through Assam and later through Manipur, but the "hinterland" was of course much less attractive to traders than the coastal regions with their easy access by sea. A tradition of Myanmar says that Tagaung was founded by Abhiraja, a prince of the Sakyans (the tribe of the Buddha), who had migrated to Upper Myanmar from Nepal in the ninth century BC. The city was subsequently conquered by the Chinese in approximately 600 BC, and Pagan and Prome were founded by refugees fleeing southward. In fact, some historians believe that, like the Myanmar, the Sakyans were a Mongolian rather than an Indo-Aryan race, and that the Buddha's clansmen were derived from Mongolian stock.

FIRST CONTACTS WITH THE BUDDHA'S TEACHINGS

The source of information for many of the events related forthwith is the *Sasanavamsa*. The *Sasanavamsa* is a chronicle written in Pali by a bhikkhu, Pannasami, for the Fifth Buddhist Council held in Mandalay in 1867. As the *Sasanavamsa* is a recent compilation, many events mentioned therein may be doubted. However, as it draws on both written records, some of which are no longer available, and on the oral tradition of Myanmar, information can be included in this account with the understanding that it is open to verification.

There are many instances in the history of Southeast Asian tribes in which a conquering people incorporates into its own traditions not only the civilization of the conquered, but also their clan gods, royal lineage, and thereby their history. This fact would explain the visits of the Buddha to Thaton and Shwesettaw in the Mon and Myanmar oral tradition, and the belief of the Arakanese that the Buddha visited their king and left behind an image of himself for them to worship. Modern historiography will, of course, dismiss these stories as fabrications made out of national pride, as the Myanmar had not even arrived in the region at the time of the Buddha. However, it is possible that the Myanmar and Arakanese integrated into their own lore the oral historical tradition of their Indian predecessors. This does not prove that the visits really took place, but it seems a more palatable explanation of the existence of these accounts than simply putting them down to historical afterthought of a Buddhist people eager to connect itself with the origins of their religion.

The *Sasanavamsa* mentions several visits of the Buddha to Myanmar and one other important event: the arrival of the hair relics in Ukkala (Yangon) soon after the Buddha's enlightenment.

THE ARRIVAL OF THE HAIR RELICS

Tapussa and Bhallika, two merchants from Ukkala, were traveling through the region of Uruvela and were directed to the Buddha by their family god. The Buddha had just come out of seven weeks of meditation after his awakening and was sitting under a tree feeling the need for food. Tapussa and Bhallika made an offering of rice cake and honey to the Buddha and took the two refuges, the refuge in the Buddha and the refuge in the Dhamma (the Sangha, the third refuge, did not exist yet). As they were about to depart, they asked the Buddha for an object to worship in his stead and he gave them eight hairs from his head. After the two returned from their journey, they enshrined the three hairs in a stupa which is now the great Shwedagon Pagoda in Yangon.

It is believed in Myanmar that the hill upon which the Shwedagon Pagoda stands was not haphazardly chosen by Tapussa and Bhallika but was, in fact, the site where the three Buddhas preceding the Buddha Gotama in this world cycle themselves deposited relics. Buddha Kakusandha is said to have left his staff on the Theinguttara Hill, the Buddha Konagamana his water filter, and Buddha Kassapa a part of his robe. Because of this, the Buddha requested Tapussa and Bhallika to enshrine his relics in this location. Tapussa and Bhallika traveled far and wide in order to find the hill on which they could balance a tree without its touching the ground either with the roots or with the crown. Eventually, they found the exact spot not far from their home in Lower Myanmar where they enshrined the holy relics in a traditional mound or stupa. The original stupa is said to have been 27 feet high. Today the Shwedagon pagoda has grown to over 370 feet.

THE BUDDHA'S VISITS TO THE REGION

The Myanmar oral tradition speaks of four visits of the Buddha to the region. While these visits were of utmost significance in their own right, they are also important in having established places of pilgrimage up to the present day.

The Visit to Central Myanmar

According to the *Sasanavamsa*, the city of Aparanta is situated on the western shore of the Irrawaddy river at the latitude of Magwe. The *Sasanavamsa* gives only a very brief summary of the events surrounding the Buddha's visit to Aparanta, presumably because these were well known and could be read in the Tipitaka and the commentaries.

Punna, a merchant from Sunaparanta, went to Savatthi on business and there heard a discourse of the Buddha. Having won faith in the Buddha and the Teachings, he took ordination as a bhikkhu. After sometime, he asked the Buddha to teach him a short lesson so that he could return to Sunaparanta and strive for arahatship. The Buddha warned him that the people of Sunaparanta were fierce and violent, but Punna replied that he would not allow anger to arise, even if they should kill him. In the Punnovada Sutta, the Buddha instructed him not to be enticed by that which is pleasant, and Punna returned and attained arahatship in his country. He won over many disciples and built a monastery of red sandalwood for the Buddha (according to some chronicles of Myanmar, the Buddha made the prediction that at the location where the red sandalwood monastery was, the great king Alaungsithu of Pagan would build a shrine). He then sent flowers as an invitation to the Buddha and the Buddha came accompanied by five hundred arahats, spent the night in the monastery, and left again before dawn.

Sakka, the king of the thirty-three devas living in the Tavatimsa plane, provided five hundred palanquins for the bhikkhus accompanying the Buddha on the journey to Sunaparanta. But only 499 of the palanquins were occupied. One of them remained empty until the ascetic Saccabandha, who lived on the Saccabandha mountain in central Myanmar, joined the Buddha and the 499 bhikkhus accompanying him. On the way to Sunaparanta, the Buddha stopped in order to teach the ascetic Saccabandha. When Saccabanda attained arahatship, he then joined the Buddha and completed the total of 500 bhikkhus who usually traveled with the Master.

On the return journey, the Buddha stopped at the river Nammada close to the Saccabandha mountain. Here, the Blessed One was invited by the Naga king, Nammada, to visit and preach to the Nagas, later accepting food from them. The tradition of Myanmar relates that he left behind a footprint for veneration near this river, which would last as long as the Sasana (i.e. 5000 years). Another footprint was left in the rock of the Saccabandha mountain. These footprints, still visible today, were worshipped by the Mon, Pyu, and Myanmar kings alike and have remained among the holiest places of pilgrimage in Myanmar. In the fifteenth century, after the decimation of the population through the Siamese campaigns, knowledge of the footprints was lost. Then, in the year 1638, King Thalun sent learned bhikkhus to the region; fortuitously, they were able to relocate the Buddha's footprints. Since then Shwesettaw, the place where the footprints are found, has once again become an important place of pilgrimage in Myanmar. And in the dry season thousands of devout Buddhists travel there to pay respects.

The Visit to Arakan

In Dhannavati, whose walls are still partially visible today, the Mahamuni temple is located on the Sirigutta hill. In this temple, for over two millennia, the Mahamuni image was enshrined and worshipped. The story of the Mahamuni image, at one time one of the most revered shrines of Buddhism, is told in the *Sappadanapakarana*, a work of a local historian.

Candrasuriya, the king of Dhannavati, on hearing that a Buddha had arisen in India, desired to go there to learn the Dhamma. The Buddha, aware of his intention, said to Ananda: "The king will have to pass through forests dangerous to travelers; wide rivers will impede his journey; he must cross a sea full of monsters. It will be an act of charity if we go to his dominion, so that he may pay homage without risking his life."

So the Buddha went there and was received with great pomp by King Candrasuriya and his people. The Buddha then taught the five and eight precepts and instructed the king in the ten kingly duties, namely, (1) universal beneficence, (2) daily paying homage, (3) the showing of mercy, (4) taxes of not more than a tenth part of the produce, (5) justice, (6) punishment without anger, (7) the support of his subjects as the earth supports them, (8) the employment of prudent commanders, (9) the taking of good counsel, and (10) the avoidance of pride. The Buddha remained for a week and on preparing for his departure the king requested that he leave an image of himself, so that they could worship him even in his absence. The Buddha consented to this and Sakka the king of the gods himself formed the image with the metals collected by the king and his people. It was completed in one week and when the Buddha breathed onto it the people exclaimed that now there were indeed two Buddhas, so alike was the image to the great sage. Then the Buddha made a prophesy addressing the image: "I shall pass into Nibbana in my eightieth year, but you will live for five thousand years which I have foreseen as the duration of my Teaching."

The Mahamuni image remained in its original location until 1784 when King Bodawpaya conquered Arakan and had the image transported to Mandalay where a special shrine, the Arakan pagoda, was built to enshrine the three-meter image. To have this image in his capital greatly added to his prestige as a Buddhist king, as it was one of the most sacred objects in the region. The king himself went out of his city to meet the approaching image with great devotion and "through the long colonnades leading to the pagoda, there used to come daily from the Myanmar palace, so long as a king reigned there, sumptuous offerings borne in stately procession, marshalled by a minister and shaded by the white umbrella."

THE MISSIONARIES OF THE THIRD BUDDHIST COUNCIL

The Third Buddhist Council was held in the reign of Emperor Asoka in the year 232 BC in order to purify the Sangha, to reassert orthodox teaching and to refute heresy. But the work of the Council did not stop there. With the support of Emperor Asoka, experienced teachers were sent to border regions in order to spread the teachings of the Buddha. This dispersal of missionaries is recorded in the *Mahavamsa*, a Sinhalese chronicle on the history of Buddhism.

When the thera Moggaliputta, the illuminator of the religion of the Conqueror, had brought the (third) council to an end and when, looking into the future, he had beheld the founding of the religion in adjacent countries, then in the month of Katthika he sent forth theras, one here and one there. The thera Majjhantika he sent to Kasmira and Gandhara, the thera Mahadeva he sent to Mahisamandala. To Vanavasa he sent the thera named Rakkhita, and to Aparantaka the Yona named Dhammarakkhita; to Maharattha he sent the thera named Mahadhammarakkhita, but the thera Maharakkhita he sent into the country of the Yona. He sent the thera Majjhima to the Himalaya country and together with the thera Uttara, the thera Sona of wondrous might went to Suvannabhumi.

According to the *Sasanavamsa*, the above mentioned regions are the following: Kasmira and Gandhara is the right bank of the Indus river south of Kabul; Mahisamandala is Andhra; Vanavasa is the region around Prome; Aparantaka is west of the upper Irrawaddy; Maharattha is Thailand; Yona, the country of the Shan tribes; and Suvannabhumi is Thaton. The *Sasanavamsa* mentions five places in Southeast Asia where Asoka's missionaries taught the Buddha's doctrine, and through their teaching many gained insight and took refuge in the Triple Gem. There are two interesting features mentioned in the text. First, in order to ordain nuns, bhikkhunis, other bhikkhunis had to be present, and secondly, the Brahmajala Sutta was preached in Thaton.

The *Sasanavamsa* goes on to describe sixty thousand women ordaining in Aparanta. It states that women could not have been ordained without the presence of bhikkhunis, as in Sri Lanka where women could only be ordained after Mahinda's sister Sanghamitta had followed her brother there. In this case, the author surmises that bhikkhunis must have followed Dhammarakkhita to Aparanta at a later stage.

The Brahmajala Sutta, which the arahats Sona and Uttara preached in Thaton, deals in detail with the different schools of philosophical and religious thought prevalent in India at the time of the Buddha. The fact that Sona and Uttara chose this Sutta to convert the inhabitants of Suvannabhumi indicates that they were facing a well-informed public, familiar with the views of Brahmanism that were refuted by the Buddha in this discourse. There can be no doubt that only Indian colonisers, not the Mon, would have been able to follow an analysis of Indian philosophy as profound as the Brahmajala Sutta.

BUDDHISM IN THE MON AND PYU KINGDOMS

While there is no conclusive archaeological proof that Buddhism continued to be practiced in southern Myanmar after the missions of the Third Council, the *Sasanavamsa* refers to an unbroken lineage of teachers passing on the Dhamma to their disciples.

THE MON

In a third century AD inscription by a South Indian king in Nagarjunakonda, the land of the Cilatas is mentioned in a list of countries visited by a group of bhikkhus. Historians believe the Cilatas or Kiratas (also mentioned by Ptolemy and in Sanskrit literature) to be identical to the Mon populations of Lower Myanmar.

The inscription states that the bhikkhus sent to the Cilata country converted the population there to Buddhism. In the same inscription, missions to other countries such as Sri Lanka are mentioned. It is generally believed that most of these countries had received earlier Buddhist missionaries sent by Buddhist kings, but as civilization in these lands was relatively undeveloped, teachings as profound as the Buddha's had probably become distorted by local religions or possibly been completely lost. It is possible that these missions did not so much re-establish Buddhism, but rather purify the type of Buddhism practiced there. Southern India was then the guardian of the Theravada faith and obviously remained in contact with countries that had been converted in earlier times but were unable to preserve the purity of the religion.

As has been already mentioned, the first datable archaeological finds of the Mon civilization stem from the Mon kingdom of Dvaravati in the South of Thailand. They consist of a Roman oil lamp and a bronze statue of the Buddha which are believed to be no later than the first or second century AD. In discussing the Mon Theravada Buddhist civilization, we cannot remain in Myanmar only. For only by studying the entire sphere of influence of the Mon in this period, can a comprehensive picture be constructed. This sphere includes large parts of present day Thailand. In fact, the Chinese Buddhist pilgrim, Yuan Chwang, who traveled to India in about 630 AD, describes a single Mon country stretching from Prome to Chenla in the east and including the Irrawaddy and Sittang deltas. He calls the country Dvaravati, but the annals of the court of China of the same period mention Dvaravati as a vassal of Thaton. We can, therefore, safely conclude that the Mon of the region formed a fairly homogenous group in which the distribution of power was obviously not always evident to the outsider.

THE PYU

Lower Myanmar was also inhabited by another ethnic group, the Pyu, who were probably closely related to the modern Myanmar. They had their capital at Sri Ksetra (near modern day Prome) and were also followers of the Theravada Buddhist faith. Chinese travelers' reports of the mid-third century AD refer to the kingdom of Lin-Yang where Buddha was venerated by all and where several thousand monks or bhikkhus lived. As Lin-Yang was to the west of Kamboja and could not be reached by sea, we can infer that the Chinese travelers must have been referring to the ancient kingdom of Prome. This is all the more likely as archaeological finds prove that only about one century later Pali Buddhist texts, including Abhidhamma texts, were studied by the Pyu.

The earliest highly developed urban settlement of the Pyu was Beikthano, near Prome. However, its importance dwindled towards the sixth century, when Sri Ksetra became the center of Pyu civilization. A major monastery built in the fourth century has been unearthed at Beikthano. The building, constructed in brick, with a stupa and shrine located nearby, is identical to the Buddhist monasteries of Nagarjunakonda, the great Buddhist center of southern India. It is situated near a stupa and a shrine, a design which is identical to the one used in South India. Bricks had been used by the Pyus since the second century AD for the construction of pillared halls, which formed the temples of their original religion. Interestingly, the Pyu bricks have always been of the exact dimensions as those used at the time of Emperor Asoka in India. But the brick laying techniques used in the monastery in Beikthano were far inferior to the ones used in their southern Indian counterparts.

For such a major edifice as the monastery at Beikthano to have been constructed, the religion must have been well established at least among the ruling class. How long it took for Buddhism to become influential in Pyu society is difficult to determine, but some historians assume that the first contacts with Asokan religious centers in India took place in the second century AD. This would allow for a period of development of two hundred years until the first important shrine was built. Despite the Indian architectural influence, the inferior brick laying techniques found in Beikthano indicate that indigenous architects and artisans, rather than imported craftsmen or Indian colonisers, were employed in the construction of monasteries and other important buildings.

It should, of course, not be forgotten that the Pyu possessed an architecture of their own and a highly developed urban culture that had evolved quite independently of Indian influences. Theravada Buddhism found a fertile ground in this highly developed civilization. It is probable that the Pyu civilization was more advanced than that of the Mon. The Pyu sites found around Prome are the earliest urban sites in Southeast Asia found to date. The urban developments and datable monuments in Thailand and Cambodia are only from the seventh century. Older artifacts may have been found in Thailand, but they were not products of indigenous people and do not prove the existence of a developed civilization.

The information we have of the state of the religion in the Mon and Pyu societies during the first four centuries AD is very limited. However, by the fifth century, with the development of religious activity in the region, information becomes more substantive. The historical tradition of Myanmar gives the credit for this religious resurgence to a well-known Buddhist scholar, Acariya Buddhaghosa.

BUDDHAGHOSA AND MYANMAR

Acariya Buddhaghosa was the greatest commentator on the Pali Buddhist texts, whose *Visuddhimagga* and commentaries to the canon are regarded as authoritative by Theravada scholars. The chronicles of Myanmar firmly maintain that Buddhaghosa was of Mon origin and a native of Thaton. They state that his return from Sri Lanka, with the Pali scriptures, the commentaries, and grammatical works, gave a fresh impetus to the religion.

However, modern historians do not accept that Buddhaghosa was from Myanmar while some even doubt his existence. Despite this contention, Eliot, in his *Hinduism and Buddhism,* gives more weight to circumstantial evidence and writes:

> The Burmese tradition that Buddhaghosa was a native of Thaton and returned thither from Sri Lanka merits more attention than it has received. It can easily be explained away as patriotic fancy. On the other hand, if Buddhaghosa's object was to invigorate Hinayanism in India the result of his really stupendous labors was singularly small, for in India his name is connected with no religious movement. But if we suppose that he went to Sri Lanka by way of the holy places in Magadha [now Bihar] and returned from the Coromandal coast [Madras] to Burma where Hinayanism afterwards flourished, we have at least a coherent narrative.

The Sinhalese chronicles, especially the *Mahavamsa,* place Buddhaghosa in the first half of the fifth century. Although he spent most of his active working life in Sri Lanka, he is also credited with imbuing new life into Theravada Buddhism in South India, and developing such important centers as Kancipura and Uragapuram that were closely connected with Prome and Thaton. Proof of this connection can be found in archeological finds in the environs of Prome which include Pali literature inscribed in the Kadambe script on gold and stone plates. This script was used in the fifth and sixth century in southern India.

All in all, Myanmar has a valid case for claiming some connection with Buddhaghosa. It is, of course, impossible to prove that he was born there or even visited there, but his influence undoubtedly led to great religious activity in the kingdoms of Lower Myanmar.

BUDDHISM IN LOWER MYANMAR: 5TH TO 11TH CENTURIES

From the fifth century until the conquest of Lower Myanmar by Pagan, there is a continuous record of Buddhism flourishing in the Mon and Pyu kingdoms. The Mon kingdoms are mentioned in travel reports of several Chinese Buddhist pilgrims and also in the annals of the Chinese court. In the fifth century, Thaton and Pegu (Pago) are mentioned in the Buddhist commentarial literature for the first time. They were now firmly established on the map as Buddhist centers of learning. Despite this, Buddhism was not without rivals in the region. This is shown, by the following event some chronicles of Myanmar mention.

A king of Pago, Tissa by name, had abandoned the worship of the Buddha and instead practiced Brahmanical worship. He persecuted the Buddhists and destroyed Buddha images or cast them into ditches. A pious Buddhist girl, the daughter of a merchant, restored the images, then washed and worshipped them. The king could not tolerate such defiance, of course, and had the girl dragged before him. He tried to have her executed in several ways, but she seemed impossible to kill. Elephants would not trample her,while the fire of her pyre would not burn her. Eventually the king, intrigued by these events, asked the girl to perform a miracle. He stated that, if she was able to make a Buddha image produce seven new images and then make all eight statues fly into heaven, she would be set free. The girl spoke an act of truth, and the eight Buddha statues flew up into the sky. The king was then converted to Buddhism and elevated the girl to the position of chief queen.

Until now, archaeological finds of Mon ruins in Myanmar are meager, but at P'ong Tuk, in southern Thailand, a Mon city, dating from the second half of the first millennium AD, has been unearthed. Here, excavations have revealed the foundations of several buildings. One contained the remains of a platform and fragments of columns similar to the Buddhist vihara at Anuradhapura in Sri Lanka; another, with a square foundation of round stones, seems to have been a stupa. Statues of Indian origin from the Gupta period (320-600 AD) were also found at the site. The Theravada Buddhist culture of the Mon flourished in both Dvaravati and Thaton. However, the Mon civilization in Thailand did not survive the onslaught of the Khmer in the eleventh century who were worshipping Hindu gods. In Myanmar, the Mon kingdom was conquered by Pagan. The Myanmar were eager to accept the Mon culture and especially their religion, while the Khmer, as Hindus, at best tolerated it.

The Pyu culture of this period is well documented because of archaeological finds at Muanggan, a small village close to the ancient ruins of Hmawza. There two perfectly preserved inscribed gold plates were found. These inscriptions reveal three texts: the verses spoken by Assaji to Sariputta *(ye dhamma hetuppabhava...)*, a list of categories of the Abhidhamma *(cattaro iddhipada, cattaro samappadhana...)*, and the formula of worship of Buddha, Dhamma, and Sangha *(iti pi so bhagava...)*. At the same site, a book with twenty leaves of gold protected with golden covers, was discovered. It contained texts such as the *paticca-samuppada* (dependent origination), the *vipassana-nanas* (stages of insight knowledge), and various other excerpts from the Abhidhamma and the other two baskets of the Buddhist scriptures. The scripts in all these documents are identical to scripts used in parts of southern India, and can be dated from the third to the sixth century AD.

In addition to these golden plates, a number of sculptures and reliefs were found in Hmawza. They depict either the Buddha or scenes from his life, for example, the birth of the Buddha and the taming of the wild elephant Nalagiri. The sculpture is similar in style to that of Amaravati, a center of Buddhist learning in South India. There were also unearthed remains of Brahman temples and sites of Mahayana worship of east Indian origin; hence it would appear that several faiths, of which the Theravada was the strongest, co-existed in Sri Ksetra, the then capital of the Pyu. The script used by the Pyu is indicative of major links with Buddhist kingdoms in South India rather than with Sri Lanka. And it can be surmised that the bhikkhus of the Deccan and other regions of southern India were the teachers of both the Mon and the Pyu in religious matters as well as in the arts and sciences.

The inscriptions show how highly developed scholarship of the Pali Buddhist texts must have been in Lower Myanmar even in these early days. Learning had gone well beyond the basics into the world of Abhidhamma studies. Pali was obviously well known as a language of learning, but unfortunately no original texts composed in Sri Ksetra or Thaton have come down to us. Interestingly, some of the texts inscribed on these gold plates are not identical to the same canonical texts as they are known today. Therefore, the Tipitaka known to the Pyu must have been replaced by a version preserved in a country that had no close contact with the Pyu. This could well have been Sri Lanka, as this country came to play an important role in the history of Buddhism in Myanmar through the friendship between the conqueror of Lower Myanmar, Anawratha, and the king who drove the Hindus from Sri Lanka, Vijayabahu.

The finds on the site of the ancient Pyu capital confirm the reports of the Chinese pilgrims and also the Tang imperial chronicles of China which state: "They (the Pyu) dislike taking life. They know how to make astronomical calculations. They are Buddhists and have a hundred monasteries, with brick of glass embellished with gold and silver vermilion, gay colours and red kino... At seven years of age the people cut their hair and enter a monastery; if at the age of twenty they have not grasped the doctrine they return to the lay state."

Both Buddhist cultures in the south of Myanmar, the Mon and the Pyu, were swept away in the eleventh century by armies of the Myanmar who had found a unifying force in their leader, the founder of Pagan and champion of Buddhism, Anawratha.

THERAVADA BUDDHISM COMES TO PAGAN

THE BEGINNINGS OF PAGAN

Pagan is believed to have been founded in the years 849-850 AD, by the Myanmar, who had already established themselves as rice growers in the region around Kyauksai near Mandalay. Anawratha began to unite the region by subjugating one chieftain after another and was successful in giving the Myanmar a sense of belonging to a larger community, a nation. The crucial event in the history of Myanmar is not so much the founding of the city of Pagan and the building of its walls and moat, but more Pagan's acceptance of Theravada Buddhism in the eleventh century. The religion was brought to the Myanmar by a Mon bhikkhu named Shin Arahan.

The religion prevailing among the Myanmar before and during the early reign of Anawratha was some form of Mahayana Buddhism, which had probably found its way into the region from the Pala kingdom in Bengal. This is apparent from bronze statues depicting Bodhisattas and especially the "Lokanatha," a Bodhisatta believed, in Bengal, to reign in the period between the demise of the Buddha Gotama and the advent of the Buddha Metteyya. Anawratha continued to cast terracotta votive tablets with the image of Lokanatha even after he embraced the Theravada doctrine.

In India, Buddhism had split into numerous schools, some of which differed fundamentally from the teachings of Pali Buddhism, which is also called Theravada Buddhism (the doctrine of the Theras). The Ari, the monks or priests of this Mahayana Buddhist form of worship, are described, in later chronicles of Myanmar, as the most shameless bogus ascetics imaginable. They are said to have sold absolution from sin and to have oppressed the people in various ways with their tyranny. Their tantric Buddhism included, as an important element, the worship of Nagas (dragons), which was probably an ancient indigenous tradition.

At this time, the beginning of the eleventh century, the Buddhist religion among the Mon in Suvannabhumi was on the decline as people were disturbed by robbers and raiders, by plagues, and by adversaries of the religion. These most probably came from the Hindu Khmer kingdom in Cambodia and the north of Thailand. The Khmer were endeavoring to add Thaton and the other Mon kingdoms of the south to their expanding empire. Shin Arahan must have feared that bhikkhus would not be able to continue to maintain their religious practice and the study of the scriptures under these circumstances. He went, therefore, upcountry where a new, strong people were developing, prosperous and secure from enemies.

It is interesting to note that in this same period, Buddhism was under attack in other places as well. The Colas, a Hindu dynasty strongly opposed to Buddhism, arose in southern India, one of the last strongholds of Theravada Buddhism. They were able to expand their rule to include most of Sri Lanka between 1017 and 1070. The great Mon city, Dvaravati, a Theravada center in southern Thailand, fell to the Khmer, the masters of the whole of Thailand, who were Shaivaite Hindus. In the north of India, Muslim armies were trying to destroy what little was left of Buddhism there. "In this perilous period," writes Professor Luce, "Buddhism was saved only by such valiant fighters as Vijayabahu in Sri Lanka and Anawratha."

SHIN ARAHAN CONVERTS THE KING

Shin Arahan arrived in the vicinity of Pagan and was discovered in his forest dwelling by a hunter. The hunter, who had never before seen such a strange creature with a shaven head and a yellow robe, thought he was some kind of spirit and took him to the king, Anawratha. Shin Arahan naturally sat down on the throne, as it was the highest seat, and the king thought: "This man is peaceful, in this man there is the essential thing. He is sitting down on the best seat, surely he must be the best being." The king asked the visitor to tell him where he came from and was told that he came from the place where the Order lived and that the Buddha was his teacher. Then Shin Arahan gave the king the teaching on mindfulness *(appamada)*, teaching him the same doctrine Nigrodha had given Emperor Asoka when he was converted. Shin Arahan then told the monarch that the Buddha had passed into Parinibbana, but that his teaching, the Dhamma, enshrined in the Tipitaka, and the two-fold Sangha consisting of those who possessed absolute knowledge and those who possessed conventional knowledge, remained.

The king must have felt that he had found what had been missing in his life and a genuine alternative to the superficial teachings of the Ari monks. He built a monastery for Shin Arahan, and according to some sources, stopped all worship of the Ari monks. Tradition has it that he had them dressed in white and even forced them to serve as soldiers in his army. The Ari tradition continued for a long time, however, and its condemnation is a feature of much later times, and not, as far as contemporary evidence shows, of the Pagan era.

The *Sasanavamsa* gives an alternate version of Anawratha's conversion according to which Shin Arahan had originally come from Sri Lanka to study the Dhamma in Dvaravati and Thaton and was on his way to Sri Ksetra in search of a text when he was taken to Anawratha by a hunter. The king asked him, "Who are you?" — "O King, I am a disciple of Gotama." — "Of what kind are the Three Jewels?" — "O King, the Buddha should be regarded as Mahosadha the wise, his doctrine as Ummagga, his order as the Videhan army."

This version is interesting in that Anawratha is portrayed as being a Buddhist with knowledge of Jataka stories, such as the Mahosadha Jataka referred to above, even before meeting Shin Arahan. This assumption that he was no stranger to Buddhism is supported by the fact that earlier kings had been followers of Buddhism in varying degrees. Caw Rahan, who died about 94 years before Anawratha's accession, is said to have built a Sima and five Pagodas, and Kyaung Pyu Min built the white monastery outside Pagan. Kyaung Pyu Min is believed to have been Anawratha's father.

ANAWRATHA ACQUIRES THE SCRIPTURES

Through Shin Arahan, Anawratha had now found the religion he had been yearning for and he decided to set out and procure the scriptures and holy relics of this religion. For he wished his kingdom to be secured on the original teachings of the Buddha. He tried to find the scriptures and relics of his new religion in different quarters. In his enthusiasm he did not limit his quest to Thaton, but also searched among the Khmer in Angkor, and in Tali, the capital of the Nanchao, a kingdom in modern day Yunnan, in China, where a tooth of the Buddha was enshrined. But everywhere he was refused. He then went to Thaton, where his teacher Shin Arahan had come from, to request a copy of the scriptures. According to the tradition of Myanmar, Anawratha's request was refused, and unable to endure another refusal he set out with his army in the year 1057 to conquer Thaton and acquire the Tipitaka by force. Before conquering Thaton, however, he had to subjugate Sri Ksetra, the Pyu capital. From there, he took the relics enshrined in King Dwattabaung's Bawbaw-gyi Pagoda to Pagan.

Some think that the aim of his campaign was mainly to add the prosperous Indian colonies of Lower Myanmar to his possessions, while others think he may have actually been called to Thaton to defend it against the marauding Khmer. Whatever the immediate cause of his campaign in the lower country, we know for certain that he returned with the king of Thaton and his court, with Mon artists and scholars and, above all, with Thaton's bhikkhus and their holy books, the Tipitaka. Suvannabhumi and its Mon population were now in the hands of the Myanmar and the Mon culture and religion were accepted and assimilated in the emergent Pagan with fervor.

Initially the fervor must have been restricted to the king and possibly his immediate entourage, yet even they continued to propitiate their traditional gods for worldly gain as the new religion was considered a higher practice. Theravada Buddhism does not provide much in the way of rites and rituals, but a royal court cannot do without them. So the traditional propitiation of the Nagas continued to be used for court ceremonials and remained part of the popular religion, while the bhikkhus were accorded the greatest respect and their master, the Buddha Gotama, was honored with the erection of pagodas and shrines.

There were contacts between the new kings of Myanmar and Sri Lanka that are recorded not only in the chronicles of the two countries but also in stone inscriptions in South India. As the Hindu Colas had ruled Sri Lanka for more than half a century, Buddhism had been weakened and King Vijayabahu, who had driven out the Vaishnavite Colas, wanted to re-establish his religion. So in 1070, he requested King Anawratha of Myanmar, who had assisted him financially in his war against the Colas, to send bhikkhus to re-introduce the pure ordination into his country. It is interesting to note that the *Culavamsa* refers to Anawratha as the king of Ramanna, which was Lower Myanmar, also called Suvannabhumi. He was approached as the conqueror and master of Thaton, a respected Theravada center, rather than as the king of Pagan, a new and unknown country. The bhikkhus who traveled to Sri

Lanka brought the Sinhalese Tipitaka back with them and established a link between the two countries which was to last for centuries.

Anawratha is mentioned in the Myanmar, Mon, Khmer, Thai, and Sinhalese chronicles as a great champion of Buddhism because he developed Pagan into a major regional power and laid the foundation for its glory. He did not, however, build many of the temples for which Pagan is now so famous as the great age of temple building started only after his reign. It is important to realize that his interest was not restricted only to Pagan. He built pagodas wherever his campaigns took him and adorned them with illustrations from the Jatakas and the life of the Buddha. Some maintain that he used only Jatakas as themes for the adornment of his religious buildings because that was all he possessed of the Tipitaka.

Such a conclusion is negative and quite superficial. After all, during Asoka's time Jatakas and scenes from the life of the Buddha were used for illustrations in Bharut and Sanchi, the great stupas near Bombay. We cannot therefore deduce that the builders of Bharut and Sanchi were acquainted only with the Jatakas. These edifying stories which teach the fundamentals of Buddhism so skillfully are singularly suited to educate an illiterate people beset by superstitions through the vivid visual means of the stone reliefs depicting these stories. It is almost unthinkable that the Mon Sangha, who taught Anawratha, had no knowledge of at least all of the Vinaya. Otherwise, they would not have been able to re-establish a valid ordination of bhikkhus in Sri Lanka.

Anawratha left behind innumerable clay tablets adorned with images of the Buddha, the king's name, and some Pali and Sanskrit verses. A typical aspiration on these tablets was: "By me, King Anawratha, this mould of Sugata (Buddha) has been made. Through this may I obtain the path to Nibbana when Metteyya is awakened." Anawratha aspired to become a disciple of the Buddha Metteyya, unlike many later kings of Myanmar who aspired to Buddhahood. Is this an indication that this warrior had remained a modest man in spite of his empire building?

PAGAN: FLOWERING AND DECLINE

Anawratha was succeeded by a number of kings of varying significance to Buddhism in Myanmar. His successors inherited a relatively stable and prosperous kingdom and consequently were able to embark on the huge temple building projects for which their reigns are still remembered.

This is the time when kings such as Kyanzitta and others built pagodas, libraries, monasteries, and ordination halls. These kings must have possessed coffers full of riches collected from their extensive kingdom which they lavished on the religion of the Buddha. Their palaces were probably built of wood as was the last palace of the Myanmar dynasty. Though the palaces must have reflected the wealth and power of the rulers, the more durable brick was not deemed necessary for such worldly buildings. This is similar to views still found in rural areas of Myanmar today. The only structure adorned to any extent in a village is the monastery and the buildings attached to it, such as the rest house. The villagers are very modest with regard to their private houses and even consider it improper to decorate them. Their monastery, however, is given every decoration affordable.

KYANZITTA STRENGTHENS THERAVADA BUDDHISM

Kyanzitta (1084-1113), who had been Anawratha's commander-in-chief and had succeeded Anawratha's son to the throne, consolidated Theravada Buddhism's predominance in Pagan. In his reign, such important shrines as the Shwezigon Pagoda, the Nanda, Nagayon, and Myinkaba Kubyauk-gyi temples were built.

With the three latter temples, Kyanzitta introduced a new style of religious building. The traditional stupa or dagoba found in India and Sri Lanka is a solid mound in which relics or other holy objects are enshrined. The area of worship is situated around them and is usually marked by ornate stone railings. In the new style of building, however, the solid mound had been hollowed out and could be entered. The central shrine was surrounded by halls which housed stone reliefs depicting scenes from the Buddha's life and Jataka stories. Kyanzitta's aim was the conversion of his people to the new faith. Whereas Anawratha had been busy expanding his empire and bringing relics and the holy scriptures to Pagan, Kyanzitta's mission was to consolidate this enterprise. Enormous religious structures such as the Nanda Temple attracted the populace and the interiors of the temples allowed the bhikkhus to instruct the inquisitive in the king's faith.

Professor Luce writes: The Nanda (temple)... he built with four broad halls. Each hall had the same 16 scenes in stone relief all identically arranged. The bhikkhus could cope with four audiences simultaneously. The scenes cover the whole life of the Buddha. When well grounded in these, the audience would pass to the outer wall of the corridor. Here, running around the whole corridor are the 80 scenes of Gotama's life up to the Enlightenment. The later life of the Buddha is shown in hundreds of other stone reliefs on the inner walls and shrines.

Kyanzitta's efforts for the advancement of Buddhism were not limited to his own country. For in one of his many inscriptions, he also mentions that he sent craftsmen to Bodhgaya to repair the Mahabodhi temple, which had been destroyed by a foreign king. The upkeep of the Mahabodhi temple became a tradition with the kings of Myanmar, who continued to send missions to Bodhgaya to repair the temple and also to donate temple slaves and land to the holiest shrine of Buddhism.

Kyanzitta also initiated an extensive review and purification of the Tipitaka by the bhikkhus. This was the first occasion in Myanmar's history when the task of a Buddhist Sangayana or Synod, comparing the Sinhalese and Suvannabhumi's Tipitaka, was undertaken. It is possible and even probable that this huge editing work was carried out along with visiting Sinhalese bhikkhus.

By nature of Myanmar's geographical position, external influences swept in predominantly from northern India, and therefore tantric Buddhism, dominant especially in Bengal, remained strong. However, Kyanzitta succeeded in firmly establishing the Pali Tipitaka by asking the bhikkhus to compare the ancient Mon Tipitaka with the texts obtained from the Mahavihara in Sri Lanka. In this way, he also made it clear that confirmation of orthodoxy was to be sought in Sri Lanka and not in any other Buddhist country. Though Mahayana practices were tolerated in his reign (his chief queen was a tantric Buddhist), they were not officially regarded as the pure religion. It is characteristic of Pagan that these two branches of Buddhism co-existed — the religion of the Theras, which was accepted as the highest religion — and the tantric practices, which included the worship of spirits or *nats* and gave more immediate satisfaction. Pagodas are often adorned with figures of all types of deities, but the deities are normally shown in an attitude of reverence towards the pagoda, a symbol of the Buddha. The ancient gods were not banished, but had to submit to the peerless Buddha. Tradition attributes to King Anawratha the observation: "Men will not come for the sake of the new faith. Let them come for their old gods, and gradually they will be won over."

An approach such as this, whether it was Anawratha's or Kyanzitta's, would suggest that the practice of the old religion of the Ari monks was allowed to continue and that the conversion of the country was gentle and peaceful as befits the religion of the Buddha. Although later Myanmar chronicles refer to the Ari monks as a debased group of charlatans who were totally rooted out by Anawratha, this is far from the truth. A powerful movement of "priests" who incorporated magic practices in their teachings continued to exist throughout the Pagan period, and though they may have respected the basic rules of the Vinaya and donned the yellow robe, their support was rooted in the old animistic beliefs of the Myanmar. It should not be forgotten that the Myanmar first started to settle in the area of Kyauksai in the sixth century AD and that the "man in the field" was in no way ready for such highly developed a religion as Theravada Buddhism. The transition had to be gradual, and the process that started remains still incomplete in the minds of many people, especially in the more remote areas of the hill country.

The example of Kyanzitta's son Rajakumar, however, shows how even in those early days the teachings of the Buddha were understood and practiced not only by the bhikkhus, but also by lay people and members of the royal court. Rajakumar's conduct is proof of his father's ability to establish men in the Dhamma and survives as a monument just as the Ananda temple does.

Rajakumar was Kyanzitta's only son and his rightful heir. Due to political misadventures Kyanzitta was separated from his wife and therefore not aware of the birth of his son for seven years. When his daughter gave birth to his grandson he anointed him as future king immediately after his birth. Rajakumar grew up in the shadow of his nephew, the crown prince, but neither during his father's reign nor after his death did he ever try to usurp the throne through intrigue or by force. He was a minister zealous in the affairs of state, prudent and wise. He was also a scholar of the Tipitaka and instrumental in its review, vigorously supporting his father in his objective to establish Buddhism. But he is best known for his devotion to his father in his last years when his health was failing. In order to restore the king's health he built five pagodas which to this day are called Min-o-Chanda, "The Welfare of the Old King." When the king was on his deathbed:

Rajakumar, remembering the many and great favors with which the king had nourished him, made a beautiful golden image of the Buddha and entering with ceremony presented it to the king, saying: "This golden Buddha I have made to help my lord. The three villages of slaves you gave me, I give to this Buddha." And the king rejoiced and said "Sadhu, sadhu, sadhu." Then in the presence of the compassionate Mahathera and other leading bhikkhus, the king poured on the ground the water of dedication, calling the earth to witness. Then Rajakumar enshrined the golden image, and built around it a cave temple with a golden pinnacle.

LATER KINGS

Rajakumar's nephew was King Alaungsithu (c.1113-67), who continued the tradition of his dynasty of glorifying the Buddha's religion by building a vast temple, the Sabbannu Temple, probably the largest monument in Pagan. During his many travels and campaigns, he built pagodas and temples throughout Myanmar. The faith that Shin Arahan had inspired in Anawratha and his successors continued to inspire Alaungsithu. Shin Arahan, who had seen kings come and go and the flowering of the religion he brought to Pagan, is believed to have died during the reign of King Alaungsithu, in about 1115.

After the death of Alaungsithu, Pagan was thrown into turmoil by violent struggles for the throne. Several kings reigned for short periods and spent most of their time and resources in power struggles. One even succeeded in alienating the great king of Sri Lanka, Parakramabahu, by mistreating his emissaries and breaking the agreements between the two countries. Eventually Parakramabahu invaded Myanmar, devastating towns and villages and killing the king. The new king, Narapati (1174-1210), blessed the country with a period of peace and prosperity. This conducive atmosphere was to allow outstanding scholarship and learning to arise in Pagan.

Kyawswa (1234-50) was a king under whom scholarship was encouraged even more, undoubtedly because the king himself spent most of his time in scholarly pursuits including memorizing passages of the Tipitaka. He had relinquished most of his worldly duties to his son in order to dedicate more time to the study of the scriptures. Two grammatical works, the *Saddabindu* and the *Paramatthabindu,* are ascribed to him. It would appear that his palace was a place of great culture and learning as his ministers and his daughter are credited with scholarly works as well.

During the twelfth century, a sect of forest dwellers also thrived. They were called *arannaka* in Pali and were identical with the previously mentioned Ari of the later chroniclers of Myanmar. This was a monastic movement that only used the yellow robes and the respect due to them in order to follow their own ideas. They indulged in business transactions and owned vast stretches of land. They gave feasts and indulged in the consumption of liquor, and, though they pretended to be practicing the teachings of the Buddha, their practices were probably of a tantric nature. It would appear that they had a considerable amount of influence at the royal court and one of the main exponents of the movement was even given the title of royal teacher. Superstition and magic were gaining dominance once again and Anawratha's and Kyanzitta's empire was slowly sliding into decadence.

The last king of Pagan, Narathihapate, whom the Myanmar know by the name Tayoupyemin (the king who fled the Chinese), repeatedly refused to pay symbolic tribute to the Mongol emperors in Peking who in 1271 had conquered neighbouring Yunnan. He even went so far as to execute ambassadors of the Chinese emperor and their retinue for their lack of deference to the king. He became so bold and blinded by ignorance that he attacked a vassal state of the Mongols. The emperor in Peking was finally forced to send a punitive expedition which defeated the Pagan army north of Pagan. The news of this defeat caused the king and his court to flee to Pathein (Bassein). As the imperial court in Peking was not interested in adding Pagan to its possessions, the Yunnan expedition did not remain in the environs. When the king was later murdered and the whole empire fell into disarray, the Yunnani generals returned, looting Pagan. The territories were divided amongst Shan chiefs who paid tribute to the Mongols.

G.E. Harvey honors the kings of Pagan with the following words: To them the world owes to a great measure the preservation of Theravada Buddhism, one of the purest faiths mankind has ever known. Brahmanism had strangled it in its land of birth; in Sri Lanka its existence was threatened again and again; east of Burma it was not yet free from priestly corruptions; but the kings of Burma never wavered, and at Pagan the stricken faith found a city of refuge.

CONTACTS WITH SRI LANKA AND THE FIRST CONTROVERSIES

The contact with Sri Lanka was very important for the growth of the religion in Pagan. As was shown previously, it started with the friendship of Anawratha and Vijayabahu, both of whom fought for Buddhism: Anawratha to establish a new kingdom, Vijayabahu to wrench an old one from the clutches of the Hindu invaders. They supported each other in their struggles and then together re-established the Theravada doctrine in their respective countries, Anawratha sending bhikkhus to Sri Lanka to revive the Sangha, while Vijayabahu reciprocated by sending the sacred texts. The continued contact between the two countries was beneficial to both: many a reform movement, purifying the religion in one country spread to the other as well. Bhikkhus visiting from one country were led to look at their own traditions critically and to reappraise their practice of the Dhamma as preserved in the Pali texts. After the fall of the main Buddhist centers in southern India, centers which had been the main allies of the Mon Theravadins in the south, Sri Lanka was the only ally in the struggle for the survival of the Theravada tradition.

Leading bhikkhus of Pagan undertook the long and difficult journey to Sri Lanka in order to visit the holy temples and study the scriptures as they had been preserved by the Sinhalese Sangha. Shin Arahan's successor as the king's teacher left the royal court for Sri Lanka, returning to Pagan only to die. He was succeeded by a Mon bhikkhu, Uttarajiva, who led a pilgrimage to Sri Lanka in 1171. This was to cause the first upheaval in the Sangha of Pagan.

Uttarajiva traveled to Sri Lanka accompanied by Chapada, a novice who remained behind on the island in order to study the scriptures in the Mahavihara, the orthodox monastery of Sri Lanka and the guardian of the Theravada tradition. After ten years, he returned to Pagan accompanied by four elders who had studied with him. The Kalyani inscription, written about three hundred years later, relates that Chapada considered the tradition of the Myanmar bhikkhus impure. He had consequently taken four bhikkhus with him because he needed a chapter of at least five theras in order to ordain new bhikkhus. It is possible that the Myanmar bhikkhus, who seemed to have formed a group separate from the Mon bhikkhus, had paid more attention to their traditional worship than was beneficial for their practice of the Dhamma. It is also possible that there was an element of nationalist rivalry between the Mon bhikkhus and the Myanmar bhikkhus. As he showed a penchant for the reform movement, the Myanmar king Narapati seems to have accepted the superiority of the Mon bhikkhus, though he did not neglect the other bhikkhus. Chapada and his companions refused to accept the ordination of the Myanmar bhikkhus as legitimate in accordance with Vinaya. They established their own ordination, following which the Myanmar bhikkhus sent a delegation to Sri Lanka to receive the Mahavihara ordination for themselves.

After Chapada's death, the reform movement soon split into two factions, and eventually each of the four remaining bhikkhus went his own way, one of them leaving the order altogether. "Thus in the town of Arimaddana (Pagan) there were four schools... Because the first of these to come was the school of the Elder Arahan from Sudhamma (Thaton) it was called the first school; while the others, because they came later, were called the later schools."

SCHOLARSHIP IN PAGAN

It is surprising how quickly a relatively simple people absorbed the great civilization that arrived in their midst so suddenly. Even before the conquest of Thaton, Pagan possessed some ornate religious buildings, which is indicative of the presence of artists and craftsmen. It is quite likely, however, that these were Indians from Bengal and the neighbouring states. The type of Buddhism that had come to Pagan from India was an esoteric religion, as some old legends indicate. It was the jealously guarded domain of a group of priests, who made no attempt to instruct the people but were happy if their superiority remained unquestioned by a superstitious populace.

The advent of Theravada Buddhism with its openness and its aim to spread understanding must have been quite revolutionary in Pagan and obviously the people were eager to acquire the knowledge offered to them by the bhikkhus. Mabel Bode says in her *Pali Literature of Burma:*Though the Burmese began their literary history by borrowing from their conquered neighbours, the Talaings (Mon) — and not before the eleventh century — the growth of Pali scholarship among them was so rapid that the epoch following close on this tardy beginning is considered one of the best that Burma has seen.

The principal works of the Pagan period still extant are Pali grammars. The most famous of these is the *Saddaniti,* which Aggavamsa completed in 1154. Uttarajiva gave a copy of this work to the bhikkhus of the Mahavihara in Sri Lanka and it "was received with enthusiastic admiration, and declared superior to any work of the kind written by Sinhalese scholars." The *Saddaniti* is still used to teach grammar in the monasteries in Myanmar and has been printed many times. B.C. Law regards it as one of the three principal Pali grammars along with the grammars by Kaccayana and Moggallana. K.R. Norman says: "The greatest of extant Pali grammars is the *Saddaniti,* written by Aggavamsa from Arimaddana [Pagan] in Burma..." Aggavamsa was also known as the teacher of King Narapatisithu (1167-1202) and was given the title Aggapandita. Unfortunately, no other works by this author are known today.

The second famous author of Pagan was Saddhammajotipala who has been previously mentioned under his clan name of Chapada. He was a disciple of Uttarajiva and is credited with a great number of works, but in the case of some it is doubtful whether he actually composed them himself or merely introduced them from Sri Lanka. His works deal not only with grammar, but also with questions of monastic discipline (Vinaya) and the Abhidhamma, which in later centuries was to become a favorite subject of Myanmar scholars. His work on Kaccayana's grammar, the *Suttaniddesa,* formed the foundation of his fame. However, his specialty would appear to have been the study of Abhidhamma, as no less than four noted works of his on the subject attained fame: *Samkhepavannana, Namacaradipani, Matikatthadipani,* and *Patthanagananaya.* According to the Pitaka-thamain, a history of Buddhism in Myanmar, he also devoted a commentary to the *Visuddhimagga* by Buddhaghosa called the *Visuddhimagga-ganthi.*There are no written records that refer to meditation being practiced in Myanmar before this century. However, his interest in the *Visuddhimagga* is indicative of an interest in meditation, if only in the theory rather than in the practice.

Another scholar of Pagan, Vimalabuddhi, also wrote a commentary concerning Abhidhamma, the *Abhidhammatthasangahatika,* in addition to another important grammatical work, the *Nyasa,* a commentary on Kaccayana's grammar.

Other grammatical works of some importance were written, but none acquired the standing of Aggavamsa's *Saddaniti.* However, a rather peculiar work worth mentioning is the *Ekakkharakosa* by Saddhammakitti. It is a work on Paii lexicography enumerating words of one letter.

SHAN RULE

UPPER MYANMAR

After Narathihapate had fled Pagan in fear of the Mongol army, he was never able to re-establish his authority, even though the Mongols supported the Pagan dynasty. The Mongol court in Peking preferred a united neighbouring country under a single ruler, but in spite of its efforts Myanmar was divided into several principalities mainly under Shan tribal leaders. These self-styled princelings paid tribute to the Chinese Mongol court and were nominally its subjects. The Shan, at this time still nomadic tribes in the north, broke into an already destabilized Myanmar like a tidal wave. They penetrated the entire region as far as the Mon country and established themselves as rulers in many towns and cities. The intrigues, fratricidal wars, and murders that make up the history of their courts are innumerable.

A division of the country into Upper and Lower Myanmar is somewhat arbitrary, as, after the fall of Pagan, the two regions were composed of many competing principalities. However, there were the two principle kingdoms of Ava in Upper Myanmar and Pago (Pegu) in Lower Myanmar. Hostilities between these two prevailed, as well as with the neighbouring smaller states including the Shan fiefs of Chiang Mai and Ayutthaya in Thailand. Intrigues within and between courts were rife. Sometimes these claimed victims only within the circle of the powerful and mighty, and sometimes whole towns were looted and destroyed, and their population massacred or carried off into slavery. But, in spite of politically unsettled conditions, the Sangha survived, because the new rulers, initially somewhat barbaric, soon accepted the religion of their subjects. Just as the Myanmar had adopted the religion and culture of the more refined Mon, so the Shan submitted to the sophisticated civilization of the peoples they subjugated. The Shan initially established their capital at Pinya in Upper Myanmar to the north of Pagan and transferred it to Ava in 1312. Ava was to remain the capital of Upper Myanmar until the eighteenth century.

The *Sasanavamsa* praises Thihathu, the youngest of three Shan brothers who wrested power from the Pagan dynasty in Upper Myanmar, as a Buddhist king who built monasteries and pagodas. He had a bhikkhu as his teacher and supported thousands of bhikkhus in his capital Pinya and later Ava. However, Pagan remained the cultural and religious capital of the region for the whole of the fourteenth century. Scholarly works were composed in its monasteries throughout this period whereas no such works are known to have been written in the new centers of power. The works of this period of scholarship were mostly concerned with Pali grammar.

Two generations later, a descendant of Thihathu secured himself a place in religious history as a great patron of scholarship. As in the courts of some previous kings, his court was also devoted to scholarly learning; and not only bhikkhus, but also the palace officials, produced treatises on religious subjects and the Pali language.

Although the political situation remained unsettled in Upper Myanmar throughout the fifteenth century, in the main, this affected only those in power and their usurpers. Consequently the Sangha appears to have flourished, while the traditional devotion to the support of the Sangha through gifts of the four requisites remained unchanged. The royal court, followed by the leading families, made great donations of monasteries, land, and revenue to the bhikkhus.

In approximately 1440, two Mahatheras from Sri Lanka settled in Ava. Here they joined a group of famous scholars, of whom Ariyavamsa was the most outstanding. The *Sasanavamsa* tells us of his great wisdom and humility in an anecdote.

The elder Ariyavamsa had studied the books of the Abhidhamma Pitaka, but felt he had not gained real understanding. Eventually he came to a bhikkhu in Sagaing who kept his mouth always filled with water in order not to have to engage in meaningless chatter. Ariyavamsa did not talk to "the Elder Water-bearer," as this bhikkhu was known in the Myanmar language, but simply performed the duties of a disciple to his teacher for two days. On the third day, the Venerable Water-bearer spat out the water and asked Ariyavamsa why he was serving him. When Ariyavamsa told him that he wanted to learn from him, the Venerable Water-bearer taught him the *Abhidhammattha-vibhavani-tika*, a subcommentary on the *Abhidhammattha-sangaha*. After two days, Ariyavamsa grasped the meaning and his teacher asked him to write a commentary on this book in order to help others to gain understanding.

During the composition of his first work, Ariyavamsa submitted his writings to the assembled bhikkhus on every Uposatha day, reading out what he had composed and asking his brethren to correct any mistakes they found. On one occasion, a visiting bhikkhu twice made a sound of disapproval during the reading. Ariyavamsa carefully noted the passages where the sound of disapproval had occurred. On reflecting on them in the evening, he found one error of grammar where he had used the wrong gender and also a repetition, an error of style. He approached the bhikkhu who had made the sounds during the reading and out of gratitude for the correction gave him his own outer robe.

Ariyavamsa composed several works in Pali: works on the Abhidhamma, on grammatical subjects, and a study of the Jatakas. But his very important contribution to Buddhism in Myanmar was the fact that all his writing was in the Myanmar vernacular. He was probably the first bhikkhu to write treatises on religious subjects in the local idiom, thus making the religion accessible to a greater number of people. The work by Ariyavamsa still known today is a commentary on the anutika (sub-commentary) of the Abhidhamma.

Towards the end of the fifteenth century, a bhikkhu by the name of Silavamsa composed several epic poems in Pali. They were, of course, of a religious nature dealing with subjects such as the life of the Buddha, or Jataka stories. This genre was later very popular in the Myanmar language and there are many poems relating Jataka stories which were sung by bards throughout the country until recently. In the *Sasanavamsa,* however, Pannasami disapproves of bhikkhus writing or reciting poetry as he considers it to be in breach of the Vinaya rules. He says that because of this, Silavamsa's name was excluded from the Theraparampara, a listing of eminent bhikkhus of Myanmar by ancient chroniclers.

LOWER MYANMAR

The Mon civilization in Lower Myanmar flourished after Pagan's importance waned, once again reliving the era of glory that it had experienced prior to Anawratha's conquest.

Wareru, the Shan ruler who had established himself in Martaban in 1287, was soon converted to Buddhism. He was a Shan peddler who had astutely wrested power from a son of the last king of Pagan, a son who had revolted against his father and founded an independent kingdom. Under Wareru's rule, scholarship in the Mon monasteries flourished and a code of law was compiled which still forms the foundation of the legal literature of Myanmar. The Mon bhikkhus based this code on ancient Hindu codes of law which had found their way into Mon tradition through Indian colonisers and merchants.

At the beginning of the fourteenth century two respected Mon theras named Buddhavamsa and Mahanaga revived the tradition of their countryman Chapada in making a pilgrimage to Sri Lanka. There, they accepted new ordination in the Mahavihara monastery, the guardian of Sinhalese orthodoxy. The bhikkhus of the Mahavihara asked those ordained in other countries to revert to the lay-state before being re-ordained as novices and full bhikkhus, as it was considered of the utmost importance that the ordination be handed down in an unbroken tradition from the time of the Buddha. This was especially significant in Myanmar where there were some reservations about the continuity of the tradition. By disrobing, a bhikkhu forgoes the seniority he has acquired through the years spent in robes and, in this case, he also states that he considers his former ordination invalid. One can imagine that such a step is not taken lightly but only after careful consideration.

THE GREAT REFORMATION OF THE SANGHA

King Dhammazedi (1472-92) takes a special place in the history of the religion in Myanmar. He unified the Sangha in the Mon country and purified the order of the bhikkhus. He recorded his great service to the country in the Kalyani inscription, which will be quoted below.

Dhammazedi was a bhikkhu of Mon origin who taught one of the queens at the royal palace in Ava. This lady, Shin Sawbu, was the daughter of the king of Pago. She had been queen to several unfortunate kings of Upper Mynamar and had beeen conveyed into the hands of the subsequent kings along with the throne. She had become disenchanted with the life of a queen and desired to return to her native land. Dhammazedi and a fellow Mon bhikkhu helped her to escape and brought her back to

Pago. Eventually she became queen of Pago, but after reigning only a few years she wished to retire and do works of merit. She found that the only people worthy of the throne of Pago were her teachers, the two bhikkhus. She let fate decide which would be the future king by concealing miniature imitations of the regalia in one of the two bowls in which she offered them their daily alms food.

She handed the throne over to Dhammazedi who had received the fateful bowl and spent the rest of her life at Dagon (Yangon) building the terrace around the Shwedagon Pagoda and gilding the sacred mound. The Shwedagon became what it is today chiefly thanks to Shin Sawbu's munificence.

Dhammazedi assumed government in Pago after leaving the Order of the bhikkhus. He moved the capital closer to the Swemawdaw Pagoda and built several pagodas and shrines. His name is also connected with a collection of wise judgments and the translation of Wareru's Code of Law into the vernacular. In 1472, Dhammazedi sent a mission to Bodhgaya to repair the temple and make plans and drawings of it.

Dhammazedi had received his education in monasteries of Ava which adhered to the Sihala Sangha. The Sihala Sangha was the faction of the Sangha of Myanmar that accepted only the Mahavihara of Sri Lanka as the ultimate authority in religious questions. King Dhammazedi knew from direct experience the state of the Sangha in Lower Myanmar and was determined to improve it. Having lived as a bhikkhu for so many years, he was also singularly qualified to change the Sangha for the better.

He chose twenty-two senior bhikkhus to lead the reform movement and informed them:

Reverend Sirs, the *upasampada* ordination of the bhikkhus of the Mon country now appears to us to be invalid. Therefore, how can the religion, which is based on such invalid ordination, last to the end of 5000 years? Reverend Sirs, from the establishment of the religion in the island of Sri Lanka up to this present day, there has been existing in this island an exceedingly pure sect of bhikkhus... Receive at their hands the *upasampada* ordination... and if you make this form of the *upasampada* ordination the seed of the religion, as it were, plant it, and cause it to sprout forth by conferring such ordination on men of good family in this Mon country... Reverend Sirs, by your going to the island of Sri Lanka, much merit and great advantage will accrue to you.

At the beginning of 1476 the chosen bhikkhus with their twenty-two disciples embarked on the journey to Sri Lanka. They sailed in two ships, one taking about two months while the other needed six full months to arrive on the shore of the Buddhist island. They received the *upasampada* ordination at the Mahavihara from 17th to 20th July 1476. The return journey of the forty-four Mon bhikkhus was not so smooth, however. One group arrived home in August 1476, while the other group took three years to return to Pago and ten of the bhikkhus died en route. Following their return, Dhammazedi had a pure ordination hall*(sima)* consecrated and made the following proclamation:

May all those who possess faith and desire to receive the bhikkhu's ordination at the hands of the bhikkhus ordained in Sri Lanka come to the Kalyani sima and receive ordination. Let those who have not faith and do not desire to receive the bhikkhus ordination of the Sinhalese, remain as they are.

In order to confer the bhikkhu ordination outside the middle country (i.e. northern India), a chapter of five bhikkhus is needed, one of whom must be qualified to serve as preceptor *(upajjhaya)* and another as teacher *(acariya)*. The latter two must have spent at least ten years in robes as fully ordained bhikkhus. So if Dhammazedi wanted to have local bhikkhus ordained in the new ordination, it was necessary to find two senior bhikkhus. Since those returning from Sri Lanka had been ordained for a period of only three years, they could not act as preceptor or teacher. Local bhikkhus who had not received the ordination of the Mahavihara in Sri Lanka were unacceptable, as otherwise the ordination would again have been invalidated by one who was not of pure descent. Fortunately, the two theras who had undertaken a pilgrimage to Sri Lanka at the beginning of the century and had received the Sinhalese ordination at that time, were still alive. As a result, one was able to act as preceptor and the other as teacher of the newly ordained bhikkhus. The stage was now set for the reformation and unification of the Mon Order of bhikkhus and soon the re-ordination of almost the entire Order of bhikkhus began. The Kalyani inscription records the number of 15,666 ordinations in hundreds of ordination halls newly constructed for the purpose.

It is interesting to note how forcefully the king reformed the Order through royal decrees that would hardly be tolerated today. He declared that all bhikkhus who were, for example, practicing medicine or other arts and crafts or who even slightly infringed on the Vinaya rules would be expelled. The king as a layman, however, did not have the power to defrock a bhikkhu who had not broken one of the four Parajika rules. Dhammazedi circumvented this by threatening to punish with royal penalties the mother, father, relatives, and lay supporters of bhikkhus whose behavior was not in accordance with the rules of the Vinaya.

It goes without saying that a king who could allow himself to take such drastic measures in regard to the Sangha must have had the support of a broad section of the Order and also the people. After years spent in robes, he was keenly aware of the problems of monastic life and because of this even senior bhikkhus respected and accepted his council. We can assume that all his actions to reform the Order were firstly discussed with his bhikkhu teachers and then implemented with their blessings. There being no such thing as a Buddhist Church with a central authority, the Sangha has little possibility to regulate itself. Only the committed support of a worldly power can protect the Order of bhikkhus from those who take advantage of the respect that is given to the yellow robe.

Dhammazedi's support for the religion was so great that his fame spread well beyond the borders of Myanmar and bhikkhus from neighbouring countries such as Thailand came to his realm to receive ordination there. Though the reform movement did not spread to Upper Myanmar and cause the same mass ordinations there, it did not remain without influence in the kingdom of Ava and other principalities, and many bhikkhus came to the Mon bhikkhus to receive the Kalyani ordination.

THE MYANMAR BUILD AN EMPIRE

SHAN VERSUS MYANMAR

The beginning of the sixteenth century was one of the most difficult periods for Buddhism in Upper Myanmar. While the religious fervor of Dhammazedi still lived on in the kingdom of Pago in Ava, Shan rulers were endeavoring to bring about the destruction of the Sangha. A Shan king named Thohanbwa (1527-1543) was particularly well-known for his barbarity. He destroyed pagodas and monasteries and robbed their treasures. Although he was a king, he was uneducated and ignorant. Hence fearing the influence of the bhikkhus and suspicious of their moves, he brought about the massacre of thousands. Under these terror regimes of the Shan rulers the Myanmar did not feel safe. Many, including learned bhikkhus, fled to Toungoo, the stronghold of the Myanmar race in the south. Despite the anarchy prevailing, some respected treatises on Pali grammar were written in Upper Myanmar in these years.

Better times, however, lay ahead for Buddhism in the Golden Land. Two successive kings of Myanmar origin from Toungoo would unite the country and fulfill the duties of Buddhist kings. The wars fought by these two kings, King Tabinshwehti (1531-50) and King Bayinnaung (1551-81), were long in duration and exceedingly cruel. They succeeded in gaining control of the Mon kingdom in Lower Myanmar and the kingdom of Ava. They conquered all of what is today Myanmar including the Shan states as far east as Chiang Mai, and made incursions into lower Thailand and Yunnan where some kings paid tribute to the Myanmar court.

Bayinnaung deferred to the Mon as far as culture and religion were concerned and dressed in Mon style. Under his royal patronage, the Mon Sangha produced scholarly works on grammar and the Abhidhamma and also helped with the collection and standardisation of a code of law based on the old Mon code compiled during Wareru's reign.

Bayinnaung not only unified the country politically, but also made Buddhist principles the standard for his entire dominion. He forbade the sacrificial slaughter of animals, a custom still practiced by the Shan chiefs, the worshippers of certain spirits, and the followers of some other religions. He built pagodas and monasteries in all the newly conquered lands and installed learned bhikkhus in order to convert the often uncivilized inhabitants to gentler ways. The main religious building of his reign is the Mahazedi Pagoda, a majestic monument to the Buddha in the capital, Pago. He also crowned the main pagodas in Myanmar with the jewels of his own crown, a custom practiced by many rulers of the country. He continued in the tradition of Dhammazedi, in supporting the Sihala Sangha and in sponsoring the ordination of many bhikkhus in the Kalyani Ordination Hall near Pago. It is said that he built as many monasteries as there were years in his life.

It remains a mystery how a king who had such deep devotion to the religion of the Buddha and who was so generous towards it could spend his life fighting campaign after campaign to expand his realm. He caused bloodshed and suffering in the conquered regions and at home people starved because farmers were drafted into the army. However this may be, Bayinnaung seems to have been able to reconcile fighting expansionist wars with being a pious Buddhist.

After King Bayinnaung, Pago rapidly lost its significance. Bayinnaung's son persecuted the Mon and consequently re-ignited racial tensions that would plague Myanmar for centuries. Later, Pago was to fall into the hands of a Portuguese adventurer who pillaged the pagodas and monasteries. Eventually the whole of Lower Myanmar, already depopulated by the incessant campaigns of Bayinnaung and his successors, was pillaged by all the surrounding kings and princelings. The country was devastated and people starved.

The *Sasanavamsa* records one major problem of the Vinaya during the sixteenth century. At the beginning of the century, the bhikkhus of Toungoo were divided over whether or not bhikkhus could partake of the juice of the toddy palm which was generally used to prepare fermented drink. The dispute was settled by a respected thera who decided that toddy juice was permissible only if it was freshly harvested.

POLITICAL INFLUENCE OF THE SANGHA IN EARLY MYANMAR

What motivated the royal court probably remained largely a mystery to the ordinary citizens, except when they were pressed into service in the king's army. There was little sense of collective responsibility as it is cultivated in today's democracies. Everyone looked after himself and his immediate circle and governments were sometimes more of a scourge than a protection. Kings did not always provide a visible administration beyond appointing governors at whose mercy local people were. These governors often endeavored to establish independence as soon as they perceived inherent weaknesses in their masters. Many accumulated great wealth for themselves.

There was, however, one element in the policy of rulers which, with a few exceptions, remained fairly stable throughout Myanmar history. Most kings supported Buddhism and the Sangha provided a framework of continuity as no other entity could. Ray writes:

They (the kings) were good Buddhists and never did they waver from their kingly duty of acting as the patron-guardian of the faith of the country. Moreover, whatever their numerical strength, the bhikkhus were real spokesmen of the people and the monasteries were the popular assemblies as it were; and each king that came to the throne sought to win the bhikkhus over to his side.

The best insurance of a peaceful life in Myanmar was to become a bhikkhu, as they were not drafted into armies or enslaved by conquerors and as long as the lay people had food to eat they were also fed. The bhikkhus not only provided a link between the people and those in power, they often played a role in the affairs of state. This is illustrated by an event which occurred in the middle of the seventeenth century and is related by the *Sasanavamsa*.

The king, Ukkamsika, popularly known as King Thalun, was a devoted Buddhist and thanks to him, learning flourished in Myanmar. The king's son, however, tried to dethrone his father, and Thalun, taken by surprise, had to flee accompanied only by two companions. Coming upon a river, the only vessel in sight was the boat of a samanera. The samanera agreed to take them onboard as passengers, and they ended up in the samanera's monastery where they revealed their true identities and asked for protection from their persecutors. They were referred to another monastery where lived a bhikkhu wise in worldly affairs. Following his advice, the bhikkhus formed a living wall around the monastery and, as no Buddhist will attack a man in robes, the rebels who had come to kill the king had to withdraw. Another example of the beneficial influence of the Sangha is their appeal for clemency to King Bayinnaung. Bhikkhus often tried to stay executions in accordance with the principles of *metta* (loving kindness) and *karuna* (compassion) and sometimes their efforts achieved success.

During one of Bayinnaung's Thai campaigns, the peasantry around Pago revolted and razed the royal city to the ground. Bayinnaung, after hurrying back from Ayutthaya, captured several thousand rebels and was ready to burn them alive. It was the custom then to burn deserters from the army alive and obviously rebellion was considered to be a crime of similar gravity. The bhikkhus of all races intervened on behalf of the poor wretches and were able to save all from the pyre, except for seventy ring leaders, the most serious offenders.

There are several instances in Myanmar history when bhikkhus also mediated between contending kings or princes and helped to avoid bloodshed. This was often the case when cities were besieged and both parties realised that they could not win. The king who was besieged would normally take the initiative and send his bhikkhus to the king in attack. Often the bhikkhus were authorized to negotiate on behalf of the monarch. An armistice agreed by or in the presence of bhikkhus was more likely to be honored than a promise given without their blessings. Therefore, if the two parties were sincere in their offers to negotiate, they usually requested bhikkhus to be mediators and judges.

THE SPREAD OF ABHIDHAMMA

The seventeenth century was a period of dynamic growth in the history of Buddhism in Myanmar. Many outstanding developments took place, and principal among these were the numerous translations of texts into the Myanmar language and the great increase in the study of the Abhidhamma. It is quite possible that the two developments were inter-connected.

In the first half of the century, Manirathana Thera translated the following texts into the Myanmar language: *Atthasalini, Sammohavinodani, Kankhavitarani, Abhidhammatthavibhavini, Sankhepavannana.* Of these five, only the *Kankhavitarani,* Buddhaghosa's commentary on the Patimokkha, is not concerned with Abhidhamma. In the second half of the century Aggadhammalankara translated Kaccayana's Pali grammar, the *Abhidhammatthasangaha, Matika, Dhatukatha, Yamaka,* and the *Patthana* into the Myanmar tongue. Later, the *Nettippakarana* was also translated.

It cannot be a coincidence that nine out of twelve translated works were texts of the Abhidhamma or its commentaries. The reason for these translations must have been a developing interest in the psychology of Buddhism among the Buddhist followers who could not themselves read Pali. Whether these were only bhikkhus or whether lay people were also interested in exploring the scriptures for themselves is difficult to determine now. However, what is known is that almost every boy and many of the girls attended monastic schools, whose curriculum was probably established by this period, if not earlier. Included in the curriculum were studies of the Mangala Sutta, Metta Sutta, Ratana Sutta, and the other parittas, as well as basic literacy which included some Pali. In addition a number of the Abhidhamma texts had to be committed to memory.

The intention behind these translations and commentaries in the Myanmar language was obviously to make the words of the Buddha accessible to a wider audience who would, then, not be solely dependent on the authority of the Pali scholars.

In the later half of the century, the bhikkhu Devacakkhobhasa designed a system for the study and teaching of the *Patthana,* the last book of the Abhidhamma, which in Myanmar is believed to be the highest teaching of the Buddha. The king at the time of Devacakkhobhasa was so impressed by the bhikkhu's proficiency in these higher teachings and by his system of instruction, that he ordered the *Patthana* to be studied in all the monasteries of Myanmar. It is not unreasonable to assume that the king himself studied these teachings. Otherwise he would hardly have been in a position to appreciate them and make them compulsory reading for the Myanmar bhikkhus.

This emphasis on Abhidhamma in general and the *Patthana* in particular has survived in Myanmar to the present day. The movement, therefore, that began in the seventeenth century is still of great significance for Buddhism there. The *Patthana,* for instance, is ubiquitous in Myanmar. The twenty-four conditions of the *Patthana* can be found printed on the fans of the bhikkhus, on calendars, and on posters. In some monasteries, the bhikkhus are woken every morning by twenty-four strokes on a hollow tree trunk, while the bhikkhu striking the tree trunk has to recite the twenty-four conditions as he does so. Even little children learn to recite the twenty-four conditions along with the suttas of protection. As the *Patthana* is the highest and most difficult teaching of the Buddha, it is believed that it will be the first to be lost. In order to slow the decline of the Sasana, many people of Myanmar, bhikkhus and lay people alike, memorize the *Patthana* and recite it daily.

In Pagan, the Jataka stories and the history of the Buddha's life were the main subjects of religious study. In later centuries, Pali grammar and the study of the Vinaya were foremost on the agenda. Dhammazedi's reform movement drew the attention back to the foundations of all monastic life, the code of conduct for the bhikkhus as laid down by the Buddha himself.

Though stricter observation of the Vinaya would have to be re-emphasised in the future, its foundation was firm enough to insure that progressive reform movements would be instigated within the Sangha and not be dependent on external impetus. How far a bhikkhu was allowed to stray from the ideal had been defined in strictures that had become integral to the Sangha. Based on this foundation of *sila* (right conduct, morality), the Sangha was now free to give increased attention to higher teachings.

The age of the Abhidhamma had dawned. The Abhidhamma remained no longer the domain of a chosen few, but began to be studied by many. The wealth of translations from the Abhidhamma would suggest that in the seventeenth century it had become so popular that it may have been taught even to lay people. The Myanmar language had developed and had been enriched with Pali terms so that it could convey the difficult concepts of Abhidhamma. civilization had matured to an extent never seen before. Myanmar was ready to study the analysis of mind and matter as taught by the Buddha. The stage was being set for the widespread practice of insight meditation *(vipassana bhavana)* in later times.

THE EIGHTEENTH AND NINETEENTH CENTURIES

In the succession of rulers of the eighteenth century some were strong and despotic, while others were ineffective and withdrawn. Some tried to expand their power and fought wars, while others appeared satisfied with existing conditions. There were several wars with Thailand and the population of Myanmar had to bear the deprivations that war invariably brings not only to the conquered, but also to the country where the conquering armies are levied.

After a war between the Mon and the Myanmar in which the Mon initially attacked and then conquered Ava itself, the Myanmar king Alaungpaya (1752-60), who believed himself a Bodhisatta, crushed Mon resistance once and for all. After Pago had fallen into his hands in 1756, Lower Myanmar was devastated and many of the Mon survivors fled to Thailand or were deported as slaves.

Like Bayinnaung, Alaungpaya established a Myanmar empire, at the same time decimating the population of the country by drafting the peasantry into the army for campaigns against Ayutthaya (Thailand) and other countries. The *Sasanavamsa* does not comment on the atrocity of war. War is perceived as it is, cruel and pitiless — but it is the affair of rulers, not of bhikkhus. The manner in which rulers conduct their affairs is entirely their responsibility. Pannasami probably took very seriously the Buddha's injunction that a member of the Sangha should not talk about rulers and royal affairs.

The *Sasanavamsa* pays much attention to a controversy which raged in monastic circles throughout the eighteenth century. At the beginning of the century, some bhikkhus began to wear their robes outside the monasteries as they were worn within them, that is, covering only one shoulder. Even when going on their daily alms round, they failed to drape the robe in the traditional way. When challenged as to the orthodoxy of this practice, they produced various interpretations and opinions, but could not validate their practice through the authority of the scriptures. Different kings endorsed one or other of the two opinions and bhikkhus of the orthodox school even died for their conviction when a king had outlawed the covering of both shoulders.

The most interesting aspect of this historical period of the religion is not so much the actual controversy as the power the king had in religious affairs. The kings of Myanmar were not normally expert in the Vinaya and yet they took the final decision in matters of monastic discipline after due consultation with the leaders of the Sangha. In the more than one hundred years that this controversy prevailed, different kings supported the orthodoxy of either view. This shows that this system is not entirely satisfactory. However, the right view which was in accordance with the Vinaya did eventually triumph due to the persistence of the majority of the Sangha. Only the worldly power was in a position to regulate the Sangha into which undesirable elements entered repeatedly. To keep the Order pure, it had to be always under careful scrutiny and bogus ascetics had to be removed. The kings of Myanmar in co-operation with the Sangharajas and the other senior bhikkhus had established a system of supervision of the bhikkhus by royal officials. In every township, the king's representatives were responsible for ensuring that the bhikkhus adhered scrupulously to the rules of the Vinaya. Bhikkhus who transgressed were taken before religious courts and punished according to the code of discipline.

The controversy concerning the correct manner of wearing the robes came up for arbitration for the last time under Bodawpaya (1782-1819), the fifth son of Alaungpaya. He decided in favor of orthodoxy and thenceforth all bhikkhus had to cover both shoulders on the daily alms round. This ruling created one unified sect throughout Myanmar under the leadership of a council of senior bhikkhus appointed by the king. These were called the Thudhamma Sayadaws and the Thudhamma sect has survived in Myanmar down to the present day.

Bodawpaya appointed a chapter of eight eminent bhikkhus as Sangharajas, leaders of the Sangha, and charged them with the duty to safeguard the purity of the Order of bhikkhus. As a direct result of the discipline and stability created by the work of these senior bhikkhus, the Sangha prospered, and consequently scholarship flourished under Bodawpaya's reign.

The name of the Mahasangharaja Nanabhivamsa is especially noteworthy in this respect. Nanabhivamsa was an eminently learned bhikkhu who had proven his wisdom even as a young man. Only five years after his ordination as a bhikkhu, he had completed a commentary *(tika)* on the *Nettippakarana.* Eight years after full ordination, at the age of twenty-eight, he became Sangharaja, and then Mahasangharaja, the title conferred by the king on the highest bhikkhu in his realm. Soon after this, he wrote his well respected "new sub-commentary" on the Digha Nikaya, the *Sadhujjanavilasini*. At the request of the king, he wrote a commentary on Buddhaghosa's *Jatakatthakatha* and several other treatises.

The king was so devoted to the head of the Sangha that he dedicated a "very magnificent five storied monastery" to him and later many other monasteries as well. According to the *Sasanavamsa*, Nanabhivamsa was not only a scholar, but also practiced the ascetic practices *(dhutanga)* sitting always alone. He divided his time between the various monasteries under his tutelage and was an indefatigable teacher of the scriptures.

Scholarship flourished in the reign of King Bodawpaya and Myanmar was able, for the first time, to return thanks to Sri Lanka for nurturing the religion in the Golden Land. The bhikkhu ordination *(upasampada)* preserved in Myanmar was re-introduced to Sri Lanka where the Sasana had been interferred with by an unwise king.

THE AMARAPURA NIKAYA IN SRI LANKA

In the later half of the eighteenth century, the *upasampada* ordination in Sri Lanka was barred to all except the members of the landed aristocracy. This was a result of royal decree probably issued with the support of at least a section of the Sangha. However, this was a flagrant defilement of the letter and the spirit of the Buddha's instructions. The conferring of the *upasampada* ordination is dependent only upon such conditions as the candidate being a man, free from government service, free of debt, free of contagious diseases, and upon his having his parents' consent, etc. Members of the lower castes had now only the possibility of becoming novices (samanera), a condition that created dissatisfaction. A sizeable section of ordained bhikkhus also disapproved of the royal order, but were in no position to defy it within the country. The only recourse for those of the lower castes desiring the higher ordination was therefore to travel to other Buddhist countries to ordain. At first, missions were sent to Thailand where Dhammazedi's reforms lived on through the ordination conferred to Thai bhikkhus in Pago and through the scores of Mon bhikkhus who had found refuge in Thailand from the Myanmar armies.

At the beginning of the nineteenth century, however, Sinhalese bhikkhus began traveling to Myanmar to find the pure ordination there. The fame of the then Mahasangharaja of Myanmar, Nanabhivamsa, influenced their choice. Scholarship had developed in all fields: Pali grammar, the Vinaya, the Suttanta, and the Abhidhamma. Myanmar had, after a long period of development, become the custodian of Buddhism.

The first delegation from Sri Lanka arrived in 1800 and was welcomed with a magnificent reception by King Bodawpaya himself. Nanabhivamsa, the wise Sangharaja, ordained the samaneras as bhikkhus and instructed them for some time in the scriptures. On returning to Sri Lanka, they were accompanied by five Myanmar bhikkhus and a letter from Nanabhivamsa to the Sinhalese Sangharaja. Five bhikkhus form a full chapter and apparently the Myanmar bhikkhus were permitted to ordain bhikkhus without class distinction. Even today, Sri Lanka possesses three schools, the Amarapura Nikaya, the Siyama Nikaya (Thai school), and the Ramanna Nikaya.

The Amarapura Nikaya was so called because King Bodawpaya had established his capital in Amarapura (between Mandalay and Ava) and the bhikkhus had received their ordination there. The Ramanna Nikaya was presumably founded by bhikkhus who had received ordination from Mon bhikkhus in the tradition of the Dhammazedi reforms and who had fled to southern Thailand from the wrath of the Myanmar kings. Both these schools were allowed to ordain bhikkhus without discriminating against the lower classes. Only the Siyama Sangha (the Thai ordination) continued to follow the royal command, and ordained only novices of the higher castes as bhikkhus. Missions from Sri Lanka continued to travel to Amarapura to consult with its senior theras and they were all given royal patronage and sent back with gifts of the Pali scriptures and commentarial texts.

BODAWPAYA'S RELATIONSHIP WITH THE SANGHA

Although King Bodawpaya would appear to have been a pious and devout king, his relationship with the Sangha was somewhat problematic. He supported it at times and even used it to extend his own glory, but at times he seemed almost jealous of the respect the bhikkhus received from the people. He realised that the bhikkhus were not respected out of fear, but were held in genuine esteem and affection by his subjects. His jealousy became apparent on different occasions.

At one time, he declared that from then on the bhikkhus were no longer to be addressed by the traditional title "Hpoungyi" meaning "The One of Great Merit." This form of address was to be reserved for the king. Then again he tried to confiscate land and other goods given to the Sangha and to pagodas by previous generations. When the Sangharajas could not answer his questions to his satisfaction, he invited the Muslim clergy for a meal to test their faith. He had heard that they were so strict in the observance of their discipline that they would rather die than eat pork. Unfortunately for them, they did not display great heroism as they all ate the pork offered to them by the king. Bodawpaya is also reputed to have been beset by a form of megalomania. He wanted to force the Sangha to confirm officially that he was the Bodhisatta of the next Buddha to come in this world cycle, the Buddha Metteyya. On this issue, however, the Sangha was not to be bent even in the face of royal wrath. The bhikkhus refused, and the king was finally forced to accept defeat. Another expression of his inflated self-esteem was the Mingun Pagoda near Sagaing. It was to be by far the biggest temple ever built. Scores of slaves and laborers worked on its construction until funds were depleted. However, it was never completed and remains today as a huge shapeless square of millions of bricks.

To his credit, King Bodawpaya imposed the morality of the Five Precepts in his whole realm and had offenders executed immediately. Capital punishment was prescribed for selling and drinking alcohol, killing larger animals such as buffaloes, spreading heretical views, and the smoking of opium. Bodawpaya ruled the country with an iron fist and brought offending lay people as well as bhikkhus to heel. His successors were benevolent, but possibly they could be so only because of the fear his rule had instilled in the populace.

THE FATE OF BUDDHISM IN UPPER AND LOWER MYANMAR

Bodawpaya's successor, Bagyidaw (1819-1837), was the first of the Myanmar kings to lose territory to the white invaders coming from the West. The Myanmar court was so out of touch with the modern world that it still believed Myanmar to be the center of the world and her army virtually invincible. Hence the king was not unduly disturbed when the British raj, governing the Indian sub-continent, declared war on the Kingdom of Ava in 1824 (Bagyidaw had moved the capital back to Ava). It came to a battle near the coast in which the Myanmar general Mahabandhula achieved little or nothing against modern British arms. The Indian colonial government occupied all of the Myanmar coast as far south as Tenasserim in 1826 and forced the treaty of Yandabo on King Bagyidaw. In the treaty, he was forced to accept the new borders established by the Indian government and pay compensation to the invaders for the annexation of the coast of Lower Myanmar.

However, Bagyidaw made a very important contribution to the development of the Sangha and to the literature of Myanmar in general. His predecessor, Bodawpaya, had united the Sangha by resolving the dispute relating to the draping of the robe over one or two shoulders. Bagyidaw saw the necessity of creating stability for the Sangha. He felt that this could be achieved to some extent by bestowing on it a sense of its own history. He commissioned a work on the history of the religion starting from the time of the Buddha, which was to show an unbroken succession of the pure tradition from teacher to pupil. Its purpose was to praise the diligent theras and expose the shameless ones.

This work, the *Thathana-lin-ga-ya-kyan,* was composed at the king's request by the ex-bhikkhu Mahadhamma-thin-gyan, a leading member of the committee appointed by King Bagyidaw to compile the famous *Hman-nan-ya-za-win, The Glass-palace Chronicle,* a secular history of Myanmar. The *Thathana-wun-tha (Sasanavamsa) -lin-ga-ya-kyan* was completed in 1831; and in 1897, it was printed in the form of a modern book for the first time in Yangon. Pannasami based his *Sasanavamsa* on this work. About forty percent of the *Sasanavamsa* is straight translation from the original work, about forty percent summaries and paraphrasing of the latter, and only some twenty percent Pannasami's own work. Pannasami states in his introduction to the *Sasanavamsa* that his treatise is based on the works of the ancients *(porana).* The concept of mental property or copyright had not been born and there was no moral need to refer the reader to sources except to give authority to a statement. The only references that would lend authority to a treatise would be the scriptures, their commentaries, and sub-commentaries, but not a work as recent as the *Thathana-wuntha-lin-ga-ya-kyan.*

The preface to the original work in Myanmar explains the reason for its compilation. The king's representative had many times pleaded with the author to write a history of the succession of [righteous] religious teachers so that the people would not become heretical. Apparently the king felt that the lack of a work recording the history of the pure religion in its entirety left scope for wrong views to arise. But with an authoritative record of the lineage of teachers, bhikkhus could not call on views of shameless bhikkhus of the past anymore in order to support their heresies. This is exactly what had happened again and again through the centuries and especially in the robe-draping dispute. The *ekamsikas*, the one-shoulder-drapers, had repeatedly dug out obscure teachers in order to support their point of view. This was to be made impossible once and for all.

Whether this has been successful is difficult to ascertain without a detailed study of the developments in the Sangha since the publication of this work. However, the fact that the original Myanmar chronicle was revised and translated into Pali for the Fifth Buddhist Council indicates that it was by this time considered a useful tool to put the king's authority behind a well-defined orthodox lineage, thus making it easy to refute heresy by referring to the historical teachers.

THARRAWADDY-MIN

King Bagyidaw never overcame his shock over the loss of part of his realm. He was declared insane and was removed from the throne by Tharawaddy-Min (1837-1846), King Mindon's father. In the reign of Tharrawaddy-Min, another mission from Sri Lanka visited Myanmar and was received by the Sangharaja Neyyadhammabhivamsa. Neyyadhamma instructed the two bhikkhus and the accompanying novice in the teachings and conferred the bhikkhu ordination on the novice. He is known for his critical emendation of the text of the *Saddhammapajjotika* and its translation into Myanmar. He was also the teacher of the later Sangharaja Pannasami, the compiler of the *Sasanavamsa* and one of the most influential theras at the time of King Mindon. Neyyadhamma showed the need for a recension of at least some of the Pali texts by editing the *Saddhammapajjotika*. His disciple, Pannasami, was to preside over the recension of the entire Tipitaka as Sangharaja under King Mindon.

PAGAN-MIN

Tharrawaddy-Min was himself deposed because of insanity by his son Pagan-Min (1846-52), the brother of Mindon-Min. Pagan-Min appointed Pannajotabhidhaja as his Sangharaja. In his tenure, scholarship received encouragement as the Sangharaja himself wrote a commentary and its sub-commentary in Myanmar on the Anguttara Nikaya. Other works of the time, all in the vernacular, are a translation of the *Saddhammavilasini* and commentaries on the Samyutta Nikaya and the Digha Nikaya. This is also the time when the author of the *Sasanavamsa* appears. He started his scholarly career with the translation into Myanmar of a commentary on the *Saddatthabhedacinta*. His next work was a comparison of the existing versions of the *Abhidhanappadipika* and the translation of his emended text.

In accord with the pre-eminence Myanmar had achieved in the Theravada Buddhist world, the kings of the country became less fierce and wars were fewer. The successors of Bodawpaya seem to have shown a genuine interest in religion as well as in improving the administration of the country. Upper Myanmar moved into a period of peace, which meant improved conditions for the bhikkhus.

The first half of the nineteenth century saw the translation of many Pali texts into the Myanmar language. Almost the whole of the Suttanta was now available in the vernacular and many commentaries and sub-commentaries on Suttanta, Abhidhamma, and the Vinaya were composed in it. This not only made it easier for bhikkhus with limited linguistic skills to study the texts, but also made them readily accessible to the laity. That people in a peaceful country have more time for the study of religion is obvious and soon Myanmar would see the first Buddhist texts printed on modern printing presses. This made it possible for a great number of people to acquire texts relatively cheaply without having to pay a scribe to copy them laboriously onto palm leaves.

Politically Pagan-Min was no luckier than Bagyidaw, as he lost the provinces of Pathein (Bassein) and Yangon (Rangoon) to the British, who were ever ready to create some pretext for war. So, in 1852, the Kingdom of Ava lost access to the sea and became increasingly dependent on the colonial power. Like his father, Pagan-Min was overthrown in a palace revolt. Although not a leader of the uprising, his brother Mindon was placed on the throne. He did not execute the deposed king as was usually the case after a revolt, but allowed him to end his days in dignity.

THE COLONIAL ADMINISTRATION AND THE SANGHA

The occupation by the British forces was of utmost significance for the Sangha as the British administration did not grant the traditional protection afforded it by a Buddhist ruler. In accordance with the colonial policy established in India, that the colonial government should be strictly secular, the new lords refused to take on the role of a Buddhist monarch and accept responsibility for the enforcing of the bhikkhus' discipline. Without this, Buddhism in Lower Myanmar soon suffered and offending bhikkhus went unpunished. The colonial administration would recognise its mistake only much later, when it was too late, and when they were not able to establish control in the Sangha any longer.

KING MINDON

Even today King Mindon's reign (1852-1877) is surrounded by the mystique of a golden era in the minds of the Myanmar people. No war occurred during the twenty-five years of his tenure and the king himself is said to have been of gentle disposition and adverse to violence. He even declared a dislike for capital punishment which was customarily inflicted by sovereigns for the slightest disobedience or even disagreement. He was not only held in esteem by his subjects, but even praised by a British envoy. The colonisers' comments on the Myanmar and their kings were usually dictated by a parochial narrow-mindedness and a simplistic view that was only widened by contact with the conquered. Therefore General Fytche's words describing King Mindon are all the more impressive: "Doubtless one of the most enlightened monarchs that has ever sat on the Burmese throne. He is polished in his manner, has considerable knowledge of the affairs of state and the history and the statistics of his own and other countries. In personal character he is amiable and kind and, according to his light, religious."

King Mindon transferred the capital from Ava to Mandalay, the last royal capital before the British annexation of the whole of Myanmar in 1886. In the early years of his reign, Mindon strove to improve monastic discipline. Although a system of official investigation of complaints relating to bhikkhus' misdemeanours existed, each king had to take his own initiative in re-establishing order in the Sangha.

Mindon found that the attitude of many members of the Sangha to their code of conduct was exceedingly lax. He therefore wanted all bhikkhus of his dominions to take a vow of obedience to the Vinaya rules in front of a Buddha image. He consulted the Sangharaja who convened an assembly of mahatheras, the Thudhamma Council. As opinions regarding the vow differed, the primate's disciple, Pannasami, had to deliver a religious address in support of the king's views. He reasoned that vows were also taken by the bhikkhus at the time of ordination and that if the king sincerely desired to improve the discipline in the Order, he should be supported. All agreed, and the vow was prescribed.

The greatest challenge King Mindon had to face as a Buddhist monarch was undoubtedly his duty to look after the spiritual welfare of his subjects not only in his own dominions, but also in the parts of Myanmar occupied by the British. Moreover, he and many of the leading sayadaws of his court were increasingly aware that the British were only waiting for an occasion to annex the whole of Myanmar. Mindon's army clearly would not be able to stand up to the might of the Indian colonial government. Therefore, it was not only important to support religious activities in the occupied territories but it was also essential to prepare the religion for the time when it would have to survive without the support of a Buddhist monarch.

The British had made it clear at the outset that they would not take over the traditional role of the Myanmar kings, that of protector of the Sasana. The new masters' religion, Christianity, rapidly gained influence through the missionary schools. The schools were popular because their education provided much assistance in securing a job and favor with the colonisers. Christian religious education was a compulsory part of their curriculum.

After the conquest of Lower Myanmar, many bhikkhus had fled north in order to remain within the jurisdiction of the Myanmar kings. Many monasteries in British Myanmar were left without an incumbent and whole villages were therefore bereft of the opportunity to receive religious and general education. King Mindon, aware of this situation, tried to convince bhikkhus to return to Lower Myanmar in order to serve their people. The king's efforts proved successful and many bhikkhus returned to their places of origin. But soon it became clear that without the king's ecclesiastic officials to control the discipline of the Sangha, many bhikkhus developed a careless attitude towards their code of discipline.

The Okpo Sayadaw, from Okpo between Yangon and Pago, had stopped many bhikkhus on their way to Upper Myanmar when the movements of bhikkhus out of the conquered territories was at its peak around 1855. He assembled the bhikkhus around himself teaching that the Sangha needed no protection from the secular power if it observed the rules of the Vinaya strictly. His monastery was the birth place of a movement of strict monastic discipline. He also emphasised that mental volition was what really mattered in the religion of the Buddha and that acts of worship done with an impure intention were worthless. He obviously felt that much of the Buddhist practice had become a ritual and that the essence had been lost. In addition to this, however, his movement also challenged the authority of the king's Council of Sayadaws, the leaders of the unified Thudhamma sect, when he declared their ordination was invalid due to a technicality. As a result, he took the higher ordination anew together with his followers.

The Okpo Sayadaw was not the only critic of the Thudhamma sayadaws. In Upper Myanmar, the Ngettwin Sayadaw criticized many religious practices and maintained that a radical reassesment of religious teachings was necessary. The Ngettwin Sayadaw was also a source of inspiration for the Okpo Sayadaw and other reformers. He had been the teacher of Mindon's chief queen and had also advised the king on many occasions. Interestingly, he was a driving force in a movement in Upper Myanmar that wanted to return to the fundamentals of the religion, but more radically than the Okpo Sayadaw. The Ngettwin Sayadaw, together with many other bhikkhus, left the royal city and went to live in the forest near Sagaing. He started to preach that meditation was essential for all bhikkhus and he required an aspirant to novicehood to prove that he had practiced meditation before he would ordain him.

All the bhikkhus around him had to spend a period of the day in meditation and he emphasised that meditation was of much greater importance than learning. He advised lay people to stop making offerings of flowers, fruits, and candles to Buddha images, but to meditate regularly on the Uposatha days. Of course, his instructions that offerings to Buddha images were fruitless and merely dirtied the places of worship, caused considerable unhappiness with the traditional Thudhamma Council and presumably with many ordinary people. However, the Ngettwin Sayadaw never strove to form a different sect by holding a separate ordination as did the Okpo Sayadaw. His reforms were within the community and within a Buddhist society that was presided over by a king. The Okpo Sayadaw had no place for royalty in his view of the world and did not hesitate to confront the system that was still alive, though obviously doomed.

Two other important sayadaws of King Mindon's reign deserve mention: the Shwegyin Sayadaw and the Thingazar Sayadaw. The Shwegyin Sayadawalso tried to reform the Sangha and his movement is still very much alive and highly respected in Myanmar today. He had studied under the Okpo Sayadaw, but when he returned to his native Shwegyin near Shwebo in Upper Myanmar, he avoided controversy in never rebelling against the Thudhamma Council. He introduced two new rules for his bhikkhus, that they must not chew betel and consume tobacco after noon. He also maintained that the Sangha must regulate itself without help from the authority, but he never doubted the validity of the traditional ordination ceremony.

The Thingazar Sayadaw was one of the most popular of the great sayadaws of his time. He was also part of the movement to return to the basics of the teachings and greatly emphasised the importance of practice as opposed to mere scholarship. Though he was greatly honored by the king and made a member of the Thudhamma Council, he preferred spending long periods in solitude in the forest. In the numerous monasteries built for him by the royal family and the nobility of the country, he insisted on the practice of the purest of conduct in accordance with the Vinaya. However, he did not involve himself in disputes with the extreme reformers or the Thudhamma council. He became very popular through the humorous tales he told in sermons preached in his frequent travels up and down the country.

King Mindon had no easy task. One section of the Sangha was pressing for far reaching reforms, yet it was the king's duty to maintain a certain continuity of the traditional ways for the benefit of the people in general. What complicated the situation was the fact that the Sangha of Lower Myanmar felt more and more independent of the Buddhist monarch and his Thudhamma council of senior mahatheras. This is illustrated graphically by the Okpo Sayadaw's declaration that the Sangha needed no regulation by the worldly power. This view gained popularity also in Upper Myanmar. Luckily, King Mindon's devotion to Buddhism was genuine and he was not deterred by the difficulties confronting him. He was determined not to allow the Sangha to split into factions that were openly opposing each other. This he achieved to some extent through careful diplomacy and through the calling of a great Synod, a Sangayana, in the royal city of Mandalay.

The Sangayana, or Buddhist Council, is the most important function of the Buddhist religion. The first Sangayana was held during the first Rains Retreat after the Parinibbana of the Buddha; the texts to be regarded as authentic were determined at this time. There had been three more Sangayanas since, according to the Theravada tradition. The council convened by the great Emperor Asoka, whose missionaries brought Buddhism to Myanmar, probably provided the most inspiration for Mindon. The Fourth Council, the one prior to Mindon's council, was held in Sri Lanka in the first century BC, at the Aluvihara near Matale, for the purpose of writing down the Tipitaka, which up to that time had been passed on orally.

King Mindon himself presided over the Fifth Buddhist Council, during which all the canonical texts were recited and the correct form was established from among any variant readings. The task took more than three years to accomplish, from 1868 to 1871. When the bhikkhus had completed their great project, the king had all of the Buddhist scriptures, the Tipitaka, engraved on 729 marble slabs. The slabs were then housed each in a separate small pagoda about three meters high with a roof to protect the inscriptions from the elements. The small shrines were built around a central pagoda, the Kuthodaw Pagoda, the Pagoda of the Noble Merit. To commemorate the great council, King Mindon crowned the Shwedagon Pagoda in Yangon with a new Hti or spire.

The Fifth Buddhist Council and the crowning of the Shwedagon Pagoda reminded all the people of Myanmar of the importance of their religion, as well as of the fact that the king and the Thudhamma Council of senior monks were still the guardians of the Sasana. The authority of the Thudhamma Council was greatly enhanced also in Lower Myanmar through the synod. Although the British had not allowed King Mindon to attend the raising of the new spire onto the Shwedagon, the crowning was a symbol of the religious unity of Myanmar which persisted in spite of the British occupation. The religion was also later to become the rallying point for the Myanmar nationalists who fought for independence from the colonisers.

King Mindon's reign produced a number of scholarly works as well as translations from the Pali. Neyyadhamma, the royal preceptor, himself wrote a sub-commentary on the Majjhima Nikaya, which had been translated by one of his disciples under his guidance. A commentary in Myanmar on the Pali Jatakas was composed by Medhavivamsa and the compiler of the *Sasanavamsa,* Pannasami, put his name to a great number of works. One of the queens of King Mindon requested Pannasami to write the *Silakatha* and the *Upayakatha.* His teacher asked him to compose the *Voharatthabheda, Vivadavinicchaya, Nagarajuppattikatha.* He also wrote a commentary on Aggavamsa's *Saddaniti.* Whether all these works were composed by Pannasami or whether they were composed under his supervision and control is difficult to assess. It is interesting to note that a majority of his works were composed in Pali, which was no doubt an attempt to encourage bhikkhus not to forgo Pali scholarship now that Myanmar translations were readily available. The calling of a great Buddhist council to purify the scriptures was part of this movement towards the revival of the study of the original texts.

During King Mindon's reign bhikkhus from Sri Lanka came to Mandalay on several occasions to solve difficult questions of Vinaya and to receive the bhikkhu ordination in Myanmar. After Mindon's death in 1877, his son Thibaw ascended the throne. He was weak and of feeble intellect, and his reign was short. In 1886, he lost his kingdom to the British empire and was exiled to India.

With the complete annexation of Myanmar by the British, a historical era came to an end. Theravada Buddhism developed in Myanmar over more than two millennia. The visits of the Buddha were the first brief illuminations in a country that was shrouded in darkness. The worship of the Buddha that is thought to have resulted from these visits and from the arrival of the hair relics, may have been merely part of a nature religion. The pure religion could not endure for long in a country which was yet on the brink of civilization. Later, however, the teachings of the Buddha were brought repeatedly to those lands by various people.

The visits of the Arahats sent out after Emperor Asoka's council are historically more acceptable than the visits of the Buddha. Their teachings were understood and perpetuated possibly in Indian settlements along the coast and later in communities of people from central Asia such as the Pyu. Through their contact with India, these cultural centers of the Pyu and Mon could remain in contact with Buddhism. At first the important centers of Theravada Buddhism were in northern India and later in South India and then Sri Lanka. Through repeated contact with orthodox bhikkhus abroad, the understanding of Buddhism grew ever stronger in the minds of the people of Myanmar. The religion was distorted dozens of times through ignorance and carelessness, but someone always appeared to correct the teachings with the help of the mainstays of the Sasana abroad. Gradually the role was reversed: instead of traveling abroad for advice, the bhikkhus of Myanmar became the guardians of Theravada Buddhist teaching and their authority was respected by all. Eventually, when Theravada Buddhism had long been lost to India and its future was uncertain in Sri Lanka, it found a secure home in Southeast Asia, especially in Myanmar.

Chapter - 4

Buddhism in Cambodia

Buddhism has existed in Cambodia since at least the 5th century CE, with some sources placing its origin as early as the 3rd century BCE. Theravada Buddhism has been the Cambodian state religion since the 13th century CE (excepting the Khmer Rouge period), and is currently estimated to be the faith of 95% of the population.

The history of Buddhism in Cambodia spans nearly two thousand years, across a number of successive kingdoms and empires. Buddhism entered Cambodia through two different streams. The earliest forms of Buddhism, along with Hindu influences, entered the Funan kingdom with Hindu merchants. In later history, a second stream of Buddhism entered Khmer culture during the Angkor empire when Cambodia absorbed the various Buddhist traditions of the Mon kingdoms of Dvaravati and Haripunchai.

For the first thousand years of Khmer history, Cambodia was ruled by a series of Hindu kings with an occasional Buddhist king, such as Jayavarman of Funan, and Suryvarman I. A variety of Buddhist traditions co-existed peacefully throughout Cambodian lands, under the tolerant auspices of Hindu kings and the neighboring Mon-Theravada kingdoms.

Unconfirmed Singhalese sources assert that missionaries of King Asoka introduced Buddhism into Southeast Asia in the 3rd century B.C. Various Buddhist sects competed with Brahamanism and indigenous animistic religions over approximately the next millennium; during this period, Indian culture was highly influential.

Th Funan Kingdom that flourished between 100 B.C. and 500 A.D. kingdom was Hindu, with the kings of Funan sponsoring the worship of Vishnu and Shiva. Buddhism was already present in Funan as a secondary religion in this era. Buddhism began to assert its presence from about year 450 A.D. onward, and was observed by the Chinese traveler I Ching toward the close of the seventh century.

The Kingdom of Chenla replaced Funan and endured from 500-700 A.D. Buddhism was weakened in the Chenla period, but survived, as seen in the inscriptions of Sambor

Prei Kuk (626 A.D.) and those of Siem Reap dealing with the erection of statues of Avalokitesvara (791 A.D.). Some pre-Angkorean statuary in the Mekong Delta region indicate the existence of Sanskrit-based Sarvastivada Buddhism. Khmer-style Buddha images are abundant from the period of 600-800 A.D. Many Mahayana bodhisattva images also date from this period, often found alongside the predominantly Hindu images of Shiva and Vishnu. An inscription from Ta Prohm temple in Bali province, dated about 625 A.D., states, that the Buddha, Dharma and Sangha are flourishing.

The transition from Hindu god-king to Mahayana Buddha-king was probably gradual and imperceptible. The cult of Shiva and Vishnu gradually blended into the cult of the Bodhisattva. The prevailing cult of Brahmanist worship of Vishnu and Shiva gave way to the worship of the Buddha and the bodhisattva Avalokitesvara.

The Buddhist Sailendra kingdom exercised suzerainty over Cambodia as a vassal state during the end of the eighth and the beginning of the ninth centuries. King Jayavarman II (802-869), the first real Khmer king of the Angkor Empire, proclaimed himself god-king and identified himself with Shiva. Nevertheless, he was increasingly friendly to and supportive of Mahayana Buddhist influence throughout his kingdom. Mahayana Buddhism became increasingly established in his empire. The form of Mahayana Buddhism that was propagated in the Srivijaya lands was similar to the Pala Dynasty Buddhism of Bengal, and of the Nalanda University in northern India.

"The Bengal University of Nalanda in Megadha (now Behar) was the theological center of Mahayana Buddhism under the protection of the Pala Dynasty [750-1060]. Shivaist interpretations of Buddhism, tinged with Tantric mysticism (that may have revived portions of pre-Aryan northeastern Indian cults) were worked out in Megadha and then were exported throughout insular and peninsular Southeast Asia, particularly to Java. Yashovarman I (889-910), who ruled from the vicinity of Rolous in the late ninth century, seems to have been a Shivite Buddhist influenced by Nalanda syncretism. His successors (notably Jayavarman IV) dedicated themselves to Vishnu and Brahma, as well as to Shiva, with whom they continued to be identified by hereditary families of priests. Rajendravarman II studied Buddhism intensely."

The Sailendra dynasty also built the fantastic Mahayana Buddhist temple Borobudur (750-850) in Java. Borobudur appears to have been the inspiration for the later fabulous Angkor building projects in Cambodia, particularly Angkor Wat and Angkor Thom.

The primary form of Buddhism practiced in Cambodia during Angkor times was Mahayana Buddhism, strongly influenced with Tantric tendencies.

"The prevalence of Tantrayana in Java, Sumatra and Kamboja [Cambodia], a fact now definitely established by modern researches into the character of Mahayana Buddhism and Sivaism in these parts of the Indian Orient. Already in Kamboja inscription of the 9th century there is definite evidence of the teaching of Tantric texts at the court of Jayavarman II. In a Kamboja record of the 11th century there is a reference to the 'Tantras of the Paramis'; and images of Hevajra, definitely a tantric divinity, have been recovered from amidst the ruins of Angkor Thom. A number of Kamboja inscriptions refer to several kings who were initiated into the Great Secret (Vrah Guhya) by their Brahmanical gurus; the Saiva records make obvious records to Tantric doctrines that had crept into Sivaism."

"But it was in Java and Sumatra that Tantrayana seems to have attained greater importance. There Mahayana Buddhism and the cult of Siva, both deeply imbued with tantric influences, are to be seen often blending with one another during this period. The Sang Hyang Kamahayanikan, consisting of Sanskrit versus explained by an Old Javanese commentary, professed to teach the Mahayana and Mantrayana."

The presence and growing influence of Buddhism continued as the Angkor empire increased in power. King Yosavarman built many Buddhist temples in 887-889, representing the mandala of Mount Meru, the mythical axis of the world. The largest of these temples is Phnom Kandal or "Central Mountain" which lies near the heart of the Angkor complex.

King Rajendravarman II (944-968) "studied Buddhism intensely. Although he decided to remain a Shivaist, he appointed a Buddhist, Kavindrarimathana, chief minister. Kavindrarimathana built shrines to Buddha and Shiva. Jayavarman V (son of Rajendravarman) also remained a devote of Shiva. He, too, permitted his own chief minister, Kirtipandita, to foster Mahayana Buddhist learning and divination."

SURAYVARMAN I

Surayvarman I (1002-1050) is considered the greatest of the Buddhist kings, excepting only Jayavarman VII.

Surayvarman was from present-day southern Thailand in the kingdom of Sri Dhammarat. He was a Tamil-Malay (Srivijaya) "usurper" to the Khmer throne, who claimed legitimate succession to the throne through his Khmer mother. His father was king of the Buddhist kingdom of Tambralingam on the Malay peninsula. He publicly venerated Shiva or Rama according to his official traditions, but was also a devout Mahayana Buddhist king.

A strong proponent of Mahayana Buddhism, he did not interfere or obstruct the growing presence and dissemination of Theravada Buddhism during his reign. "Indeed, inscriptions indicate he sought wisdom from wise Mahayanists and Hinayanists and at least somewhat disestablished the Sivakaivalya family's hereditary claims to being chief priests (purohitar). Surayvarman's posthumous title of Nirvanapada, 'the king who has gone to Nirvana' is the strongest evidence that he was a Buddhist."

JAYAVARMAN VII

Jayavarman VII (1181-1215), the most significant Khmer Buddhist king, worked tirelessly to establish Buddhism as the state religion of Angkor. Jayavarman VII was a

Mahayana Buddhist, and he regarded himself to be a Dharma-king, a bodhisattva, whose duty was to "save the people" through service and merit-making, liberating himself in the process. Jayavarman withdrew his devotion from the old gods and began to identify more openly with Buddhist traditions. His regime marked a clear dividing line with the old Hindu past. Before 1200, art in the temples mostly portrayed scenes from the Hindu pantheon; after 1200, Buddhist scenes began to appear as standard motifs.

During Jayavarman VII's reign, there was a shift away from the cult of devaraja god-king, toward the cult of the Sangha, the cult of monks. In former times, great effort and resources were invested into building temples for elite brahman priests and god-kings. Under Jayavarman, these resources were redirected to building libraries, monastic dwellings, public works, and more "earthly" projects accessible to the common people.

While Jayavarman VII himself was Mahayana Buddhist, the presence of Theravada Buddhism was increasingly evident. "This Singhalese-based Theravada Buddhist orthodoxy was first propagated in Southeast Asia by Taling (Mon) monks in the 11th century and together with Islam in the 13th century in southern insular reaches of the region, spread as a popularly-based movement among the people. Apart from inscriptions, such as one of Lopburi, there were other signs that the religious venue of Suvannabhumi were changing. Tamalinda, the Khmer monk believed to be the son of Jayavarman VII, took part in an 1180 Burmese-led mission to Sri Lanka to study the Pali canon and on his return in 1190 had adepts of the Sinhala doctrine in his court. Chou Ta-Laun, who led a Chinese mission in to Angkor in 1296-97 confirms the significant presence of Pali Theravada monks in the Khmer Capital."

DECLINE OF ANGKOR AND THE EMERGENCE OF A THERAVADA KINGDOM

After the 13th century Theravada Buddhism became the state religion of Cambodia. King Jayavarman VII had sent his son Tamilinda to Sri Lanka to be ordained as a Buddhist monk and study Theravada Buddhism according to the Pali scriptural traditions. Tamalinda then returned to Cambodia and promoted Buddhist traditions according to the Theravada training he had received, galvanizing and energizing the long standing Theravada presence that had existed throughout the Angkor empire for centuries.

During the time Tamalinda studied at the famous Mahavihara Monastery in Sri Lanka (1180-1190), a new dynamic type of Theravada Buddhism was being preached as the "true faith" in Sri Lanka. This form of Buddhism was somewhat militant and highly disciplined in reaction to the wars with the Tamil that nearly destroyed Buddhism in Sri Lanka in the 9th and 10th centuries. As Theravada Buddhism struggled for survival in Sri Lanka, it developed a resiliency that generated a renaissance throughout the Buddhist world, and would eventually spread across Burma, Chang Mai, the Mon kingdoms, Lana, Sukothai, Laos, and Cambodia.

In the 13th century, wandering missionaries from the Mon-Khmer-speaking parts of Siam, Burma, Cambodia, and Sri Lanka played an important part in this process.

When Prince Tamalinda returned after ten years of ordination, he was a Thera, a senior monk, capable of administering ordination into this vigorous Theravada lineage, which insisted on orthodoxy and rejected Mahayana "innovations" such as tantric practices.

The mass conversion of Khmer society to Theravada Buddhism amounted to a nonviolent revolution every all level of society. All monumental building projects that had characterized the Angkor empire came to a sudden end. Scholars struggle to account for this sudden and inexplicable transformation of Khmer civilization. Theravada Buddhism succeeded because it was inclusive and universal in its outreach, recruiting the disciples and monks from not only the elites and court, but also in the villages and among the peasants, enhancing its popularity among the Khmer folk.

"The post-Angkor period saw the dramatic rise of the Pali Theravada tradition in Southeast Asia and concomitant decline of the Brahmanic and Mahayana Buddhist religious traditions. A 1423 Thai account of a mission to Sri Lanka mentions eight Khmer monks who again brought orthodox Mahavihara sect of Singhalese order to Kampuchea. This particular event belied, however, the profound societal shift that was taking place from priestly class structure to a village-based monastic system in Theravada lands. While adhering to the monastic discipline, monks developed their wats, or temple-monasteries, not only into moral religious but also education, social-service, and cultural centers for the people. Wats became the main source of learning and popular education. Early western explorers, settlers, and missionaries reported widespread literacy among the male populations of Burma, Thailand, Kampuchea, Laos, and Vietnam. Until the 19th century, literacy rates exceeded those of Europe in most if not all Theravada lands. In Kampuchea, Buddhism became the transmitter of Khmer language and culture."

The Theravada revolution was therefor a grassroots movement of the Khmer people rejecting the oppressive burden of maintaining the god-king religion of Hinduism and Mahayana Buddhism. The monumental temples that had countless thousands of slaves attached to them were gradually abandoned to the jungles.

With the rise of Siam in the west and Vietnam in the east, the classical Angkor empire disappeared and the beginning of present day Cambodia began. Cambodia became from this time forward a Theravada Buddhist nation.

BUDDHIST MIDDLE AGES

The Jinakalamali gives an account of the cultural connections between Cambodia and Sri Lanka in the fifteenth century. It states that 1967 years after the Mahaparinibbana of the Buddha, eight monks headed by Mahananasiddhi from Cambodia with 25 monks from Nabbispura in Thailand came to Sri Lanka to receive the umpasampada ordination at the hands of the Sinhalese Mahatheras.

As Angkor collapsed under the advancing jungles, the center of power of the Theravada Cambodia moved south toward present day Phnom Penh. Phnom Penh was originally a small riverside market center where the Mekong River and the Tonle Sap River converge.

Phnom Penh was founded when Lady Penh found a "four-faced Buddha" floating down the river on a Koki tree during the flooding season. She retrieved the Buddha image and had the Wat Phnom constructed to house the image. The four-faced Buddha [Buddha facing the four directions] is important in Khmer Buddhist iconography, signifying the establishment of the kingdom of the Buddha of the Future, Maitreya, who is often identified with the Buddha-king of Cambodia.

After 1431 when the Cambodian kings permanently abandoned Angkor due to a Siamese invasion, the royal court was located on Udon Mountain, a few miles north of Phnom Penh. Siamese incursions from the west and Vietnamese invasions from the east weakened the Khmer empire. The Vietnamese invaders attempted to suppress Theravada Buddhism and force the Khmer people to practice Mahayana Buddhism. The Siamese, on the other hand, would periodically invade Cambodia and attempt to drive out the "unbelievers" in an attempt to protect the Theravada religion. This power-struggle between the two ascendant powers continued until the arrival of the Europeans in the 16th century.

COLONIAL ERA

Buddhism continued to flourish in Cambodia in the sixteenth century. King Ang Chan (1516-1566), a relative of King Dhammaraja, was a devout Buddhist. He built pagodas in his capital and many Buddhist shrines in different parts of Cambodia. In order to popularize Buddhism, King Satha (1576-1549), son and successor of King Barom Reachea, restored the great towers of the Angkor Wat, which had become a Buddhist shrine by the sixteenth century.

Each successive wave of European influence was accompanied by Catholic missionaries, but Theravada Buddhism proved surprisingly resistant to foreign attempts to convert the Khmer people. During the colonial period, the peace was periodically breached by outbreaks of religiously-motivated violence including periodic millenarian revolts.

During the seventeenth, eighteenth, and nineteenth centuries, Thailand's involvement in Cambodian politics extended Thai influence into religious matters as well. On King Norodom's invitation, monks from the Thai Dhammayuttika Nikaya established a Dhammayuttika presence in Cambodia. The newly-formed Thommayut order benefited from royal patronage, but frequently came into conflict with the existing Mohanikay (Mahanikaya) lineage. The Thommayut were sometimes accused of holding loyalty to the Thai court, rather than to the Khmer nation.

During the era of French rule, convulsions of violence, led by Buddhist holy men, would periodically break out against the French. Significant advances were made in the education of Cambodian monks, both in specifically Buddhist topics and more general studies. Primary education of Cambodian children continued to take place at temple schools. Monks were also encouraged to become involved in community development projects.

KHMER ROUGE ERA

In 1975 when the communist Khmer Rouge took control of Cambodia, they tried to completely destroy Buddhism and very nearly succeeded. By the time of the Vietnamese invasion in 1979, nearly every monk and religious intellectual had been either murdered or driven into exile, and nearly every temple and Buddhist temple and library had been destroyed.

The Khmer Rouge policies towards Buddhism- which included the forcible disrobing of monks, the destruction of monasteries, and, ultimately, the execution of uncooperative monks effectively destroyed Cambodia's Buddhist institutions. Monks who did not flee and avoided execution lived among the laity, sometimes secretly performing Buddhist rituals for the sick or afflicted.

Estimates vary regarding the number of monks in Cambodia prior to the ascension of the Khmer Rouge, ranging between 65,000 and 80,000. By the time of the Buddhist restoration in the early 1980s, the number of Cambodian monks worldwide was estimated to be less than 3,000. The patriarchs of both Cambodian nikayas perished sometime during the period 1975-78, though the cause of their deaths is not known.

Due to their association with the Thai monarchy, monks of the Thommayut order may have been particularly targeted for persecution.

POST-KHMER ROUGE ERA

Today Buddhism is struggling to re-establish itself although the lack of Buddhist scholars and leaders and the continuing political instability makes the task difficult.

Following the defeat of the Khmer Rouge by forces of the Vietnamese government, Buddhism initially remained officially suppressed within Cambodia. Following challenges to the legitimacy of the Vietnamese-backed People's Republic of Kampuchea, policies towards Buddhism began to liberalize starting in the summer of 1979. A group of monks who had been exiled and re-ordained in Vietnam during the Khmer Rouge period were sent to Cambodia, and in 1981 one of their number, Venerable Tep Vong, was elected the first sangharaja of a new unified Cambodia sangha, officially abolishing the division between the Thommayut order and the Mohanikay. The ordination of new monks was sponsored by the government as a public show of piety and lifted restrictions on ordination.

Following the withdrawal of the Vietnamese military, the newly-renamed Cambodian People's Party sought to align itself with the Buddhist sangha, declaring Buddhism to be Cambodia's 'state religion' in a 1991 policy statement In 1991, King

Sihanouk returned from exile and appointed a new sangharaja for each of the Thommayut and Mohanikay orders, effectively marking the end of the unified system created under Vietnamese rule in 1981.

THE CAMBODIAN SANGHA

Since 1855, the Buddhist monastic community in Cambodia has been split into two divisions, excepting a brief period of unification between 1981 and 1991: the Maha Nikaya and the Dhammayuttika Nikaya. The Maha Nikaya is by far the larger of the two monastic fraternities, claiming the allegiance of a large majority of Cambodian monks. The Dhammayuttika Nikaya, despite royal patronage, remains a small minority, isolated somewhat by its strict discipline and connection with Thailand.

The Maha Nikaya monastic hierarchy- headed by the *sanghreach* (sangharaja)- has been closely connected with the Cambodian government since its re-establishment in the early 1980s. High-ranking officials of the Maha Nikaya have often spoken out against criticism of the government and in favor of government policies, including calling for the arrest of monks espousing opposition positions. Officials from the Maha Nikaya hierarchy appoint members to lay committees to oversee the running of temples, who also act to ensure that temples do not become organizing points for anti-government activity by monks or lay supporters Nevertheless, divisions within the Maha Nikaya fraternity do exist.

MODERNISTS AND TRADITIONALISTS

Divisions within the sangha between "modernists" and "traditionalists" were recorded in Cambodia as early as 1918. Broadly speaking, "modernists" have attempted to respond to Western criticism of Buddhist institutions by re-interpreting Buddhist teachings- particularly those related to philosophy and meditation- in light of both modern secular knowledge and the textual source of Theravada teachings- the Pali Canon. "Traditionalist", on the other hand, prefer to stick to the practices and teachings handed down through the monastic oral tradition, which have traditionally centered on the performance of merit-making ceremonies and the attainment of "heightened states" through concentration meditation. Traditionalists have tended to reject modern interest in vipassana meditation as a foreign affectation, and have focused on the rote memorization and recitation of Pali passages rather than attempts to study, translate, and interpret the contents of the Pali tripitaka.

For many years, Maha Ghosananda remained the most visible and recognizable figure of the Maha Nikaya modernists. Through his Dhammayatra program and other attempts to use the influence of the sangha to effect social change in Cambodian society, Maha Goshananda brought to Cambodia a form of Engaged Buddhism not previously seen among Cambodian religious institutions. This form of modernist, Engaged Buddhism has proved very popular with Western Buddhists and NGO's, who have lent their support and funding to efforts by Maha Goshananda and other modernist leaders.

High officials of the Cambodian government, by contrast, have tended to support the most conservative of the Maha Nikaya monks, particular the members of a segment known as the *boran*, an ultra-conservative movement that touts the worldly efficacy of the rote recitation of various Pali and Khmer prayers and discourses. Monks in the *boran* movement do not typically possess a significant knowledge of Pali, instead focusing on the rote memorization and recitation of certain verses and scriptures considered powerful. *Boran* monks maintain that by sponsoring recitations of these verses, lay supporters can accrue great merit that will result in immediate, worldly benefits, such as financial or career success. A large number of senior Cambodian officials (including Hun Sen) have patronized *boran* temples, providing for extensive expansions and rich decoration of the most popular temples. *Boran* monks also teach the efficacy of 'group repentance' rituals, where through the recitation of Pali texts the karmic fruit of earlier misdeeds can be avoided or moderated. These rituals, which developed from New Years repentance ceremonies, have become very popular among certain segments of Cambodian society, and have been conducted by the current Maha Nikaya sangharaja, Tep Vong.

The Dhammayuttika order in Cambodia seems to occupy a middle position between the Maha Nikaya modernists and traditionalists. Like the Dhammayuttika order in Thailand, they place a higher premium on scriptural study and knowledge of the Pali language than the monks of the traditionalist camp. At the same time, they have not embraced the modernist/Engaged notion of monks as agents of social development, preferring instead to stick closely to traditional monastic roles of study, meditation, and providing merit-making opportunities for lay supporters.

"YOUNG MONKS" MOVEMENT

Another division in the Cambodian sangha can be seen in what has been called the "young monks" movement, a small group of politically active monks (primarily Maha Nikaya) voicing public opposition to the current government. The "young monks" are primarily junior members of the clergy, drawn from temples in and around Phnom Penh. Unlike the Engaged modernists, their interest is not in using the authority of the sangha to aide social development programs, but rather to express direct opposition to government policies and corruption. Since the 1993 UN-monitored elections, monks have been permitted to vote in Cambodia (a move opposed by some senior monks). While this has not resulted in any large-scale mobilization of the sangha as a political force, it has drawn some young monks farther into participation in parliamentary politics. Many of these young monks are associated with opposition figure Sam Rainsy and his political party, the SRP.

Members of the young monks movement have participated in and organized public demonstrations in Phnom Penh, aimed at drawing attention to perceived government misdeeds. The Maha Nikaya hierarchy has condemned this form of political activism, calling for the arrest of some monks and defrocking others.

KHMER NATIONALISM AND BUDDHISM

Cambodian Buddhism was instrumental in fomenting Khmer national identity and the independence movement in the 20th century, leading to Cambodian independence as a sovereign state. In their attempt to separate the Khmer people from their cultural allegiance to the neighboring Theravada kingdom of Siam, the French "protectors" nurtured a sense of Khmer identity by emphasizing Khmer-language studies and Khmer Buddhist studies. They established Pali schools within Cambodia to keep the Cambodian monks from traveling to Siam for higher education. These Khmer-language study centers became the birthplace of Cambodian nationalism.

CAMBODIAN ADAPTATIONS

Cambodian Buddhism has no formal administrative ties with other Buddhist bodies, although Theravada monks from other countries, especially Thailand, Laos, Burma, and Sri Lanka, may participate in religious ceremonies in order to make up the requisite number of clergy. Cambodian Buddhism is organized nationally in accordance with regulations formulated in 1943 and modified in 1948. During the monarchical period, the king led the Buddhist clergy. Prince Sihanouk continued in this role even after he had abdicated and was governing as head of state. He appointed both the heads of the monastic orders and other high-ranking clergy. After the overthrow of Sihanouk in 1970, the new head of state, Lon Nol, appointed these leaders.

Two monastic orders constituted the clergy in Cambodia. The larger group, to which more than 90 percent of the clergy belonged, was the Mohanikay. The Thommayut order was far smaller. The Thommayut was introduced into the ruling circles of Cambodia from Thailand in 1864; it gained prestige because of its adoption by royalty and by the aristocracy, but its adherents were confined geographically to the Phnom Penh area. Among the few differences between the two orders is stricter observance by the Thommayut bonzes (monks) of the rules governing the clergy. In 1961 the Mohanikay had more than 52,000 ordained monks in some 2,700 wats, whereas the Thommayut order had 1,460 monks in just over 100 wats. In 1967 more than 2,800 Mohanikay wats and 320 Thommayut wats were in existence in Cambodia. After Phnom Penh, the largest number of Thommayut wats were found in Batdambang, Stoeng Treng, Prey Veng, Kampot, and Kampong Thum provinces.

Each order has its own superior and is organized into a hierarchy of eleven levels. The seven lower levels are known collectively as the thananukram; the four higher levels together are called the rajagana. The Mohanikay order has thirty-five monks in the rajagana; the Thommayut has twenty-one. Each monk must serve for at least twenty years to be named to these highest levels.

The cornerstones of Cambodian Buddhism are the Buddhist bonze and the wat. Traditionally, each village has a spiritual center—a wat—where from five to more than seventy bonzes reside. A typical wat in rural Cambodia consists of a walled enclosure containing a sanctuary, several residences for bonzes, a hall, a kitchen, quarters for nuns, and a pond. The number of monks varies according to the size of the local population. The sanctuary, which contains an altar with statues of the Buddha and, in rare cases, a religious relic, is reserved for major ceremonies and usually only for the use of bonzes. Other ceremonies, classes for monks and for laity, and meals take place in the hall. Stupas containing the ashes of extended family members are constructed near the sanctuary. Fruit trees and vegetable gardens tended by local children are also part of the local wat. The main entrance, usually only for ceremonial use, faces east; other entrances are located at other points around the wall. There are no gates.

Steinberg notes the striking ratio of bonzes to the total population of Cambodia. In the late 1950s, an estimated 100,000 bonzes (including about 40,000 novices) served a population of about 5 million. This high proportion undoubtedly was caused in large part by the ease with which one could enter and leave the sangha. Becoming a bonze and leaving the sangha are matters of individual choice although, in theory, nearly all Cambodian males over sixteen serve terms as bonzes. Most young men do not intend to become fully ordained bonzes (bhikkhu), and they remain as monks for less than a year. Even a son's temporary ordination as a bonze brings great merit to his parents, however, and is considered so important that arrangements are made at a parent's funeral if the son has not undergone the process while the parent was living. There are two classes of bonzes at a wat—the novices (samani or nen) and the bhikkhu. Ordination is held from mid-April to mid-July, during the rainy season.

Buddhist monks do not take perpetual vows to remain monks, although, in fact, some become monks permanently. Traditionally, they became monks early in life. It is possible to become a novice at as young an age as seven, but in practice thirteen is the earliest age for novices. A bhikkhu must be at least twenty. The monk's life is regulated by Buddhist law, and life in the wat adheres to a rigid routine. A bhikkhu follows 227 rules of monastic discipline as well as the 10 basic precepts. These include the five precepts that all Buddhists should follow. The five precepts for monastic asceticism prohibit eating after noon, participating in any entertainment (singing, dancing, and watching movies or television), using any personal adornments, sleeping on a luxurious bed, and handling money. In addition, a monk also is expected to be celibate. Furthermore, monks supposedly avoid all involvement in political affairs. They are not eligible to vote or to hold any political office, and they may not witness a legal document or give testimony in court. Since the person of a monk is considered sacred, he is considered to be outside the normal civil laws and public duties that affect lay people. Some of these practices have changed in the modern period, however, and in the 1980s Buddhist monks have been active even in the PRK government.

Women are not ordained, but older women, especially widows, can become nuns. They live in wat and play an important role in the everyday life of the temple. Nuns shave their heads and eyebrows and generally follow the same precepts as monks. They may prepare the altars and do some of the housekeeping chores.

ROLE OF BUDDHISM IN CAMBODIAN LIFE

Buddhist monks traditionally were called upon to perform a number of functions in Cambodian life. They participated in all formal village festivals, ceremonies, marriages, and funerals. They also might have participated in ceremonies to name infants and in other minor ceremonies or rites of passage. Monks did not lead the ceremonies, however, because that role was given to the achar, or master of ceremonies; the monk's major function was to say prayers of blessing. They were often healers and, in traditional Khmer culture, they were the practitioners whose role was closest to that of modern psychiatrists. They might also have been skilled in astrology. The monk traditionally occupied a unique position in the transmission of Khmer culture and values. By his way of life, he provided a living model of the most meritorious behavior a Buddhist could follow. He also provided the laity with many opportunities for gaining merit. For centuries monks were the only literate people residing in rural communities; they acted as teachers to temple servants, to novices, and to newly ordained monks. Until the 1970s, most literate Cambodian males gained literacy solely through the instruction of the sangha.

After independence from France, young Cambodian intellectuals changed their attitude toward the clergy. In describing a general shift away from Buddhism in the late 1950s and the early 1960s, Vickery cites the early work of anthropologist May Mayko Ebihara and his own observations. He suggests that the Khmer Rouge was able to instill antireligious feelings in younger males because the latter were losing interest in becoming monks even during their teenage years, the traditional temporary period of service. The monks themselves had abandoned some of their traditional restrictions and had become involved in politics. At intervals during the colonial period, some monks had demonstrated or had rebelled against French rule, and in the 1970s monks joined pro-government demonstrations against the communists.

Anticlerical feelings reached their highest point among the Khmer Rouge, who at first attempted to indoctrinate monks and to force them to pass anticlerical ideas on to the laity. Under the Khmer Rouge regime, monks were expelled forcibly from the wats and were compelled to do manual labor. Article 20 of the 1976 Constitution of Democratic Kampuchea permitted freedom of religion but banned all reactionary religions, that were "detrimental to the country." The minister of culture stated that Buddhism was incompatible with the revolution and was an instrument of exploitation. Under this regime, to quote the Finnish Inquiry Commission, "The practice of religion was forbidden and the pagodas were systematically destroyed." Observers estimated that 50,000 monks died during the Khmer Rouge regime. The status of Buddhism and of religion in general after the Vietnamese invasion was at least partially similar to its status in pre-Khmer Rouge times.

According to Michael Vickery, who has written positively about the PRK, public observance of Buddhism and of Islam has been reestablished, and government policies allow Cambodians freedom to believe or not to believe in Buddhism. Vickery cites some differences in this reestablished Buddhism. Religious affairs are overseen by the PRK's Kampuchean (or Khmer) United Front for National Construction and Defense, the mass organization that supports the state by organizing women, youths, workers, and religious groups. In 1987 there was only a single Buddhist order because the Thommayut order had not been revived. The organization of the clergy also had been simplified. The sangharaja (primate of the Buddhist clergy) had been replaced by a prathean (chairman).

Communities that wanted a wats had to apply to a local front committee for permission. The wat were administered by a committee of the local laity. Private funds paid for the restoration of the wats damaged during the war and the Khmer Rouge era, and they supported the restored wats. Monks were ordained by a hierarchy that has been reconstituted since an initial ordination in September 1979 by a delegation from the Buddhist community in Vietnam. The validity of this ordination continues to be questioned. In general, there are only two to four monks per wat, which is fewer than before 1975. In 1981 about 4,930 monks served in 740 wats in Cambodia. The Buddhist General Assembly reported 7,000 monks in 1,821 active wats a year later. In 1969 by contrast, observers estimated that 53,400 monks and 40,000 novice monks served in more than 3,000 wats. Vickery sums up his observations on the subject by noting that, "The government has kept its promise to allow freedom for traditional Buddhism, but does not actively encourage it."

Martin offers another, more pessimistic, view of the religious situation in the late 1980s. In a 1986 study, she asserts that the PRK showed outsiders only certain aspects of religious freedom; she also states that the few wats that were restored had only two or three old monks in residence and that public attendance was low. The monks were allowed to leave the wats only for an hour in the mornings, to collect their food, or during holy days. Lay people who practiced their faith were about the same ages as the monks, and they were allowed to visit the wats only in the evenings. A government circular had also instructed civil servants to stop celebrating the traditional New Year Festival. Some traditional Buddhist festivals still were tolerated, but the state collected a 50 percent tithe on donations. Martin believes that Buddhism was threatened externally by state repression and by nonsupport and internally by invalid clergy. She noted that the two Buddhist superiors, Venerable Long Chhim and Venerable Tep Vong, were both believed to be from Vietnam. Venerable Tep Vong was concurrently the superior of the Buddhist clergy, vice president of the PRK's Khmer National Assembly, and vice president of the KUFNCD National Council. She quoted a refugee from Batdambang as having said, "During the meetings, the Khmer administrative authorities, accompanied by the Vietnamese experts, tell you, `Religion is like poison, it's like opium; it's better to give the money to the military, so they can fight'."

Buddhism is still strong among the various Cambodian refugee groups throughout the world, although some younger monks, faced with the distractions of a foreign culture, have chosen to leave the clergy and have become laicized. In the United States in 1984, there were twelve Cambodian wats with about twenty-one monks. In the 1980s, a Cambodian Buddhist wat was constructed near Washington, D.C., financed by a massive outpouring of donations from Cambodian Buddhists throughout North America. This wat is one of the few outside Southeast Asia that has the consecrated boundary within which ordinations may be performed.

Most of the major Cambodian annual festivals are connected with Buddhist observances. The chol chnam (New Year Festival) takes place in mid-April; it was one of the few festivals allowed under the Khmer Rouge regime. The phchun ben, celebrated in September or in October, is a memorial day for deceased ancestors and for close friends. Meak bochea, in January or February, commemorates the last sermon of the Buddha. Vissakh bochea, in April or in May, is the triple anniversary of the birth, death, and enlightenment of the Buddha. The chol vossa takes place in June or in July; it marks the beginning of a penitential season during which the monks must remain within the temple compounds. The kathen marks the end of this season; celebrated in September, it features offerings, especially of robes, to the monks. The kathen was still celebrated in the PRK in the late 1980s.

Cambodian Buddhism exists side-by-side with, and to some extent intermingles with, pre-Buddhist animism and Brahman practices. Most Cambodians, whether or not they profess to be Buddhists (or Muslims), believe in a rich supernatural world. When ill, or at other times of crisis, or to seek supernatural help, Cambodians may enlist the aid of a practitioner who is believed to be able to propitiate or obtain help from various spirits. Local spirits are believed to inhabit a variety of objects, and shrines to them may be found in houses, in Buddhist temples, along roads, and in forests.

Several types of supernatural entities are believed to exist; they make themselves known by means of inexplicable sounds or happenings. Among these phenomena are khmoc (ghosts), pret and besach (particularly nasty demons, the spirits of people who have died violent, untimely, or unnatural deaths), arak (evil spirits, usually female), neak ta (tutelary spirits residing in inanimate objects), mneang phteah (guardians of the house), meba (ancestral spirits), and mrenh kongveal (elf-like guardians of animals). All spirits must be shown proper respect, and, with the exception of the mneang phteah and mrenh kongveal, they can cause trouble ranging from mischief to serious life-threatening illnesses. An important way for living people to show respect for the spirits of the dead is to provide food for the spirits. If this food is not provided, the spirit can cause trouble for the offending person. For example, if a child does not provide food for the spirit of its dead mother, that spirit can cause misfortunes to happen to the child.

Aid in dealing with the spirit world may be obtained from a kru (shaman or spirit practitioner), an achar (ritualist), thmup (witch, sorcerer or sorceress), or a rup arak (medium, usually male). The kru is a kind of sorcerer who prepares charms and amulets to protect the wearer from harm. He can cure illnesses, find lost objects, and prepare magic potions. Traditionally, Cambodians have held strong beliefs about protective charms. Amulets are worn routinely by soldiers to ward off bullets, for example. The kru are believed to have the power to prepare an amulet and to establish a supernatural link between it and the owner. A kru may acquire considerable local prestige and power. Many kru are former Buddhist monks.

Another kind of magical practitioner is the achar, a specialist in ritual. He may function as a kind of master of ceremonies at a wat and as a specialist in conducting spirit worship rituals connected with life-cycle ceremonies. Rup arak are mediums who can be possessed by supernatural beings and communicate with the spirit world. The thmup are sorcerers who cause illnesses.

Fortunetellers and astrologers—haor teay—are important in Cambodian life. They are consulted about important decisions such as marriages, building a new house, or going on a long journey. They are believed to be able to foretell future events and to determine lucky or unlucky days for various activities.

Villagers are sensitive to the power and to the needs of the spirit world. According to observations by an American missionary in the early 1970s, villagers consulted the local guardian spirit to find out what the coming year would bring, a new province chief held a ceremony to ask the protection of the spirits over the province, and soldiers obtained magic cloths and amulets from mediums and shamans to protect them from the bullets of the enemy. Before embarking on a mission against enemy forces, a province chief might burn incense and call on a spirit for aid in defeating the enemy. Examples of Brahman influences were various rituals concerned with the well-being of the nation carried out by the ruler and the baku (a Brahman priestly group attached to the royal court). These rituals were reportedly stopped after Sihanouk's ouster in 1970.

Chapter - 5

Buddhism in Thailand

Buddhism in Thailand is largely of the Theravada school. Nearly 95% of Thailand's population is Buddhist of the Theravada school, though Buddhism in this country has become integrated with folk beliefs such as ancestor worship as well as Chinese religions from the large Thai-Chinese population. Buddhist temples in Thailand are characterized by tall golden stupas, and the Buddhist architecture of Thailand is similar to that in other Southeast Asian countries, particularly Cambodia and Laos, with which Thailand shares cultural and historical heritage.

Thailand is perhaps the only country in the world where the king is constitutionally stipulated to be a Buddhist and the upholder of the Faith. For centuries Buddhism has established itself in Thailand and has enriched the lives of the Thais in all their aspects. Indeed, without Buddhism, Thailand would not be what it is today. Owing to the tremendous influence Buddhism exerts on the lives of its people, Thailand is called by many foreigners "The Land of Yellow Robes," for yellow robes are the garments of Buddhist monks. In view of the increasing interest the world is taking in Buddhism and in view of the fact that Thailand is one of the countries where Buddhism still exists as a living force it will not, perhaps, be out of place to know something of the story of how this great faith reached that country.

Thai Buddhism was based on the religious movement founded in the sixth century B.C. by Siddhartha , later known as the Buddha, who urged the world to relinquish the extremes of sensuality and self-mortification and follow the enlightened Middle Way...... The focus of this religion is on man, not gods; the assumption is that life is pain or suffering, which is a consequence of craving, and that suffering can end only if desire ceases. The end of suffering is the achievement of nirvana (in Theravada Buddhist scriptures, nibbana), often defined as the absence of craving and therefore of suffering, sometimes as enlightenment or bliss.

By the third century B.C., Buddhism had spread widely in Asia, and divergent interpretations of the Buddha's teachings had led to the establishment of several sects.

The teachings that reached Ceylon (present-day Sri Lanka) were given in a final written form in Pali (an Indo-Aryan language closely related to Sanskrit) to religious centers there in the first century A.D. and provided the Tipitaka (the scriptures or "three baskets"; in Sanskrit, Tripitaka) of Theravada Buddhism. This form of Buddhism reached what is now Thailand around the sixth century A.D. Theravada Buddhism was made the state religion only with the establishment of the Thai kingdom of Sukhothai in the thirteenth century A.D.

The details of the history of Buddhism in Thailand from the thirteenth to the nineteenth century are obscure, in part because few historical records or religious texts survived the Burmese destruction of Ayutthaya, the capital city of the kingdom, in 1767. The anthropologist-historian S.J. Tambiah, however, has suggested a general pattern for that era, at least with respect to the relations between Buddhism and the sangha on the one hand and the king on the other hand. In Thailand, as in other Theravada Buddhist kingdoms, the king was in principle thought of as patron and protector of the religion (sasana) and the sangha, while sasana and the sangha were considered in turn the treasures of the polity and the signs of its legitimacy. Religion and polity, however, remained separate domains, and in ordinary times the organizational links between the sangha and the king were not close.

Among the chief characteristics of Thai kingdoms and principalities in the centuries before 1800 were the tendency to expand and contract, problems of succession, and the changing scope of the king's authority. In effect, some Thai kings had greater power over larger territories, others less, and almost invariably a king who sought successfully to expand his power also exercised greater control over the sangha. That control was coupled with greater support and patronage of the ecclesiastical hierarchy. When a king was weak, however, protection and supervision of the sangha also weakened, and the sangha declined. This fluctuating pattern appears to have continued until the emergence of the Chakkri Dynasty in the last quarter of the eighteenth century.

By the nineteenth century, and especially with the coming to power in 1851 of King Mongkut, who had been a monk himself for twenty-seven years, the sangha, like the kingdom, became steadily more centralized and hierarchical in nature and its links to the state more institutionalized. As a monk, Mongkut was a distinguished scholar of Pali Buddhist scripture. Moreover, at that time the immigration of numbers of Mon from Burma was introducing the more rigorous discipline characteristic of the Mon sangha. Influenced by the Mon and guided by his own understanding of the Tipitaka, Mongkut began a reform movement that later became the basis for the Dhammayuttika order of monks. Under the reform, all practices having no authority other than custom were to be abandoned, canonical regulations were to be followed not mechanically but in spirit, and acts intended to improve an individual's standing on the road to nirvana but having no social value were rejected.

This more rigorous discipline was adopted in its entirety by only a small minority of monasteries and monks. The Mahanikaya order, perhaps somewhat influenced by Mongkut's reforms but with a less exacting discipline than the Dhammayuttika order, comprised about 95 percent of all monks in 1970 and probably about the same percentage in the late 1980s. In any case, Mongkut was in a position to regularize and tighten the relations between monarchy and sangha at a time when the monarchy was expanding its control over the country in general and developing the kind of bureaucracy necessary to such control. The administrative and sangha reforms that Mongkut started were continued by his successor. In 1902 King Chulalongkorn (Rama V, 1868-1910) made the new sangha hierarchy formal and permanent through the Sangha Law of 1902, which remained the foundation of sangha administration in modern Thailand.

BUDDHISM IN THAILAND AND ITS PAST

Different opinions exist about when, exactly, Buddhism reached that part of the world now officially known as Thailand. Some scholars say that Buddhism was introduced to Thailand during the reign of Asoka, the great Indian emperor who sent Buddhist missionaries to various parts of the then known world. Others are of the view that Thailand received Buddhism much later. Judging from archaeological finds and other historical evidence, however, it is safe to say that Buddhism first reached Thailand when the country was inhabited by a racial stock of people known as the Mon-Khmer who then had their capital, Dvaravati, at a city now known as Nakon Pathom (Sanskrit: Nagara Prathama), about 50 kilometers to the west of Bangkok. The great pagoda at Nakon Pathom, Phra Pathom Chedi (Prathama cetiya), and other historical findings in other parts of the country testify to this fact as well as to the fact that Buddhism, in its varied forms, reached Thailand at four different periods, namely:

I. Theravada or Southern Buddhism

II. Mahayana or Northern Buddhism

III. Burma (Pagan) Buddhism

IV. Ceylon (Lankavamsa) Buddhism

We shall now proceed to study each of these periods in detail.

THERAVADA OR SOUTHERN BUDDHISM

That the first form of Buddhism introduced to Thailand was that of Theravada (The Doctrine of the Elders) School is proved by various archaeological remains unearthed in the excavations at Nakon Pathom, such as the Dharma Chakra (Wheel of Law), the Buddha footprints and seats, and the inscriptions in the Pali language, all of which are in rocks. Such objects of Buddhistic veneration existed in India before the introduction of the Buddha image, which appeared later as a result of Greek influence. Buddhism, therefore, must have reached Thailand during the 3 century B.C., and it must have been more or less the same form of Buddhism as was propagated by the great Buddhist Emperor Asoka.

This form of Buddhism was known as Theravada or Hinayana (The Lower Vehicle) in contradistinction to the term Mahayana (The Higher Vehicle); the two schools having sprung up soon after the passing away of the Buddha. When worship of the Buddha image became popular in India, it also spread to other countries where Buddhism had already been introduced. This is borne out by the fact that many Buddha images, especially those of the Gupta style, had been found in the ruins of Nakon Pathom and the neighboring cities. Judging from the style of the Buddha images found, it can also be assumed that the early Buddhist missionaries to Thailand went from Magadha (in Bihar state, India).

To support the view that the first form of Buddhism introduced to Thailand was that of the Theravada School as propagated by Emperor Asoka, we have evidence from the Mahavamsa, the ancient chronicle of Ceylon. In one of its passages dealing with the propagation of the Dhamma, the Mahavamsa records that Asoka sent missionaries headed by Buddhist elders to as many as nine territories. One of these territories was known as Suvarnabhumi where two Theras (elder monks), Sona and Uttara, were said to have proceeded.

Now opinions differ as to where exactly this land of Suvarnabhumi is. Thai scholars express the opinion that it is in Thailand and that its capital was at Nakon Pathom, while scholars of Burma say that Suvarnabhumi is in Burma, the capital being at Thaton, a Mon (Peguan) town in eastern Burma near the Gulf of Martaban. Still other scholars of Laos and Cambodia claim that the territory of Suvarnabhumi is in their lands. Historical records in this connection being meager as they are, it would perhaps be of no avail to argue as to the exact demarcation of Suvarnabhumi.

Taking all points into consideration, one thing, however, seems clear beyond dispute. That is Suvarnabhumi was a term broadly used in ancient times to denote that part of Southeast Asia which now includes Southern Burma, Thailand, Laos, Cambodia and Malaya. The term Suvarnabhumi is a combination of the words *suvarna* and *bhumi*. Both are Sanskrit words; the former means gold and the latter stands for land. Suvarnabhumi therefore literally means Golden Land or Land of Gold. Keeping in view the abundance of nature in that part of Asia just referred to, the term seems but appropriate.

The reason why scholars of Thailand express the view that the capital of Suvarnabhumi was at Nakon Pathom was because of the archaeological finds unearthed in the area surrounding that town. Nowhere in any of the countries mentioned above, not even at Thaton in Burma, could one find such a large and varied number of ancient relics as were found at Nakon Pathom. By age and style these archaeological objects belong to the times of Emperor Asoka and the later Guptas. Even the Great Stupa (Phra Pathom Chedi) at Nakon Pathom itself is basically identical with the famous Sañchi Stupa in India, built by Asoka, especially if one were to remove the *shikhara* or upper portion.

Many Thai archaeologists are of the opinion that the shikhara was a later addition to the pagoda, a result, so to say, of the blending of the Thai aesthetic sense with Indian architectural art. Moreover, the name Pathom Chedi (Pali: Pathama Cetiya) means "First Pagoda" which, in all probability, signifies that it was the first pagoda built in Suvarnabhumi. This would easily fit in with the record of the Mahavamsa — that Theras Sona and Uttara went and established Buddhism in the territory of Suvarnabhumi at the injunction of Emperor Asoka. Taking cognizance of the fact that Asoka reigned from 269 to 237 B.C., we can reasonably conclude that Buddhism first spread to Thailand during the 3 century B.C. It is interesting to note in this connection that the history of the penetration of Indian culture to Southeast Asia also started more or less during the same period.

MAHAYANA OR NORTHERN BUDDHISM

With the growth of Mahayana Buddhism in India, especially during the reign of King Kanishka who ruled over Northern India during the second half of the first century A.D., the sect also spread to the neighboring countries, such as Sumatra, Java, and Kambuja (Cambodia). It is probable that Mahayana Buddhism was introduced to Burma, Pegu (Lower Burma) and Dvaravati (now Nakon Pathom in Western Thailand) from Magadha (in Bihar, India) at the same time as it went to the Malay Archipelago. But probably it did not have any stronghold there at that time; hence no spectacular trace was left of it.

Starting from the beginning of the fifth century A.D. Mahayana Buddhist missionaries from Kashmir in Northern India began to go to Sumatra in succession. From Sumatra the faith spread to Java and Cambodia. By about 757 A.D. (Buddhist Era: 1300) the Srivijaya king with his capital in Sumatra rose in power and his empire spread throughout the Malay Peninsula and Archipelago. Part of South Thailand (from Surasthani downwards) came under the rule of the Srivijaya king. Being Mahayanists, the rulers of Srivijaya gave much encouragement and support to the propagation of Mahayana Buddhism. In South Thailand today we have much evidence to substantiate that Mahayana Buddhism was once prevalent there. This evidence is in the form of stupas or chetiyas and images, including votive tablets of the Buddhas and Bodhisattas (Phra Phim), which were found in large number, all of the same type as those discovered in Java and Sumatra. The chetiyas in Chaiya (Jaya) and Nakon Sri Thammarath (Nagara Sri Dharmaraja), both in South Thailand, clearly indicate Mahayana influence.

From 1002 to 1182 A.D. kings belonging to the Suryavarman dynasty ruled supreme in Cambodia. Their empire extended over the whole of present-day Thailand. Being adherents of Mahayana Buddhism with a strong mixture of Brahmanism, the Suryavarman rulers did much to propagate and establish the tenets of the Northern School. There is an interesting stone inscription, now preserved in the National Museum at Bangkok, which tells us that in about 1017 A.D. (B.E. 1550) there ruled in Lopburi, in central Thailand and once a capital city, a king from Nakon Sri Thammarath who traced his ancestry to Srivijaya rulers. The king had a son who later became the ruler of Kambuja

(Cambodia) and who, more or less, kept Thailand under the suzerainty of Cambodia for a long time. During this period there was much amalgamation of the two countries' religions and cultures. The stone inscription under consideration probably refers to one of the Suryavarman kings who had blood relationship with the Srivijaya rulers.

From the inscription just referred to we also learn that at that period the form of Buddhism prevalent in Lopburi was that of Theravada, and that Mahayana Buddhism, already established in Cambodia, became popularized in Thailand only after Thailand had come under the sway of Cambodia. There are no indications, however, that the Mahayana School superseded the Theravada in any way. This was due to the fact that Theravada Buddhism was already on a firm basis in Thailand when the Mahayana School was introduced there. That there were monks of both schools, Theravada and Mahayana, in Lopburi during those days, is indicated in a stone inscription in the Cambodian language, found in a Brahmanic Temple within the vicinity of Lopburi city itself.

Much of the Brahmanic culture which survives in Thailand till today could be traced to its origin from Cambodia during this period. Many of the Cambodian kings themselves were zealous adherents of Brahmanism and its ways of life. This period, therefore, can be termed Mahayana Period. Sanskrit, the sacred language of the Hindus, took its root deep in Thailand during these times.

BURMA (PAGAN) BUDDHISM

In 1057 A.D. King Anuruddha (Anawratha) became powerful in the whole of Burma, having his capital at Pagan (Central Burma). Anuruddha extended his kingdom right up to Thailand, especially the Northern and Central parts, covering areas now known as Chiengmai, Lopburi, and Nakon Pathom. Being a Theravada Buddhist, Anuruddha ardently supported the cause of Theravada which Burma, like Thailand, at first received directly from India through missionaries sent by Emperor Asoka. However, at the time under consideration, Buddhism in India was already in a state of decline, and as contact between Burma and India was then faint, Theravada Buddhism, as prevalent in Burma at that time, underwent some changes and assumed a form somewhat different from the original doctrine. This, at a later stage, became what is known in Thailand as Burma (Pagan) Buddhism. During the period of King Anuruddha's suzerainty over Thailand, Burmese Buddhism exercised great influence over the country, especially in the North where, owing to proximity, the impact from Burma was more felt.

It is significant that Buddhist relics found in North Thailand bear a striking Theravada influence, whereas those found in the South clearly show their Mahayana connections dating back from Srivijaya days. To a great extent this is due to the fact that, in their heyday of suzerainty over Thailand, the Burmese under Anuruddha were content with Upper Thailand only, while leaving the South practically to be ruled by their Khmer (Cambodian) vassals whose capital was at Lopburi.

From the beginning of the 2 century B.C. the Thai people, whose original homeland was in the valleys between the Huang Ho and the Yangtze Kiang in China, began to migrate southwards as a result of constant friction with the neighboring tribes. In the course of their migration which lasted for several centuries, they became separated into two main groups. One group went and settled in the plains of the Salween River, Shan States, and other areas and spread on as far as Assam. This group of Thais is called Thai Yai (Big Thai). The other main group moved further South and finally settled in what is today termed Thailand. The latter group of Thais is called Thai Noi (Small Thai). The Thais in present-day Thailand are actually the descendants of these migrant Thais. Of course, in the course of their migration which, as said above, continued off and on for a long time, there had been a great deal of mixture of blood through intermarriage which was only natural. We should always bear in mind that there are several ethnic groups scattered through the length and breadth of Southeast Asia from times immemorial. But even today we can trace the language affinity of the Thais living in widely scattered areas such as Assam, Upper Burma, Southern China, Shan States, Laos, North Vietnam, and Thailand.

After struggling hard for a long time the Thais were able to establish their independent state at Sukhothai (Sukhodaya) in North Thailand. This was probably about 1257 A.D. (B.E. 1800). It was during the period of their movement southwards that the Thais came into contact with the form of Buddhism as practiced in Burma and propagated under the royal patronage of King Anuruddha. Some scholars are of the opinion that as Mahayana Buddhism had spread to China as early as the beginning of the Christian Era, the Thais, while still in their original home in China, must have already been acquainted with some general features of Buddhism. As the Thai migrants grew in strength their territory extended and finally they became the masters of the land in succession to Anuruddha, whose kingdom declined after his death.

During the succeeding period, the Thais were able to exert themselves even more prominently in their southward drive. Thus they came into close contact with the Khmers, the erstwhile power, and became acquainted with both Mahayana Buddhism and Brahmanism as adopted and practiced in Kambuja (Cambodia). Much of the Brahmanic influence, such as religious and cultural rites, especially in the court circles, passed on from Cambodia to the Thais during this period, for Hinduism was already firmly established in Cambodia at that time. Even the Thai scripts, based on Cambodian scripts which, in turn, derived their origin from India, were invented by King Ram Kamhaeng of Sukhothai during the period under consideration.

Of the period under discussion it may be observed in passing that Northern Thailand, from Sukhothai District upwards, came much under the influence of Burma (Pagan) Buddhism, while in the central and southern parts of the country many Mahayana beliefs and practices, inherited from the days of the Suryavarmans and the Srivijayas, still persisted.

CEYLON (LANKAVAMSA) BUDDHISM

This is the most important period in the history of the spread of Buddhism to Thailand, for it witnessed the introduction to that country of that form of Buddhism which remains dominant there until today.

About 1153 A.D. (B.E. 1696) Parakramabahu the Great (1153-1186 A.D.) became king of Ceylon, known in ancient days as Lanka. A powerful monarch and a great supporter of Theravada Buddhism, Parakramabahu did much to spread and consolidate the Dhamma of the Lord in his island kingdom. He it was who caused (according to some scholars of Southern Buddhism) the Seventh Buddhist Council to be held under the chairmanship of Kassapa Thera, of Dimbulagala in order to revise and strengthen the Doctrine and the Discipline (Dhamma and Vinaya).

As a result of the efforts of King Parakramabahu the Great, Buddhism was much consolidated in Ceylon and the news spread to neighboring lands. Buddhist monks from various countries, such as Burma, Pegu (Lower Burma), Kambuja, Lanna (North Thailand) and Lanchang (Laos) flocked to Ceylon in order to acquaint themselves with the pure form of the Dhamma. Thailand also sent her Bhikkhus to Ceylon and thereby obtained the *upasampada vidhi* (ordination rite) from Ceylon, which later became known in Thailand as Lankavamsa. This was about 1257 A.D. (B.E. 1800). Apparently the early batches of Bhikkhus, who returned from Ceylon after studies, often accompanied by Ceylonese monks, established themselves first in Nakon Sri Thammarath (South Thailand), for many of the Buddhist relics bearing definitely Ceylonese influence, such as stupas and Buddha images, were found there. Some of these relics are still in existence today.

News of the meritorious activities of these monks soon spread to Sukhothai, then the capital of Thailand, and King Ram Kamhaeng who was ruling at the time, invited those monks to his capital and gave them his royal support in propagating the Doctrine. This fact is recorded in one of the King's rock inscriptions, dated about 1277 A.D. Since then Ceylon (Sinhala) Buddhism became very popular and was widely practiced in Thailand. Some of the Thai kings, such as King Maha Dharmaraja Lithai of Sukhothai dynasty and King Borom Trai Lokanath of the early Ayudhya Period, even entered the Holy Order or Bhikkhu Sangha according to the ordination rite of Lankavamsa Buddhism by inviting a patriarch from Ceylon, Maha Sami Sangharaja Sumana by name, to be the presiding monk over his upasampada (ordination) ceremony. Many monasteries, stupas, Buddha images and even Buddha footprints, such as the well-known one at Sraburi in central Thailand, were built in accordance with the usage popular in Ceylon. The study of Pali, the language of Theravada or Southern Buddhism, also made great progress, and in all matters dealing with the Dhamma the impact of Ceylon was perceptibly felt.

However, there had been no antagonism between the different forms of Buddhism already in existence in Thailand and the Lankavamsa which had been introduced later from Ceylon. On the contrary they seemed to have amalgamated peacefully, and all had adjusted themselves to one another's benefit. This is evident in all religious rites and ceremonies of Thailand. Indeed, somewhat characteristic of the Buddhists, there had been a spirit of forbearance in all matters. For instance, even today Brahmanic rites thrive side by side with Buddhistic ceremonies in Thailand and Cambodia, especially in the royal courts.

History repeats itself. Years after, when in Ceylon under King Kirtisri (1747-1781 A.D.) the upasampada ordination was lost due to a decline of Buddhism and upheavals in the country, Thailand (during the reign of King Boromkot, 1733-1758 A.D.) was able to repay the debt by sending a batch of Buddhist monks, under the leadership of Upali and Ariyamuni Theras, who in the course of time established in Ceylon what is known as the *Siyamopali Vamsa* or *Siyam Nikaya*, or Siamese Sect, which still is a major sect in that country. Upali worked and died in Sri Lanka, the country he loved no less than his own.

Today, for all purposes, Thailand can be termed a Theravada Buddhist country. There are, of course, a few Mahayana monks and monasteries, but they are mostly confined to foreign communities, chiefly the Chinese. All, however, live at peace and cooperate with one another.

BUDDHISM IN THAILAND: ITS PRESENT

According to the census taken in 1960 the population of Thailand numbers 25,519,965. Of this number 94% are Buddhists (the rest are mostly Muslims and Christians). This fact itself demonstrates more than anything else how influential Buddhism is in Thailand. In their long history of existence the Thais seem to have been predominantly Buddhists, at least ever since they came into contact with the tenets of Buddhism. All the Thai kings in the recorded history of present-day Thailand have been adherents of Buddhism. The country's constitution specifies that the King of Thailand must be a Buddhist and the Upholder of Buddhism.

The term "The Land of Yellow Robes" has not been inappropriately applied to Thailand, for two things strike most foreigners as soon as they set foot in that country. One is the Buddhist temple with its characteristic architecture, and the other is the sight of yellow-clad Buddhist monks and novices who are to be seen everywhere, especially in the early hours of dawn when they go out in great numbers for alms. The two sights inevitably remind the foreigners that here is a country where Buddhism is a dominant force in the people's life. Indeed, to the Thai nation as a whole, Buddhism has been the main spring from which flow its culture and philosophy, its art and literature, its ethics and morality, and many of its folkways and festivals.

For clarity and convenience we shall divide the study of the present state of Buddhism in Thailand into two parts, namely the Bhikkhu Sangha or the Holy Order, and the Laity.

THE BHIKKHU SANGHA OR THE HOLY ORDER

The Bhikkhu Sangha or the Holy Order of Buddhist monks has been in existence in Thailand ever since Buddhism was introduced there. According to the 1958 census there were in the whole kingdom of Thailand 159,648 monks; 73,311 novices; and 20,944 monasteries or temples. These are scattered throughout the country, particularly more numerous in the thickly populated areas. The Bhikkhu Sangha of Thailand, being of Theravada or Southern School, observes the same set of discipline (Vinaya) as the Bhikkhu Sanghas in other Theravada countries such as Ceylon, Burma, Laos, and Cambodia.

In spite of the fact that the government allots a yearly budget for the maintenance and repair of important temples and as stipends for high ranking monks, almost the entire burden for the support of the Sangha and the upkeep of the temples rests with the public. A survey entitled "Thailand Economic Farm Survey" made in 1953 by the Ministry of Agriculture of the Government of Thailand gives the religious cash expenses of the average Thai rural family per year as ranging from 5 to 10 per cent of its total annual cash income. It may be added here that the report concerns the average Thai rural family, and not the urban dwellers, the majority of whom, in Thailand as elsewhere, are less inclined to religion than the country folks.

Two Sects or Nikayas

There are two sects or Nikayas of the Buddhist Order in Thailand. One is the Mahanikaya, and the other is the Dhammayuttika Nikaya. The Mahanikaya is the older and by far the more numerous one, the ratio in the number of monks of the two sects being 35 to 1. The Dhammayuttika Nikaya was founded in 1833 A.D. by King Mongkut, the fourth ruler of the present Chakri Dynasty who ruled Thailand from 1851 to 1868 A.D. Having himself spent 27 years as a Bhikkhu, the King was well versed in the Dhamma, besides many other branches of knowledge, including Pali, the canonical language of Theravada Buddhism. The express desire of the King in founding the Dhammayuttika sect was to enable monks to lead a more disciplined and scholarly life in accordance with the pristine teachings of the Buddha. The differences between the two Nikayas are, however, not great; at most they concern only matters of discipline, and never of the Doctrine. Monks of both sects follow the same 227 Vinaya rules as laid down in the Patimokkha of the Vinaya Pitaka (the Basket of the Discipline), and both receive the same esteem from the public. In their general appearance and daily routine of life too, except for the slight difference in the manners of putting on the yellow robes, monks of the two Nikayas differ very little from one another.

Organization of the Sangha

Formerly, and in accordance with the Administration of the Bhikkhu Sangha Act (B.E. 2484, A.D. 1943), the organization of the Sangha in Thailand was on a line similar to that of the State. The Sangharaja or the Supreme Patriarch is the highest Buddhist dignitary of the Kingdom. He is chosen by the King, in consultation with the Government, from among the most senior and qualified members of the Sangha. The Sangharaja appoints a council of Ecclesiastical Ministers headed by the *Sangha Nayaka*, whose position is analogous to that of the Prime Minister of the State. Under the Sangha Nayaka there function four ecclesiastical boards, namely the Board of Ecclesiastical Administration, the Board of Education, the Board of Propagation and the Board of Public Works.

Each of the boards has a Sangha Mantri (equivalent to a minister in the secular administration) with his assistants. The four boards or ministries are supposed to look after the affairs of the entire Sangha. The Ecclesiastical Ministerial Council which, by the way, corresponds to the Cabinet, consists of ten members, all senior monks of the Sangha. In addition to this, there is a Consultative Assembly (*Sangha Sabha*), equivalent to the National Assembly, the members of which number 45, selected from various important monasteries. The Sangha Sabha acts as an Advisory Body to the Ecclesiastical Ministerial Council. Below the Sangha Sabha the administration of the Sangha continues to correspond to the secular administration of the country. All monks and novices (*samaneras*) have to live in monasteries which are scattered throughout the country. Each monastery has its abbot appointed by the Ecclesiastical Ministerial Council in consultation with local people. It may be pointed out here that all religious appointments in Thailand are based on scholarly achievements, seniority, personal conduct and popularity, and contacts with monks further up in the Sangha.

There is a Department of Religious Affairs in the Ministry of Education which acts as a liaison office between the Government and the Sangha. In general the Department of Religious Affairs works in cooperation with the Ecclesiastical Ministerial Council on all matters affecting the Sangha. For instance, it issues all legal directives concerning the entire community of monks; it keeps record of the Sangha's property, such as lands etc.; it maintains facts and figures with respect to monks and monasteries. The Religious Affairs Department also prepares the annual budget for the upkeep of the Sangha functionaries and the maintenance and repair of temples etc. It may be added here that all temples and monasteries are State property.

In 1962, the Administration of the Bhikkhu Sangha Act of 1943 was abolished; a new one was enacted instead. By virtue of the new act, the posts of Sangha Nayaka, Sangha Mantris, and Sangha Sabha were abolished. In place of these there is a *Mahathera Samagama* (Council of the Elders) headed by the Sangharaja himself and consisting of not less than four and not more than eight senior monks (*mahatheras*) of the two sects (*nikayas*). The Mahathera Samagama, in collaboration with the Department of Religious Affairs, directly governs the entire Sangha.

Education of Monks

As is well known, the original idea of men's entering monkhood during the Buddha's time or shortly later, was to attain liberation from worldly existence in accordance with the teaching of the Master. Such an idea, of course, springs from man's feeling of aversion to things mundane. In other words, in those far-off days, men entered monkhood with the sole intention of ridding themselves of life's miseries and of obtaining spiritual freedom or Nirvana. Instances of such self-renunciation are found in the holy books of the

Buddhists. With the passage of time, as is only natural, many of the ideals and practices of the early followers of the Buddha underwent modifications. Today, over 2,500 years after the passing away of the Buddha, though the ideal of becoming a Bhikkhu still remains very lofty among Buddhists of all lands, in practice it must be admitted that there have been many deviations from the Master's original admonitions with regard to the whys and wherefores of man's entering monkhood.

Generalization of any subject matter is often dangerous but it will not be far from truth to say that today, in Thailand as in other Buddhist countries, the practice of Buddhist males entering monkhood is to a considerable extent prompted rather by the dictation of custom, the wish for education and other external considerations than by the desire to attain emancipation. Yet there are also many who join the Sangha through genuine love for a religious life and religious studies, or out of the wish to be of service to Buddhism and their country. Finally, in the Thai Sangha also those are not entirely lacking whose life is vigorously devoted to the aim of ultimate emancipation and to the guidance of others towards that goal. There have been, and still are, saintly and able meditation masters in Thailand, with a fair number of devoted disciples in Sangha and laity. There are also still monks — the so-called *thudong* bhikkhus — who follow the ancient way of austere living embodied in the "strict observances" or *dhutangas*.

In view of the above facts, there are two categories of Buddhist monks in Thailand. One comprises those who become monks for long periods, sometimes for life, and the other those who enter the Order temporarily. To serve in the monkhood even for a short period is considered a great merit-earning attainment by the Thai Buddhists. Even kings follow this age-old custom. For instance, the present ruler, H.M. King Bhumibol Adulyadej, also observed the custom for a period of half a month some time ago. Government officials are allowed leave with full pay for a period of four months in order to serve in monkhood. The idea is to enable young men to gain knowledge of Buddhism and thereby to become good citizens.

Life as a monk gives them practical experience of how an ideal Buddhist life should be. In rural districts the general tendency is still to give more deference to those who have already served in monkhood. Such people are supposed to be more "mature" than those who have not undergone the monk's life. Moreover, in Thailand *wats* (monasteries and temples) used to be and are still regarded as seats of learning where all men, irrespective of life's position, could go and avail themselves of education benefits. This is especially so in the case of economically handicapped males of the countryside. Instances are not lacking in which people have climbed high up on life's status ladder after obtaining education while in monkhood. There are neither religious restrictions nor social disapproval against monks' returning to lay life if and when they find themselves unable to discharge their duties as monks.

Cases exist in which, for some reason or the other, men have entered monkhood more than once, although such practice cannot be said to be in the esteem of the public. Looked at from this viewpoint, the institution of entering monkhood in Thailand, apart from being a way of gaining moral and spiritual enlightenment, is a social uplift method by which those not so fortunately placed in life could benefit. Judged from the ideal of adopting a monk's life as enunciated by the Buddha, whether or not such practice is commendable, is a different story. The fact is that even today when modernism has penetrated deep into Thailand, about one half of the primary schools of the country are still situated in wats. With sex and crimes on the increase in the country, the cry for living a better Buddhist life is being heard more and more distinctly in Thailand today.

The traditional education of monks and novices in Thailand centers mainly on the studies of the Buddhist Doctrine (Dhamma) and Pali, the language in which the Theravada scriptures are written. Of the former, the study of the Doctrine, there are three grades with examinations open to both monks and laymen. Those passing such examinations are termed *Nak Dhamm,* literally meaning one who knows the Dhamma. The latter, i.e., the study of Pali, has seven grades, starting with the third and ending with the ninth grade. Students passing Pali examinations are called *parian* (Pali: *pariñña* = penetrative knowledge); in the Thai language the word *parinna* is used to mean academic degree. For example, monks and novices passing the first Pali examination are entitled to write "P. 3" after their names.

Generally the Dhamma and the Pali studies go hand in hand and take at least seven years to complete. The stiffness of the two courses, especially that of the Pali language, can be guessed from the fact that very few students are able to pass the highest grade, the Parian 9, in any annual examination. In the good old days when living was less competitive than now, passing of even the lower Dhamma and Pali examinations used to be of much value in securing good government posts. But now things are quite different; even those successful in the highest Pali examination, the 9 Grade, find it difficult to get suitable employment.

Of late there has developed a new outlook in the education of monks in Thailand. With the rapid progress of science and with the shrinking of the world, Buddhist leaders of Thailand, monks as well as laymen, are awakened to the necessity of imparting broader education to members of the Sangha, if the Sangha is to serve the cause of Buddhism well, "for the gain of the many, for the welfare of the many." As a result of the new outlook there now function in Bangkok two higher institutes of learning exclusively for monks and novices. One is the Mahachulalongkorn Rajvidyalaya, and the other is the Mahamongkut Rajvidyalaya. Both are organized on a modern university footing and both seem to be making satisfactory progress towards that direction. Inclusion in the curriculum of some secular subjects not incompatible with monks' discipline (Vinaya) is among the notable features of these two institutes; the aim is to give an all-round education to monks in order to enable them to be of better service to the cause of Buddhism amidst modern conditions.

So much for the education of 'long-term' monks. As for those who enter the Order temporarily, mostly for a period of three rainy months during the Vassa, or Buddhist Lent, the education is brief and devoted to the main tenets and features of Buddhism only. As pointed out above, such people enter monkhood either by their own genuine desire for knowledge of the Dhamma, by the dictum of custom or, as generally is the case, by the two reasons combined. Monks of this category return to lay life again as soon as the Lent is over. This is the reason why accommodations in monasteries (wats) are usually full during the Lenten period. Nowadays, owing to the pressure of modern life, the custom of temporarily entering monkhood is not so rigorously observed by people living in urban areas as by those in the countryside. The custom has its parallel in Burma, Cambodia, and Laos where Theravada Buddhism prevails.

Wats and Monks

The word "wat" means monastery and temple combined. It is the residence of monks and novices. There are about 21,000 wats in the whole of Thailand. In Bangkok alone there are nearly two hundred wats. Some big wats in Bangkok have as many as 600 resident monks and novices. Wats are centers of Thai art and architecture. Thai culture, to a considerable extent, flows from wats. Wat-lands and constructions thereon are donated by royalty, wealthy people and the public in general. The wat is the most important institution in Thai rural life. The social life of the rural community revolves around the wat. Besides carrying out the obvious religious activities, a wat serves the community as a recreation center, dispensary, school, community center, home for the aged and destitute, social work and welfare agency, village clock, rest-house, news agency, and information center.

A wat is headed by a *Chao Avas* (the abbot) who is responsible for the maintenance of the wat discipline, the proper performance of religious services and rituals, and the general welfare of the inmates. Besides monks and novices, there are also the "temple boys" in wats, who assist monks and novices in various ways, such as bringing and arranging food, cleaning dormitories, washing yellow robes, etc. Usually these boys are related to resident monks in one way or another, and their stay is free of charge. Most of them are students whose homes are far away and who would, otherwise, find it impracticable to get education. This is especially so in Bangkok where accommodation is difficult to get and where all higher seats of learning of the country are situated. The census taken in 1954 reveals that there are as many as 119,044 temple boys in Thailand, which indeed is not a small figure. The institution of the wat, in itself a gift of Buddhism, therefore contributes in no small measure to the social welfare and progress of the Thai Buddhists. The benefits in this respect, of course, are more apparent among the lower strata of society than in the case of the fortunate few on the top.

Apart from engaging themselves in doctrinal studies and observing disciplinary rules (Vinaya) in general, monks are expected to be "friends, philosophers, and guides" of the people. Preaching to masses face to face or over the radio is one of the commonest ways by which monks help the promotion of moral stability among various members of the society. It may not be out of place to reiterate the fact that Buddhism lays great stress on the necessity of leading a morally good life in order to obtain happiness in life here and hereafter. In most of the ceremonies and rituals, whether private or public, monks' cooperation and benediction are indispensable. Indeed, in the life of the average Thai Buddhists, from the cradle to the grave, monks are persons to whom they constantly turn for moral support.

The role of monks in rural districts is even more important, for there the local wat is not only the religious but also the social center of the community. It is at the wat that people come together and experience a sense of comradeship. Religious rituals and ceremonies held at wats are always accompanied by social activities: they are occasions for people, especially the young, to enjoy themselves in feast, fun and festivities. This aspect of the religious service helps the common folks to relax and satisfies their needs for recreation. Not a few matrimonial alliances started from contacts at wat premises. Acting as a moral and ethical example, monks are the most venerated persons in the countryside Thai society, remaining very close to the hearts of the people. In times of crisis, it is to monks that people bring their problems for counsel and encouragement. With few exceptions, the Sangha has well justified this attitude of respect and honor shown to it on the part of the laity and, on the whole, has lived up to the dignity of the Faith.

THE LAITY

Throughout its over 2,500 years of existence Buddhism has been closely connected with the lay community. In Pali the word for a male lay devotee is *upasaka*; *upasika* is its female equivalent. In the history of Buddhism, right from the time of its founder, there had been numerous upasakas and upasikas whose faith in the Teachings of the Master had contributed largely to the dissemination of the Doctrine. Names of the Buddha's munificent followers like Anathapindika, Visakha, Asoka, Kanishka, etc., are on the lips of Buddhists even today. Without the patronage of Emperor Asoka, Buddhism probably could not have spread so far and the course of its history might have been different.

In India, the land of its birth, as well as in most of the countries where its Message has been accepted, Buddhism has received unstinted support from people of all classes, especially the ruling class. History of the movements of Buddhism in China, Japan, Burma, Ceylon, Tibet, etc., amply justifies this statement. In the case of Thailand too, ever since its introduction to that country, Buddhism has been warmly received and patronized by kings and commoners alike. It is well-known that many of the Thai rulers, not satisfied with being mere lay-devotees, got themselves ordained into monkhood and became famous for their erudition in the Dhamma. King Mongkut, Rama IV, probably stands out as most distinguished among this class of royal devotees. The custom of Thai males entering the Sangha also contributes much to the better understanding and cooperation between the lay community and the monkhood. After all, personal experience is better than mere theoretical knowledge.

The Buddha himself, in one of his discourses, exhorted his followers to discharge their duties well so as to enable the Dhamma to endure long in the world. One of the duties of the lay followers, as taught by the Master, is to look after the needs of monks. Hence it is the traditional practice with lay followers in all Buddhist countries, especially those following Theravada Buddhism, to see that monks do not suffer from lack of the four requisites, namely food, clothing, shelter, and medicine. Although in the present age of competitive economy, when life in any field is not so easy, nobody can say in fairness that monk-life in Thailand suffers greatly from shortage of the above four requisites. As Bhikkhus are not allowed to follow any occupational activities, it is clear that they entirely depend on the laity for their existence. In return for this spontaneous support offered them by the public, monks are expected to live exemplary lives for the benefit of themselves as well as of those who look to them as teachers and guides. We have already seen what moral influence monks have upon the people.

Cooperation between the laity and the Bhikkhu Sangha in Thailand is close and spontaneous. To a very great extent this is due to the fact that in an average Thai family some of its members are certain to be found who have for some time served in the Sangha. To the masses yellow robes are symbol of the Master, and Bhikkhus are upholders of the Dhamma, to be deferred to in all circumstances. It is interesting to note that Bhikkhus or Samaneras found guilty of committing crimes are formally divested of their yellow robes before legal action is taken against them by the State, and this is done invariably under permission of the chief monk or the abbot.

"To do good" (*kusala kamma*) is a cardinal point in the teachings of Buddhism. Consequently the idea of performing meritorious deeds is very deeply ingrained in the minds of Buddhists. Ways of doing good or making merit (*puñña*) among the Thai Buddhists are numerous. A man gains merit each time he gives alms to monks or contributes to any religious rituals. To get ordination into monkhood even for a short period, of course, brings much merit. Besides, there are other ways of merit-earning, such as releasing caged birds or freeing caught fishes, plastering gold leaf on Buddha statues or religious monuments, contributing to the construction of a new temple or the repair of an old one, etc. "The Law of Karma" that each action has its corresponding result and the belief in rebirth are two important factors in molding such attitude towards life among the Buddhists.

Though *Nibbana* (Sanskrit: Nirvana), the highest bliss in Buddhism, is aspired to by all good Buddhists, the vast majority of them still think it is not so easy to reach and that they will be reborn again in this world, in heaven or some other world, or — at the very worst — in hell. Hence, as long as they live they must try to do good in order to ensure good results in this very life as well as in the life to come. "Be a light unto yourself. Each man must strive for his own salvation" — these were the Master's words. In view of this, Theravada Buddhism is often said to have individualistic temper. Nevertheless, it is very tolerant, as the long history of its existence will prove. Indeed, the characteristic tolerance of Buddhism, for instance in Thailand, has always permitted the absorption of many beliefs and practices from other sources which have often served to supplement or expand its concepts or to fill gaps.

Animism and Brahmanism may be cited in this connection; the two being important supplements of popular Buddhism in Thailand. A foreign writer has rightly observed that the attitude of the Thai masses towards their religion is of an easy-going nature. They do not bother to distinguish among the various components of their religion; for them it is all of a piece. Only the sophisticated few are concerned with doctrinal logic and purity. Of course, they too know much about its legends, its festivals, its ideals, and its general message that "good will render good." On the whole it can be said that the Thais enjoy their religion. Religious observances are to them as social and recreational as sacred occasions. And for the vast majority, Buddhism suffices in that it enables them to feel and believe and enjoy.

BUDDHIST ORGANIZATIONS AND THE REVIVAL OF BUDDHISM

Organizations among the lay Buddhists of Thailand are recent establishments. Prominent and oldest among them is perhaps the Buddhist Association of Thailand, under Royal Patronage, which now is about 30 years old, having been established in 1933. Having its head office in Bangkok, it maintains branch organizations in almost all major districts of Thailand. Its membership is open to both sexes, irrespective of class, creed, and color. The aim and object of the Buddhist Association of Thailand is to promote the study and practice of Buddhism and to propagate its message in and outside Thailand. Besides arranging regular lectures and discussions on topics concerning the Dhamma, the Association also publishes a monthly journal in the Thai language on the teachings of the Buddha.

Another organization is the Young Buddhists Association which came into being at the close of the Second World War. As its name implies, the Young Buddhists Association takes care of the interest of the young in matters concerning Buddhism. Its primary object is to encourage the young to imbibe the tenets of Buddhism and to live a virtuous life. Chief among its activities are arranging regular lectures and discussions on the Dhamma, issuing publications on subjects dealing with Buddhism in general, and sponsoring meetings of the young on the platform of Buddhism. The Young Buddhists Association also has branches in the districts.

As said earlier the end of the Second World War saw a great revival of interest in Buddhism throughout the world. Even in countries like Thailand where the Doctrine of the Awakened One has been traditionally accepted for generations, people seem to be increasingly eager to know more about the Dhamma. Strange as it may seem, this is partly due to the interest the Occidental World has taken in Buddhism. In times past religion has been more or less regarded in Thailand as "solace of the old." But with the impact of the West in most matters and with the general interest shown towards Buddhism by Western intelligentsia, the Buddhists of Thailand, especially the younger generations who came into contact with the West, began to evince an inquisitive attitude towards their religion — a heritage which they have all along accepted as their own but which they have cared little to know about its true value. This is no attempt to belittle the exceedingly great importance the Thais attach to their religion. But human nature being what it is, the saying "Familiarity breeds contempt" is in most cases not very far wrong. In the Thai language also we have a proverb *"klai kleua kin dang"* which may be rendered in English as "to have the folly to resort to alkali when one is in possession of salt."

Having taken root on the soil of Thailand for centuries Buddhism has naturally attracted many appendages to its fold, some of which are not quite in conformity with the teachings of the Master as contained in the Canon (Tipitaka). Many leaders of Buddhistic thought in Thailand have, therefore, come forward to try to purify the Dhamma of the many impurities that have crept into it. Notable among the reformatory groups are the Dhammadana Association in Jaiya, South Thailand, under the leadership of Buddhadasa Bhikkhu, and the Buddha Nigama of Chiengmai (North Thailand) started by Paññananda Bhikkhu. The two organizations are showing good efforts in the field of awakening the Buddhists of Thailand to the pristine teachings of the Buddha as treasured in the Pali Tipitaka. The mission is admittedly a difficult one but already a promising start has been made in this direction. Much will also no doubt depend on how things transpire in other spheres of human activities, chiefly economic, social and political. The present is an age of conflict — conflict between mind and body, between spirit and matter. Man must find harmony between the two if peace be his aim in life. And to this task of finding harmony within man Buddhism could contribute in no small measure.

INFLUENCES

Three major forces have influenced the development of Buddhism in Thailand. The most visible influence is that of the Theravada school of Buddhism, imported from Sri Lanka. While there are significant local and regional variations, the Theravada school provides most of the major themes of Thai Buddhism. By tradition, Pâli is the language of religion in Thailand. Scriptures are recorded in Pâli, using either the modern Thai script or the older Khom and Tham scripts. Pâli is also used in religious liturgy, despite the fact that most Thais understand very little of this ancient language. The Pâli Tipitaka is the primary religious text of Thailand, though many local texts have been composed in order to summarise the vast number of teachings found in the Tipitaka. The monastic code (Patimokkha) followed by Thai monks is taken from the Pâli Theravada—something that has provided a point of controversy during recent attempts to resurrect the bhikkhuni lineage in Thailand.

The second major influence on Thai Buddhism is Hindu beliefs received from Cambodia, particularly during the Sukhothai period. Vedic Hinduism played a strong role in the early Thai institution of kingship, just as it did in Cambodia, and exerted influence in the creation of laws and order for Thai society as well as Thai religion. Certain rituals practiced in modern Thailand, either by monks or by Hindu ritual specialists, are either explicitly identified as Hindu in origin, or are easily seen to be derived from Hindu practices. While the visibility of Hinduism in Thai society has been diminished substantially during the Chakri dynasty, Hindu influences, particularly shrines to the god Brahma, continue to be seen in and around Buddhist institutions and ceremonies.

Folk religion—attempts to propitiate and attract the favor of local spirits known as *phi*—forms the third major influence on Thai Buddhism. While Western observers (as well as urbane and Western-educated Thais) have often drawn a clear line between Thai Buddhism and folk religious practices, this distinction is rarely observed in more rural locales. Spiritual power derived from the observance of Buddhist precepts and rituals is employed in attempting to appease local nature spirits. Many restrictions observed by rural Buddhist monks are derived not from the orthodox Vinaya, but from taboos derived from the practice of folk magic. Astrology, numerology, and the creation of talismans and charms also play a prominent role in Buddhism as practiced by the average Thai—topics that are, if not proscribed, at least marginalized in Buddhist texts.

Additional, more minor influences can be observed stemming from contact with Mahayana Buddhism. Early Buddhism in Thailand is thought to have been derived from an unknown Mahayana tradition. While Mahayana Buddhism was gradually eclipsed in Thailand, certain features of Thai Buddhism—such as the appearance of the bodhisattva Lokesvara in some Thai religious architecture, and the belief that the king of Thailand is a bodhisattva himself—reveal the influence of Mahayana concepts. The only other bodhisattva prominent in Thai religion is Maitreya; Maitreya is derived from a verb meaning to beam, emit, radiate, broadcast. Statues of Phra Sangkrachai can be found in most Thai Buddhist temples and on amulets as well. Thais sometimes pray to be reborn during the time of Maitreya, or dedicate merit from worship activities to that end.

In modern times, additional Mahayana influence has stemmed from the presence of Chinese immigrants in Thai society. While some Chinese have "converted" to Thai-style Theravada Buddhism, many others maintain their own separate temples in the East Asian Mahayana tradition. The growing popularity of the goddess Kuan Yin in Thailand (a form of Avalokitesvara) may be attributed to the Chinese Mahayanist presence in Thailand.

GOVERNMENT TIE

While Thailand is currently a constitutional monarchy, it inherited a strong Southeast Asian tradition of Buddhist kingship that tied the legitimacy of the state to its protection and support for Buddhist institutions. This connection has been maintained into the modern era, with Buddhist institutions and clergy being granted special benefits by the government, as well as being subjected to a certain amount of government oversight.

In addition to the ecclesiastic leadership of the *sangha*, a secular government ministry supervises Buddhist temples and monks. The legal status of Buddhist sects and reform movements has been an issue of contention in some cases, particularly in the case of Santi Asoke, which was legally forbidden from calling itself a Buddhist denomination, and in the case of the ordination of women- monks attempting to revive the Theravada bhikkhuni lineage have been prosecuted as though attempting to impersonate members of the clergy.

In addition to state support and recognition—in the form of formal gifts to monasteries made by government officials and the royal family (for example, Kathin)—a number of special rights are conferred upon Buddhist monks. They are granted free passage on public transportation, and most train stations and airports have special seating sections reserved for members of the clergy. Conversely, ordained monastics are forbidden from standing for office or voting in elections.

In 2007, calls were made by some Thais for Buddhism to be recognized in the new national constitution as a state religion. This suggestion was initially rejected by the committee charged with drafting the new constitution. This move prompted a number of protests from supporters of the initiative, including a number of marches on the capital and a hunger strike by twelve Buddhist monks. Some critics of the plan, including scholar and social critic Sulak Sivaraksa, have claimed that the movement to declare Buddhism a national religion is motivated by political gain, and may be being manipulated by supporters of ousted Prime Minister Thaksin Sinawatra.

The Constitution Drafting Committee later voted against the special status of Buddhism, provoking the religious groups. The groups condemned the Committee and the constitution draft. On August 11, Sirikit, the Queen of Thailand, expressed her concern over the issue. According to her birthday speech, Buddhism is beyond politics. Some Buddhist organizations announced the break of the campaigns a day after.

ORDINATION AND CLERGY

Like in most other Theravada nations, Buddhism in Thailand is represented primarily by the presence of Buddhist monks, who serve as officiants on ceremonial occasions, as well as being responsible for preserving and conveying the teachings of the Buddha.

Up until the latter half of the 20th century, most monks in Thailand began their careers by serving as *dek wat* (literally, 'child[ren] of the wat'). *Dek wat* are traditionally no younger than eight, and do minor housework around the temple. The primary reason for becoming a *dek wat* is to gain a basic education, particularly in basic reading and writing and the memorization of the scriptures chanted on ritual occasions. Prior to the creation of state-run primary schools in Thailand, village temples served as the primary form of education for most Thai boys. Service in a temple as a *dek wat* was a necessary prerequisite for attaining any higher education, and was the only learning available to most Thai peasants. Since the creation of a government-run educational apparatus in Thailand, the number of children living as *dek wat* has declined significantly. However, many government-run schools continue to operate on the premise of the local village temple.

After serving (typically for four years or more) as a *dek wat*, a future monk typically ordains as a novice *samanen*, but often shortened to *nen*. Novices live according to the Ten Precepts, as do monks, but are not formally required to follow the full range of monastic rules found in the Patimokkha (Buddhist monastic code). There are a few other significant differences between novices and monks. Novices often are in closer contact with their families, spending more time in the homes of their parents than monks. Novices do not participate in the recitation of the monastic code (and the confessions of violations) that take place on the uposatha days. Novices technically do not eat with the monks in their temple, but this typically only amounts to a gap in seating, rather than the separation observed between monks and the laity.

Young men typically do not live as a novice for longer than one or two years. At the age of 20, they become eligible to receive upasampada, the higher ordination that establishes them as a full bhikkhu. A novice is technically sponsored by his parents in his ordination, but in practice in rural villages the entire village participates by providing the robes, alms bowl, and other requisites that will be required by the monk in his monastic life.

Temporary ordination is the norm among Thai Buddhists. Most young men traditionally ordain for the term of a single rainy season (known in Pâli as *vassa*, and in Thai as *phansa*). Those who remain monks beyond their first *vassa* typically remain monks for between one and three years, officiating at religious ceremonies in surrounding villages and possibly receiving further education in reading and writing (possibly including the Kham or Tham scripts traditionally used in recording religious texts). After this period of one to three years, most young monks return to lay life, going on to marry and begin a family. Young men in Thailand who have undergone ordination are seen as being more suitable partners for marriage; unordained men are euphemistically called 'raw', while those who have been ordained are said to be 'cooked'. A period as a monk is a prerequisite for many positions of leadership within the village hierarchy. Most village elders or headmen were once monks, as were most traditional doctors, spirit priests, and some astrologists and fortune tellers.

Monks who do not return to lay life typically specialize in either scholarship or meditation. Those who specialize in scholarship typically travel to regional education centers to begin further instruction in the Pâli language and the scriptures, and may then continue on to the major monastic universities located in Bangkok. The route of scholarship is also taken by monks who desire to rise in the ecclesiastic hierarchy, as promotions within the government-run system is contingent on passing examinations in Pâli and Buddhist philosophy.

Monks who specialize in meditation typically seek out a known master in the meditation tradition, under whom they will study for a period of years. 'Meditation monks' are particularly revered in Thai society as possessing great virtue and as potential sources of supernatural powers. Ironically, monks of the Thai Forest Tradition often find themselves struggling to find time and privacy to meditate in the face of enthusiastic supporters seeking their blessings and attention.

TEMPLES

In Thailand, a temple is much more than a place to worship, The *wat* is the center of village life, serving as a school, orphanage, theatre, meeting hall, crematorium, youth club, playground - even sometimes a market, political center or restaurant. Although one's behavior must always be correct and polite in a temple, there is no feeling of remoteness or superiority in a Thai *wat* it is a repository for all aspects of the life and spirit, as well as the spirituality of the community it serves.

Thais love to "make merit" with Buddha by donation religious objects to temples. These are always accepted, which means that temples are cluttered with religious bric-a-brac. The richer the populace the more extensive and impressive the objects donated. Recently, a poor lady won six million *baht* in the national lottery. She spent all the money on the building of a new temple, so staying poor but making enough merit to assure her of a good reincarnation at her death. Truly a long term investment!

Although *wats* are exclusively Buddhist, there are elements of pre-Buddhist, Hindu beliefs in most temples. Hindu gods such as Shiva may have their statues included, and Thais combine Buddhism with ancient Animist beliefs so that temples have become centers of local superstition as well as Buddhism. For many visitors, *wats* can become too much. Having seen a few, they merge in the mind's eye into an unfathomable riot of strange sculptures and bright colors.

Without some understanding of the design and function of the various parts, the brain can switch off and "no more temples" is the unfortunate response.

A *wat* is a complex of several buildings. There is no fixed pattern, but in general the largest and most central building is the *wiharn*. This building will have one or more Buddha statues at the far end (Buddhas should always face east), before a large open area for the general public. In this area people come to worship, and to receive instructions from the monks. The chief monk (or Abbot) may have a special low dias of ornamented wood to the left of the altar area. The walls of the *wiharn* are usually decorated with murals depicting the life of Buddha. These vary from exquisite ancient depictions to ugly modern ones.

To one side of the *wiharn* there will usually be one or more *chedis*. These conical structures of brick, coated with plaster painted white or covered in brass or gold, are said to resemble piles of rice. When asked at his death how he should be remembered, Buddha replied "Make piles of rice to remember me by". *Chedis* contain the bones or other relics of religious leaders. The most prestigious (giving the temple the name of *Wat Prathat* or *Wat Mahathat*) contain relics of Buddha himself. Many Thais, on cremation have their remains interred into the side of a *chedi*, identified by a small plaque set into the surface.

The *bot* is the building where monks are ordained. It may contain the most sacred Buddha sculpture, but is often closed when not in use, and the building may be quite small, tucked away in a corner. The area of consecrated ground is marked by eight black stones around the corners and axes of the *bot*.

Most temples also contain a library, usually a decorated wooden building raised on a podium, and a *sala* where novice monks or orphaned children are educated by ordained monks. It is customary to have a *bothi* tree within the temple grounds. It was under this thick trucked tree with heart shaped leaves that Buddha became "enlightened". To one side of the temple grounds, identified by the saffron robes hanging out of windows, are the monks' quarters. Monks administer, clean and look after the *wat*, as well as teaching and meditating in it.

All temples are covered in small, highly reflective mosaics of colored glass. Their significance is to drive away evil spirits - if they approach too close they will see their reflection and be frightened away. There are other precautions to ward off bad spirits, including the monster figures often guarding doorways. Many temples are approached by long flights of steps, guarded at the base by pairs of fearsome serpent heads (*nagas*) whose long scaly backs form the walls on either side of the steps.

The *naga* is a serpent which can change shape at will. One guarded Buddha in the wilderness by growing seven heads to form an umbrella over Buddha's head, and promised to give his body for use by Buddha for all time. Candle holders near the altar within the *wat* are normally made in the form of a *naga.*

Singhas are very popular in Northern Thailand. These are stylized lion statues, and originate in Burmese folklore. They represent strength and power and are usually depicted with mouth half open, seated outside temple door, or devouring a frightened victim. The *Kala* is a monster that devours itself, representing the relentless passage of time. It is usually shown without its lower jaw, which it has already eaten. Originally a Hindu god, it is often seen above windows and doors.

Kinnari are beautiful women above the waist, but with the wings and legs of a bird. They are companions to the gods, and are Himalayan and Animist in concept. Ornate *Kinnari* are popular in Chiang Mai temples. The *Hongse* is a mythical swan-like creature, the mount of the god Brahma. It is often seen in the Northern Thailand as a decoration for ornamental gates or standing on a tall pole in front of the *wiharn.*

All temples contain at least one, and usually many, Buddha images. They can be made from a wide range of materials, but are commonly brick based and covered in cement or plaster stucco. Smaller or more venerable statues will be made of molded bronze, brass or gold. In front of the main image in every temple will be an arrangement of offerings, including lotus blossoms covered in a tea cozy like hood of dried flowers, bronze or copper money trees and commonly a host of lesser Buddha statues, donated by worshippers to make merit.

The physical features of Buddha are largely determined by convention. These vary over time and from place to place. All Buddha's though, have certain features in common. There is a lotus bud on the head to symbolize enlightenment, and very long earlobes which show he was of a royal family who wore such heavy earrings that the ears became lengthened. The fingers are, in most styles, of equal length, as are the toes.

Some statues of Buddha are very different. The Chinese favor an obese, pot bellied Buddha. One at *Doi Tung* has a large deep navel in which visitors are invited to toss coins. This Buddha is associated with happiness, wealth, food and plenty. A fine example towers over the food market at Chiang Rai. An emaciated statue refers to Buddha's experiment as an ascetic - when he decided that total self denial was unnecessary, and developed the idea of 'the middle path'.

Buddha may be pictured in number of different poses. Most usually he is seated cross legged, which indicated meditation. If the right hand is raised, palm outwards, this indicates that Buddha is imploring peace. With left hand raised, palm up, he is teaching. If two fingers are held up, he is blessing. If both bands are down, then Buddha has achieved enlightenment.

The reclining Buddha, in which he is seen resting on a cushion with one arm holding his head, refers to the death of Buddha - the point at which he achieved nirvana.

The walking Buddha refers to walking meditation - regarded as very difficult by most monks. Standing with both hands raised, palms outwards, is a sign of power and refers to a legend in which Buddha stopped the sea from engulfing a village by adopting this pose.

All Buddha images are designed according to precise convention. The sculptor has no artistic freedom in which to work. The changes through time and place of the statues is a catalogue of cultural evolution, not artistic development.

POSITION OF WOMEN

Unlike in Myanmar (Burma) and Sri Lanka, the female Theravada bhikkhuni lineage was never established in Thailand. As a result, there is a wide-spread perception among Thais that women are not meant to play an active role in monastic life; instead, they are expected to live as lay followers, making merit in the hopes of being born in a different role in their next life. As a result, lay women primarily participate in religious life either as lay participants in collective merit-making rituals, or by doing domestic work around temples. A small number of women choose to become Mae Ji, non-ordained religious specialists who permanently observe either the eight or ten precepts. Mae Ji do not generally receive the level of support given to ordained monks, and their position in Thai society is the subject of some discussion.

Recently, there have been efforts to attempt to introduce a bhikkhuni lineage in Sri Lanka as a step towards improving the position of women in Thai Buddhism. Unlike similar efforts in Sri Lanka, these efforts have been extremely controversial in Thailand. Women attempting to ordain have been accused of attempting to impersonate monks (a civil offense in Thailand), and their actions have been denounced by many members of the ecclesiastic hierarchy. Most objections to the reintroduction of a female monastic role hinge on the fact that the monastic rules require that both five ordained monks and five ordained bhikkhunis be present for any new bhikkhuni ordination. Without such a quorum, critics say that it is not possible to ordain any new Theravada bhikkhuni. The Thai hierarchy refuses to recognize ordinations in the Taiwanese tradition (the only currently existing bhikkhuni ordination lineage) as valid Theravada ordinations, citing differences in philosophical teachings, and (more critically) monastic discipline.

Chapter - 6

Buddhism in Vietnam

When Buddhism spreads to Vietnam, the Dharma, adapting to the times and the capacities of the people, consists of two traditions, the Northern and the Southern. The Southern tradition (Theravada) emphasizes everyday practical realities and swift self-emancipation, leading to the fruits of the Arahats or Pratyeka Buddhas. The Northern tradition (Mahayana, or Great Vehicle) teaches all-encompassing truths and stresses the goal of liberating all sentient beings, leading to the complete Enlightenment of the Tathagatas. With both traditions now existing in Vietnam, we can explain how Buddhism came to Vietnam.

Intent to give readers the overview of Buddhism in Vietnam, here we focus mainly on the great times and significant events that have great impacts on Vietnamese Buddhist history so that one may see clearly how Buddhism has made great contributions to the founding, and protecting of the country.

THE BEGINNING OF BUDDHISM IN VIETNAM

How did the Buddhism come to Vietnam? Many people at first believe that it came from China. The reason is that China is a big neighbor and Vietnam was influenced strongly by Chinese politics as well as culture for many centuries. Actually, it's not true. Buddhism came to Vietnam directly from India.

In the past, Vietnam was very much like the intersection between India and China (That's why the French call this country as Indochina). At that time, either walking, or by boat, people made a trip from India to China or vice versa, in doing so they must cross Vietnam. Vietnam, therefore, was a good place to stop by for foreign business people as well as Buddhist monks.

Back to 3rd century BC, after King Asoka organized the Third Council -a Conference to Collect the Dharma- at Pataliputra, India, he sent 9 Buddhist monk delegates overseas. The monks went from Afghanistan to the Mediterranean to teach Dharma. One of these, lead by Sona and Uttara went to Burma then Indochina, including Viet Nam.

Now, in Haiphong -60miles north east of HaNoi- there is a memorial tower to commemorate King Asoka that was built by local Vietnamese Buddhists at that time to express their gratitude to King Asoka. From that evidence, we may come up with conclusion that Buddhism came to Vietnam as early as 300 years BC, even before China.

Then in 2nd century (168-189), Buddhism in Vietnam became more popular and developed with the contribution of three great Buddhist monks who came from India: MARAJIVAKA, K'ANG SENG HOUEI, TCHI KIANG LIANG and a local scholar, MECU -FO (MAU - BAC or MAU - TU in Vietnamese). Because MECU FO played a very important role in developing the Buddhism in Vietnam, we may want to take a close look at him.

MECU - FO was born in between the time 165 -170 in TS'ANG-WU. Many Chinese historians now acclaimed that he was Chinese, but in fact he was Vietnamese or might have been born and raised in a great Chinese-Vietnamese family. To support that theory, we knew that TS'ANG-WU, now consists of KWANG-TUNG and KWANG-SI provinces, originally was a part of Vietnam which was invaded and annexed to China under Han Dynasty, 111 BC. MECU - FO was a talented scholar who understood the philosophies of both great Chinese philosophers Lao Tseu and Confucius well, so that in any debate, he easily made the comparison between those Chinese philosophy traditions and Buddhism and gained the respect among the Chinese scholars at that time. His famous book, "Reason and Doubt" was considered as the first one written at that time about Buddhism, not only in Vietnam but also in East Asia.

MECU FO was mandarin. He took advantage of his position to teach his people about Buddhism. Because of his important contribution, Vietnamese Buddhists always consider him as a first lay man to help build a Buddhist stronghold in Southeast Asia, particularly, in Luy Lau, the capital of Vietnam at that time.

THE LY (1010-1225) AND TRAN (1225-1400) DYNASTIES: THE GOLDEN AGE OF BUDDHISM

For almost 10 centuries, Vietnam was dominated by Chinese. Under the Chinese cruel rule, Vietnamese people were suffering a lots. The Chinese which employed the "Sinicization" -the cultural invasion- tried to uproot the Vietnamese traditions and in the long run, transformed the Vietnamese to become Chinese and annex Vietnam to be one of its province. Many historians now look back into the past still wonder how Vietnam can survive and still exist under such aggressive policy. For us, the answer would be Buddhism. Yes, it's no doubt that Vietnamese people have absorbed the Buddha teaching for many centuries. Buddhism was very much like a glue to tighten them together to live in peace and happiness. Strongly believe in Buddha teaching, especially the universal Law of Cause and Effect, Vietnamese people believe that the evil power someday would be eroded.

During the Chinese rule, there were many revolt attempts to liberate the country including the famous one led by TWO SISTERS TRUNG in the early years of First century.

The Buddhist temples or what we now call the Buddhist communities-by that time certainly played a key role in those movements. It's easy to understand why, because that's the common place to gather and mobilize people. That's why now Vietnamese Buddhist are always proud to say that Buddhism is people's religion. (What's happened to Vietnam in the past is exactly the same thing like the Tibetan Buddhist movements to liberate their country from Chinese at the present time).

Finally, in 939 NGO QUYEN, a Vietnamese general, led the Vietnamese people to fight and win the big battle against the Chinese army on the BACH DANG river, Vietnam then became an independent state. But from independence to a strong, healthy country, it took almost one century. For that period, especially under DINH Dynasty, Vietnamese Buddhists with many excellent monks worked closely with the current government helping to build the kingdom. In return, the emperor, DINH TIEN HOANG, is a Buddhist himself, was helping to organize the Shangha and named KHUONG VIET, the highest ranking monk as his national security adviser. He also named the Most Venerable PHAPTHUAN as his Secretary of State. This was the first time in Vietnamese history, the emperor declared Buddhism as a national religion.

The young nation, of course, had to deal with many problem, domestic as well as foreign matters. But, the critical problem was the pressure from its big neighbor, China. For that period, Vietnam was always under the threat of Chinese invasion. The threat became more clearer when the Chinese government (under SONG Dynasty) in 968 sent a diplomatic delegate to visit Vietnam. Actually, the visiting delegate carried a spy mission. Its purpose was to estimate how strong the kingdom was, in order to make the final decision whether or not to launch the attack. To reach the capital of Vietnam at that time, the delegation must crossed the HONG river and the first Vietnamese that they met were a ferry-man.

During the conversation on the boat, the Chinese were impressed by that guy. They couldn't believe that in a small country like Vietnam, even the ferry-man was very smart and educated, who had deep knowledge about everything, able to discuss with them in any topics, including writing a poem just in seconds. The ferry-man, one may have guessed, was actually the Most Venerable PHAP THUAN, Secretary of State in disguise. Later on, when they met the Vietnamese counterpart, led by the Most Venerable KHUONG VIET, they knew exactly that the country was well prepared, therefore, it's too risky for them to launch the invasion. The kingdom was safe. That's the first time in Vietnamese history, we won a diplomatic war against China. Both KHUONG VIET and PHAP THUAN, the highest ranking monks of the Vietnamese Buddhist -the Sangha-with their diplomatic skills saved the new independent kingdom from invasion.

More than 30 years later, the Chinese began to build up the military force on its border with Vietnam. Facing with the near invasion, the country was in panic. The royal families and the army had no choice but to work together to elect the good leader to lead the country through that difficult time. LY CONG UAN, the Commander in

Chief of the army, a talent, kind and high moral general was enthroned to become the new emperor. That's the birth of the LY DYNASTY (1010).

LY CONG UAN was Buddhist, actually a Buddhist monk when he was young. He was raised by Zen Master VAN HANH in a Buddhist temple since he was 3 years old. Looking into the political atmosphere at that time, we knew that VAN HANH was not only his religious master, but also his mentor. Therefore, when becoming an emperor, he asked The Venerable VAN HANH to become his national advisor. Under his rein, about 300 Buddhist temples were built, and in the capital, the Sangha with his help, was well organized which had about 1000 excellent monks. Like ASOKA of India, the emperor applied Buddha teaching into every aspects to govern the country. With full of compassion, the first thing the Emperor did was to give the order to burn all kinds of fishing nets, to set free all kind of birds. He also freed all the inmates from the previous dynasty. For people who felt mistreat by the local government, he allowed them to go to the capital to see him directly.

Influenced deeply by Buddhism, the next emperor was very kind too. The killings of animals, especially, cows and buffaloes were forbidden. He once woke up at midnight in a very cold winter. He saw his lovely daughter was trembling in the cold, and felt very sorrow, not for his daughter but for his all people. He said, "Oh! My daughter who has all kind of fine winter clothing was still tremble like that. How do my people who don't have enough clothing?"

The LY Dynasty lasted more than two centuries. With good advice from VAN HANH at the very first beginning and many excellent monks later on, Vietnam rapidly became a strong, and civilized state. This is the first time in history, under LY dynasty, Vietnam had built the justice system that tend to educate the criminals rather than punish them. Also this is the first time, Vietnam had its first university which produced many talented scholars as well as public administrators who working for the royal government. Under LY dynasty, the military was also very strong. Employed by the strategy "The best defense is offense", Vietnamese army, the first time in history, crossed the border and strike two provinces of southern China where the Chinese was building the logistic systems in preparation to invade Viet Nam. Vietnam won that war.

That's the golden time in Vietnam history, also the golden time of Buddhism in Viet Nam. Then came the TRAN dynasty. Like the LY dynasty, all emperors of TRAN Dynasty were Buddhists who understood the Buddha teaching well. The Buddhism under TRAN dynasty went to the next stage, the highest level of development. The first emperor, TRAN THAI TONG (1225-1258) dedicated to being a monk rather than a king. So, one night, like what Buddha had done more than thousand years ago, he abdicated the throne, escaped from his family and went into hiding up in the mountain to practice Buddhism. The next day, the powerful prime minister lead the royal family members and all the members of the Imperial Court left the capital to look for him. Finally they found him and asked him to return to the capital to govern his country. The emperor refused. Knowing that they had no power to persuade him, all the people threatened to commit the suicide. The emperor had no choice but to return.

At that time, the Mongolian became a super power in the world stage. By then, half of the world already felt into the Mongolian hands: Central Asia, Russia, Hungary, Poland, Yugoslavia, Iran... then China. After dominating China, Mongolian look into Vietnam. Then 30,000 troops of Mongolian cavalry -very well known at that time- crossed the border and attacked Vietnam the first time on January 17, 1258. Emperor TRAN THAI TONG -the one who wanted to be a Buddhist monk - now commanded the Vietnamese army to fight back. It took about 2 weeks, the Mongolian was defeated.

Angry over the defeat, the Mongolian took the revenge. The second invasion was well prepared, began on August 1284, with 200,000 strong troops under the command of a Mongolian prince. This time, the commander of Vietnamese army was Emperor TRAN NHAN TONG, also a devout Buddhist. The second invasion was not luckier than the first time. After 6 months that both sides had engaged into the fierce battles, the Mongolian was defeated and there was only a few thousands survived to back home.

For Mongolian, especially Emperor Koubilai, the defeat was so unbelievable and unbearable. It's too shameful for the Mongolian empire, therefore, only two months after the defeat, Koubilai giving the order to mobilize all of his best units, ready to take the revenge. On December 25, 1287, 500,000 Mongolian troops under the command of the same Prince, one more time, crossed the border to invade Viet Nam the third time. Again, Emperor TRAN NHAN TONG led the Vietnamese army to fight back and defeat the Mongolian. This time it took for only 4 months. Like last time, there were only few thousands Mongolian survived to comeback. After the third try, the Mongolian quitting the idea to invade Vietnam. Vietnam then began enjoying the peaceful time for about two centuries.

After fulfilling the duties to protect the country and his people, Emperor TRAN NHAN TONG abdicated the throne to become a monk. He went to the YEN TU mountain to practice Buddhism. There he founded TRUC LAM (Bamboo Forest) Meditation School, the first Vietnamese Zen tradition that attracted thousands of followers at that time. TRAN NHAN TONG used most of his time to go to the country side, giving Buddha teaching to people. He organized many Buddhist conferences, wrote many books about Buddhism. After years of teaching, one day he came back to YEN TU mountain and asked his most senior, favorite student to come to see him. That night, after giving his student last lesson, he told him: "It's time for me to leave", then went to Nibbana peacefully. TRAN NHAN TONG was a big name in Vietnamese history as well as Buddhist history.

Vietnamese people as well as Vietnamese Buddhists enjoyed the golden time under TRAN Dynasty which prolonged about two centuries. One may recognize that in this historical period, the country 's intellectual class was mainly consists of Buddhist monks. It's easy to understand why. Under policy of exterminating Vietnamese culture, Chinese which dominated Vietnam for almost 10 centuries, had forbid to establish the local education system in Vietnam. Buddhist temples, therefore, were only places where people can go to get education. As a result , Buddhist Church had produced many talent scholars as well as public administrators to form a backbone of country's intellectual class at that time. That's the fruit of about one thousand years under Chinese non-educational system policy. The interesting thing was, though Buddhism obviously played the important role in shaping the country, it had never seek to influence the government or discriminate the other religions to gain the supremacy. Buddhism, Confucianism, and Taoism together coexisted in harmony under the LY-TRAN dynasties.

BUDDHISM SPREAD INTO THE SOUTH

King Nguyen Phuc Chu (1691-1725), a Bodhisattva in Precepts, played a big role to prosper Buddhism in the South. A historical turn in Vietnam's history had began with the power struggle between the two brothers - Nguyen Hoang and his brother in law, Trinh Kiem- within a powerful family under the Le dynasty. At that time, the king had no power, the real power was at Trinh Kiem' hands, acting as country's prime minister. To avoid persecuting and possible murdering by his brother in-law, Nguyen Hoang left the kingdom seeking refuge in the South where the territory which Vietnam gained from Champa from Tran dynasty had not been developing yet. Officially, he came there as the governor of the new land which was consists of four provinces: Quang Binh, Quang Tri, Thuan Hoa (Hue), and Quang Nam (DaNang). Going with him are loyal followers and whoever wanted to seek the opportunities to build new lives in the new land. Thus, Nguyen Hoang was considered as a pioneer of a movement that Vietnam's history call "Southern Forward Campaign" aiming at expanding Vietnam territory to the South. He later found a Southern kingdom named DAI VIET -Great Vietnam- and claimed independent to the North that led to a war between two clans, the "Trinh-Nguyen Civil War" in Vietnamese history, that prolonged more than two centuries.

Nguyen Hoang was a devout Buddhist. After resettling in Quang Tri and moving to Hue later, he knew that a new country needs a new spirit so he relied in Buddhism to boost the country's moral. That's why he build many temples and promoted some Buddhist monks to the rank of State monks to taking care of religious affairs. The kingdom at that time, in fact, was in a state of war, facing two enemies at both ends, Champa in the South and Trinh in the North but Nguyen's dynasty had exempt young Buddhist monks from draft, that showed how favor of state toward Buddhism. Nguyen Hoang died in 1613. His son, Nguyen Phuoc Nguyen was enthroned. Nguyen was also a devout Buddhist and best known in history as a compassionate king who governed the country with loving and tolerance, that's why people loved him so much and called him "Chua Sai" -The Monk King.

But until NGUYEN PHUC CHU took power, then Buddhism in Southern kingdom got a big boost. King NGUYEN PHUC CHU (1691-1725) was enthroned at the age of seventeen and was a strong devout Buddhist more than any of his predecessors. Not satisfied with the present condition of Vietnam Buddhism, and upsetting about the Shangha where many Buddhist monks lacking of Dharma knowledge and not keeping precepts seriously, though very busy with national defense matters, he set a high priority to improve Shangha. Therefore, in 1695, he invited a well known Chinese monk of Kwang Tung, China, The Most Venerable THICH DAI SAN, came to Hue to help him reorganize and upgrade the Shangha. Ven. DAI SAN arrived in Hue in January of 1696, going with him was a fleet of monks and followers numbered at about hundred. King NGUYEN PHUC CHU was very happy to see him and said to him at the first meeting: "Most of monks don't follow the precepts completely. I will summon all of them here so you may work with them on this matter. Let's prepare to ordain them all and giving precepts. .. You, Sir, may make a public announcement about this event which will open on April 1 till Buddha Birthday (April 8) of this year". After three months working with the King and few Vietnamese state monks, THICH DAI SAN opened a Grand Bikkhus Ordained in Hue which had more than 1,400 Vietnamese monks took part. That would be a big mass ordain in Vietnamese Buddhist history, especially in Vietnam Southern state. Monks over the country had to participate this event in order to get the Precepts Certificate which carried a King seal that recognizes them as Buddhist monks, that could exempt them from military draft, public works and paying taxes.

King NGUYEN PHUC CHU, his family, and most of high ranking public administrators from Royal Court also asked Ven. THICH DAI SAN to be their spiritual master, and all of them got Bodhisattva in precepts from DAI SAN. Ven. THICH DAI SAN claimed that he is the 29th patriarch of Chinese TaoTong Zen School and because it's a great honor for him to have a King as student, he passed the position to King NGUYEN PHUC CHU as his successor, the 30th patriarch of TaoTong Zen School. King NGUYEN PHUC CHU also sent his men to China to buy thousand copies of Sutras, Vinaya ... to store in every temple's libraries. Under his directions, many temples were built or upgraded, such as Kinh Thien Temple (Quang Binh, 1716), Hoang Giac (Quang Dien, 1721),... and the famous one, THIEN MU temple, was refurbished in 1714 . The temple had a new big bell which its lovely sound may reach as far as ten miles away, best known in history as well as Vietnamese literature as "The Sound of Thien Mu 's Bell". To mark the celebration of the renovation temple, the King and family vowed to eat vegetarian foods strictly for one month; also to show his compassionate heart by giving foods, rice, money for the poor over the country.

Thus, one can see, King NGUYEN PHUC CHU has made a great contribution in establishing, expanding Buddhism to the South. More than one century, he and his predecessors have worked hard to prosper Buddhism and unofficially make it to become the state religion in his kingdom. That's we are not wonder why Hue -the capital- as well as Quang Tri province were considered as the root, the stronghold of Vietnamese Buddhist from that time up to now which has produced many great, talent monks in the Vietnamese modern time. We may compare his works with two famous kings in Buddhist history, King Asoka of India and King TRAN NHAN TONG of Vietnam. Under his rein, Vietnamese also accomplished the "Southern Forward Campaign", took control over last piece of land of Champa Kingdom, now Binh Thuan province, in 1692 and began set foot on Cambodia territory in 1698.

BUDDHISM IN THE CONTEMPORARY TIME

Vietnam had been endured the French colonist for almost a century, since 1858. During that time, suspicious of potential threats to their power, the French was pursuing a persecuted policy toward Buddhism by limited the Buddhist clergy and curbed the construction of temples. Moreover, at the first place, the purpose of the French invasion was also to spread Christianity into Viet Nam. Therefore, no wonder why they favored Catholics and discriminated Buddhism. For example, in 1950, the French colonist government in Vietnam issue Decree #10 which imposed a "private" status on Buddhism. Thus Buddhism now was considered as a club, not a religion, which required to obtain official permission to conduct any public activities.

There were many movements attempted to liberate the country. Finally, what we called "The First Vietnam War" -the war between Vietnam and France- ended in 1954. The Geneva Accord divided Vietnam into two countries, which put the North under Communists control and the South to the nationalists which was led by BAO DAI, the last emperor of Vietnam. BAO DAI then assigned NGO DINH DIEM, a Catholic, as his prime minister to form a new government in South Vietnam. NGO DINH DIEM later overthrew BAO DAI to become the head of state.

President Diem applied exactly the same discrimination policy of the French toward Buddhism. Decree #10 of French colonist was reinforced. His older brother, NGO DINH THUC, the most powerful member of the NGO family and also a Catholic Archbishop, was assigned to Hue, Central of Vietnam, which is considered as a Buddhist stronghold in Vietnam.

Then on May 8, 1963, while the Buddhists in Hue prepared to celebrate Buddha's Birthday, one urgent order came from the central government that prohibited them to display the International Buddhist Flag. Coincidentally, a Vatican delegate visited Hue at the same time and people believed that archbishop THUC was behind that order because it irritated him to see the city of Hue -where, over 95% of population is Buddhist- covered with Buddhist Flags, during the visit of Vatican delegate. This act of discrimination upset many local Buddhists. Thousands of them then rallied in front of the local government radio station to listen to the Buddhist leader's address, the formal conduct to celebrate Buddha 's Birthday that has repeated every year. But this time, they hoped to hear some explanations regarding the government 's discrimination order too. Worried that the Buddhist leader might use the broadcasting system to criticize the government and mobilize his Buddhist followers to take the action, the director of radio station canceled the address. He then telephoned the local chief army for help. Five armored cars were dispatched to the scene to disperse the gathering with the result of 9 Buddhists lying dead in blood.

Vietnamese Buddhists had no choice but to stand up to condemn the killings and struggle for the religious freedom. The movement quickly gained the momentum and spread rapidly to the whole country. On May 25, 1963, 10 Buddhist delegates from both traditions in Vietnam held an emergency meeting in Saigon to discuss the situation. As a result, a "Committee To Protect Buddhism" was formed to lead the movement. The committee, on behalf of Vietnamese Buddhists, filed 5 - points petition asking the government to terminate the persecution against Buddhism. Since then, many rallies, demonstrations, hunger strikes took place everywhere. Then came a big thing: On June 11, the Most Venerable THICH QUANG DUC was self-immolated on a busy intersection of Saigon to protest. His last words, a respectful plea to Diem, asking the president to show "charity and compassion" to all religions. Next morning, a photograph of a Vietnamese Buddhist monk, who sat calmly on the street, pressed his palm together in prayer as a sheet of flame covered his orange robe, appeared almost on every newspapers' front page in the world. The international communities were shaken of that event but not DIEM regime. Instead Madame NHU, his sister in law, was considered as the First Lady -because DIEM never got marry- mocked the self-immolation as "barbecue" when asked by foreign journalists.

In a desperate action to save his power, Diem made a serious mistake: He ordered his loyal forces attacked all Buddhist temples over the country on the midnight of August 21, 1963. Thousands of monks, nuns, layman leaders were arrested. The assault turned the country to a big mess. People poured into streets to demonstrate against DIEM regime. Many high ranking officials among DIEM loyalists quitting their posts to protest the violent assaults. Among them were his foreign minister, VU VAN MAU; the ambassador to the United States, TRAN VAN CHUONG, father of Madame NHU. The respected figures of Catholics also resigned to raise the voice of dissidents, among them was father CAO VAN LUAN, rector of HUE university. Many scholars, professors, intellectual people expressed the same views and followed his path.

Finally, United States -the main supporter of South Vietnam- was tired of Diem's stubborn, gave the green light to the generals to overthrow Diem. The coup-d'etat led by Gen. DUONG VAN MINH was successful which toppled Diem regime on November 1, 1963.

The fall of DIEM regime opened a new chapter to Buddhism in Vietnam. A Buddhist Conference was held in Saigon on December 31, 1963. Ten delegates which represent both Buddhist traditions in Vietnam, Mahayana and Therevada, discuss the way to unify the Buddhists. The five days meeting ended with the birth of " Unified Vietnamese Buddhist Church" (UVBC), the only organization to represent the Buddhism in Vietnam at that time.

When Communist North took over the whole country in 1975, they outlawed the UVBC. [...] In 1981, encouraged and sponsored by state, some high ranking monks from UVBC departed the old organization and worked with Buddhist monks from the North to form a new Buddhist organization: Vietnamese Buddhist Church, which is now recognized by the state and acclaimed to represent the Vietnamese Buddhist interests of the whole country.

ZEN IN VIETNAM

From Buddha teaching, Buddhism has 84 thousand ways to attain enlightenment. Zen is one of them. In Buddhist history, the first patriarch of Zen would be the Elder Mahakasyapa, a great disciple of Buddha. One may remember that when Buddha was about to enter final nirvana, one day, before the assembly of the Shangha, he held up a flower. No one in the assembly knew what He meant except the Most Venerable Mahakasyapa who smiled slightly at him. Buddha knew that only Mahakasyapa who can get true Dharma from him without scriptural teaching. He became the first patriarch of Zen and from him, it passed down through twenty-eight generations in India to Bodidharma, who brought Zen teaching to China.

Zen is considered as the separate transmission of the mind-source beyond the verbal teachings and for most of people, Zen is a myth. To most Westerners, Vietnamese Buddhism, especially Vietnamese Zen, has been considered as continuation of Chinese Zen. It's true if we consider Zen must be come from a traditional sectarian school with distinctive doctrines, practices... But it's totally wrong if we think about Zen as a form of meditation in which we learn to understand, to face and live in the real world then we have the so-called Zen tradition of Vietnam. Zen by that definition has become the art of living, culture... It's very much like when we think about Japanese Zen, we think about the art of drinking tea...

Back to the golden age of Buddhism in Vietnam, Ly and Tran dynasties, we have many eminent Zen masters. Traditionally, before passing away, a Zen master left a poem for their students. It may be in the forms of instructional verse or an expression of the spiritual understanding, experience and attitudes toward life. The writing of Buddhist poetry -or Zen poetry- became a familiar practice among Vietnamese Zen masters which has continued up to modern times. These poems have become very popular and have been learned by hearts by many generations of Vietnamese Buddhists. Even Vietnamese Buddhist influenced strongly by Mahayana tradition, Zen in Vietnam has different characteristic. It showed that Buddhism has adapted well to the cultural atmosphere of a new country in which it was propagated. It clearly reflected the attitudes of the Vietnamese people towards life: always optimist and positive.

Let's begin with King TRAN NHAN TONG, the founder and patriarch of TRUC

LAM ZEN School. His famous poem, "Cu Tran Lac Dao" -Living in this world, enjoying with the Tao(*)" is a good example to show the spirit of Vietnamese Zen: living in a simple, easy going way, that's Zen.

Satisfied with your present condition and live, enjoy Tao;

Eating when hungry, resting when fatigue;

You already have a great fortune, don't need to seek elsewhere;

View things with empty mind, that's Zen.

That's TRAN NHAN TONG's message. You just live just that. You already have a good fortune, so what you need is to return to yourself and working with your mind. Whenever you view things with empty mind, you are walking into the opened door of Enlightenment.

TRUC-LAM ZEN of Vietnam was considered as the mature of Vietnamese Buddhist Thoughts which was cultivated for almost three centuries from Ly to Tran dynasty. Among the great Buddhist monks from Ly dynasty who may have the last long impact on the following Vietnamese Buddhist generations were Van Hanh and Man Giac. Let's examine one of the poem written by Zen master Van Hanh:

The life span of body is like a lightning, it exists then disappears in a short moment

It's like all plants and trees -fresh in the spring but fading in autumn

Trust in your destiny, unafraid of raising or falling, ups or downs

They are like a drop of morning dew on the blade of grass

This poem carries a very simple idea and easy to understand. You don't need to be scholar or Zen master to understand this, however this poem displays one of the principal virtues of a Bodisattva, the Buddhist spirit of no-fear in the face of the impermanence of the phenomenal world. Van Hanh, one of the most beloved eminent monks in the hearts and mind of Vietnamese Buddhist, before passing away, taught his disciples the last lesson: Don't be afraid of the constantly changing of the phenomenal world. Why don't you see yourself as a drop of morning dew? At the present moment, it 's bright under the sunrise as a diamond. But in the next moment it will vaporize in to the air or it will disappear onto the ground to complete a transforming. Your life is just that.

Zen master Man Giac, a respected and popular monk whose disciples including the Emperor and the Empress, wrote:

When spring goes, the hundred flowers wither

when spring comes, the hundred flowers blossom

Things go on, lives passed before our eyes

The childhood fades then old age comes someday

Don't think that as spring ends, all flowers go away

A plum flower blossomed in my garden last night

Like Van Hanh, in this poem Man Giac refers to the flow of natural events as emblematic of ultimate realty. Once we realize that the phenomenal world is impermanent, we will experience no fear at any changing or unstable world.

Today we are living in a stressful world where people have to work very hard physically and mentally. The keen competition happens every where. The daily life of one person is full of mental frustration, worries, miseries, anxieties, tension and fear. Meditation, therefore, is the remedy for many physical and mental sicknesses. Since we can not withdraw from the society, since we cannot withdraw from the madding crowd to live in a forest or an ivory tower, we have to find the way to face, to understand, and to balance our mind with the material world in order to have a peaceful and happy life. Meditation would be the best answer.

To practice meditation, one must have strong determination, effort and patient. Some one says practicing meditation is like swimming in a river against the current. One must not lose the patience. There are many ways to practice Zen but first of all, we need to have an object to focus, to think deeply in order to control the jumping mind. A Buddhist may take Buddha or Kwan-Yin image as an object. A Christian may take Jesus Christ image to think. The old and traditional way is concentrating on the breath by counting the length of inhaling and exhaling. Whatever the method may be, if anyone tries to practice meditation, they could control the mind easily and find the relaxation whenever it's necessary. That means they have a great deal of both physical and mental health.

Living in the modern world, time is very valuable. People may be afraid that they don't have time to practice Zen. But unless we want practicing Zen in order to attain the Enlightenment, we may practice Zen everywhere, at anytime we want. Then, Vietnamese Zen may offer you something. Let's think about those poems of the great Vietnamese Zen masters above. We are in the Spring time. Let's think about plum flowers have blossomed in your garden last night. And think about yourself too, you are a flower in a wonderful world. The flowers are always smiling.

THERAVADA BUDDHISM IN VIETNAM

Buddhism came to Vietnam in the first century CE. By the end of the second century, Vietnam developed a major Buddhist centre in the region, commonly known as the Luy-Lau centre, now in the Bac-Ninh province, north of the present Hanoi city. Luy-Lau was the capital of Giao-Chi, former name of Vietnam, and was a popular place visited by many Indian Buddhist missionary monks on their way to China, following the sea route from the Indian sub-continent by Indian traders. A number of Mahayana sutras and the Agamas were translated into Chinese scripts at that centre, including the sutra of *Forty Two Chapters*, the *Anapanasati*, the *Vessantara-jataka*, the *Milinda-panha*, etc.

In the next 18 centuries, due to geographical proximity with China and despite being annexed twice by the Chinese, the two countries shared many common features of cultural, philosophical and religious heritage. Vietnamese Buddhism has been greatly influenced by the development of Mahayana Buddhism in China, with the dominant traditions of Ch'an/Zen, Pure Land, and Tantra.

The southern part of the present Vietnam was originally occupied by the Champa (Cham) and the Cambodian (Khmer) people who followed both a syncretic Saiva-Mahayana Buddhism and Theravada Buddhism, although Champa probably had a Theravada presence from as early as the 3rd century CE, whilst Cambodia received the Theravada as late as the 12th century. The Vietnamese started to conquer and absorbed the land in the 15th century, and the current shape of the country was finalised in the 18th century. From that time onward, the dominant Viet followed the Mahayana tradition whilst the ethnic Cambodian practiced the Theravada tradition, and both traditions peacefully co-existed.

In the 1920s and 1930s, there were a number of movements in Vietnam for the revival and modernisation of Buddhist activities. Together with the re-organisation of Mahayana establishments, there developed a growing interest in Theravadin meditation and also in Buddhist materials based on the Pali Canon. These were then available in French. Among the pioneers who brought Theravada Buddhism to the ethnic Viet was a young veterinary doctor named Le Van Giang. He was born in the South, received higher education in Hanoi, and after graduation, was sent to Phnom Penh, Cambodia, to work for the French government.

During that time, he developed a growing interest in Buddhism. He started to study and practice the Pure Land and Tantric ways but was not satisfied. By chance, he met the Vice Sangharaja of the Cambodian Sangha and was recommended a book on the Noble Eightfold Path written in French. He was struck by the clear message in the book, and decided to try out the Theravada way. He learnt meditation on the breath (*Anapanasati*) from a Cambodian monk at the Unalom Temple in Phnom Penh and achieved deep samadhi states. He continued the practice and after a few years, he decided to ordain and took the Dhamma name of Ho-Tong (*Vansarakkhita*).

In 1940, upon an invitation by a group of lay Buddhists led by Mr Nguyen Van Hieu, a close friend, he went back to Vietnam and helped to establish the first Theravada temple for Vietnamese Buddhists, at Go Dua, Thu Duc (now a district of Saigon). The temple was named Buu-Quang (*Ratana Ramsyarama*). Later, the Cambodian Sangharaja, Venerable Chuon Nath, together with 30 Cambodian bhikkhus established the *Sima* boundary at this temple. The temple was destroyed by French troops in 1947, and was rebuilt in 1951.

In 1949-1950, Venerable Ho-Tong together with Mr Nguyen Van Hieu and supporters built a new temple in Saigon, named Ky-Vien Tu (*Jetavana Vihara*). This temple became the centre of Theravada activities in Vietnam, which continued to attract increasing interest among the Vietnamese Buddhists. In 1957, the Vietnamese Theravada Buddhist Sangha Congregation (Giao Hoi Tang Gia Nguyen Thuy Viet Nam) was formally established and recognised by the government, and the Theravada Sangha elected Venerable Ho-Tong as its first President, or Sangharaja.

During that time, Dhamma activities were further strengthened by the presence of Venerable Narada from Sri Lanka. Venerable Narada had first came to Vietnam in the 1930s and brought with him Bodhi tree saplings which he planted in many places throughout the country. During his subsequent visits in the 1950s and 1960s, he attracted a large number of Buddhists to the Theravada tradition, one of whom was the popular translator, Mr Pham Kim Khanh who took the Dhamma name of Sunanda. Mr Khanh translated many books of Venerable Narada, including *The Buddha and His Teachings, Buddhism in a Nutshell, Satipatthana Sutta, The Dhammapada, A Manual of Abhidhamma, etc.* Mr Khanh, now in his 80s, lives in the USA and is still active in translating Dhamma books of well-known meditation teachers from Thailand, Burma and Sri Lanka.

From Saigon, the Theravada movement spread to other provinces, and soon, a number of Theravada temples for ethnic Viet Buddhists were established in many areas in the South and Central parts of Vietnam. As at 1997, there were 64 Theravada temples throughout the country, of which 19 were located in Saigon and its viccinity. Beside Buu-Quang and Ky-Vien temples, other well known temples are Buu-Long, Giac-Quang, Tam-Bao (Da-Nang), Thien-Lam and Huyen-Khong (Hue), and the large Sakyamuni Buddha Monument (Thich-Ca Phat Dai) in Vung Tau.

In the 1960s and 1970s, a number of Vietnamese bhikkhus were sent overseas for further training, mostly in Thailand and some in Sri Lanka and India. Recently, this programme has been resumed and about 20 bhikkhus and nuns are receiving training in Burma.

Historically, there has been a close relationship between the Cambodian and the Vietnamese bhikkhus. In fact, in 1979, after the Khmer Rouge were driven out of Phnom Penh, a group of Vietnamese bhikkhus led by Venerables Buu-Chon and Gioi-Nghiem came to that city to re-ordain 7 Cambodian monks, and thus re-established the Cambodian Sangha which had been destroyed by the Khmer Rouge when they were in control.

Dhamma literature in the Vietnamese language comes from two main sources: the Pali Canon and the Chinese *Agamas*, together with a large collection of Mahayana texts. Since 1980s, there has been an ongoing programme to publish these materials by scholar monks of both Mahayana and Theravada traditions. So far, 27 volumes of the first 4 *Nikayas*, translated by Venerable Minh-Chau, and the 4 *Agamas*, translated by Venerables Tri-Tinh, Thien-Sieu and Thanh-Tu, have been produced. Work is under way to translate and publish the 5th Nikaya. In addition, a complete set of the *Abhidhamma*, translated by Venerable Tinh-Su, has been printed, together with the *Dhammapada*, the *Milinda-Panha*, the *Visudhi-Magga*, the *Abhidhammatthasangaha* and many other work.

In summary, although Buddhism in Vietnam is predominantly of the Mahayana form, the Theravada tradition is well recognised and is experiencing a growing interest especially in the practice of meditation, in Nikaya-Agama literature and in Abhidhamma studies.

MODERN BUDDHISM IN VIETNAM

Starting in 1920, after the manner of similar events in Nationalist China, a new movement was launched simultaneously in the three main regions of Viet Nam: North, Centre and South. The movement aimed at a regeneration of Buddhism and even serious obstacles were not able to stop it. But it was not until 1931 that the first Association of Buddhist Studies was founded at Saigon Similar associations were founded in 1932 and Hanoi in 1934.

Each association naturaly had its own programme but, composed as they were of both monks and laymen, it was their task to improve conditions in the monasteries, tighten up discipline, instruct a new generation of monks, who should be both devout and well educated and finally to ensure a wide diffusion of the Doctrine in the language of the country and not, as in the past, through the medium of Chinese characters. With such aims in view many magazines and translations from the Buddhist Canon, both Theravadin (Southern) and Mahayanist (Northern), were published. It is paradoxical that while *Zen* lost its influence it was Amidism that took its place, which it retains at the time of writing.

This movement to revive Buddhism met with success and there was a change of opinion among the intellectuals, who were disillusioned with Western materialism. Many joined the movement and supported it not only financially but also with their help in the work of Buddhist instruction. Unfortunately the second World War just about put a stop to all these efforts but they began again in 1948 when the situation seemed a little clearer. At Hanoi the communities of monks broken up by the war were reformed and the Buddhist community was reorganized, together with the Association of laymen. A year later, thanks to the initiative of Venerable TÑ Liên and Trí H£i and the strong support of the laity, an orphanage, a school, a printing press and social works to help the victims of the war raging in the countryside, were also established at Hanoi. Ruined temples in several places were rebuilt or restored; old publications reappeared and authors and translators went back to work with energy.

Two year later a new Association of Buddhist Studies came into existence at Saigon, to replace the previous one that was no longer active. On May 6th, 1951, a national Buddhist Congress was held and attended by about fifty monks and laymen. Important resolutions were passed, concerning the unification of the three Associations, the reorganisation in depth of the Sangha, the standardisation of ceremonies. Buddist instrution for adults and the formation of Buddist youth movements. The Congress further ratified the support given by Venerable TÑ Liên, delegate from the North, to the World Fellowship of Buddhists, which came into existence as a result of the first World Congress held at Colombo in 1950.

The second World Congress, held at Tokyo in September 1952, gave to Vietnamese Buddhism, now unified, an opportunity to show its vigour. The Singhalese delegation to this Congress were taking a relic of the Buddha to Japan, aboard the French steamer «La Marseillaise», which had to stop for a day at Saigon. It was decided to accord a devout reception to this relic and under the auspices of unified Vietnamese Buddhism 50,000 people, who had assembled in less than six days, gave the capital of Vietnam an impressive view of faith, devotion and discipline such as had not been seen before.

This peaceful demonstration had happy results. From the North to the South a reinvigorated Buddhism, warmly acclaimed, was able to broaden its scope and offset the effect of unorthodox sects. Since then social works, shools for monks, private schools under Buddhist auspices and youth organizations have increased and flourished. Progress was made in making known Buddhist thought and it was only the partition of the country into two zones by the Geneva Agreement that hindered still more far-reaching results.

INFLUENCE OF BUDDHISM ON THE LIFE AND THOUGHT OF THE VIETNAMES

In theory there are three main religions in Vietnam: Taoism, Confucianism and Buddhism; but in fact there is only one, which is an amalgam of these three doctrines, each of which represents a particular aspect of the whole. This state of affairs makes it difficult, if not impossible, to distinguish three separate religious communities among the Vietnamese. There are perhaps some people who follow either Taoism or Buddhism but they are in a minority. The bulk of the population remains unprejudiced and is not interested in sectarian distinctions. A Buddhist family for example will visit Taoist temples and perform the rites belonging to the Confucian cult of ancestors.

Though this confusion sometimes fosters superstitious practices and ignorance it also has its good points and exerts a tolerant influence on life and thought.

Many scholars are really products of Buddhism, though they do not deny the principles of Confucianism. Even if there is no direct borrowing of ideas many Buddhist concepts such as impermanence, *karma* (action), causality, rebirth and earthly sufferings are found in their writings, so that there can be little doubt about their common origin.

Buddhism has had a particularly strong effect on morals and behaviour. Even uneducated Vietnamese and non-Buddhists fear the results of bad actions conceiving them in the symbolism of the «Ten Hells» and this fear often makes them avoid such actions, encouraging them instead to be kind. Strengthened by the Five Precepts, or basic morality of Buddhism, it is part of the reason for the gentle manners, which came to pervade Vietnamese life, thanks firstly to the opportunity for happiness out of the ordinary inherent in Amidism. Vegeterianism is followed by the laity on specific dates. and is the standard diet for monks. It has the merit of mitigating the sanguinary instinct common to all.

The influece of the three religions is clear in the artistic field, where that of Buddhism is predominant. Architecture, painting and sculpture are often inspired by two of the key ideas of Buddhism, which are Purity and Compassion. The flower of the lotus is a frequent motif and the various representations of Avalokiteshvara are greatly venerated, especially by women.

CONCEPTION AND PRACTICE OF BUDDHISM IN VIETNAM

Though the movement for reform which started in 1920 achieved good results it is still far from reaching the goal put forward by its sponsors. The efforts of these enthusiasts succeeded to some extent in throwing light on the essence of Buddhism and ridding it of certain excrescences. Vietnamese Buddhism remains faithful to the Mahayana tradition, of which the emphasis is on Compassion, as is well known, represented by the Bodhisattva doctrine, based on the exhortation of the Buddha: For this reason the supporters of the movement, monks and laity alike, continually try and improve their spiritual life and translate into action the truths that they have found in the texts. They now see ceremonies and moral precepts for what they are: means to attain wisdom and peace of mind, but not ends in themselves. They have a clear conception of Mahayana symbolism and understand its essence. If they subscribe without reservation to the orthodoxy extolled by the Theravadins, who have had a group in Saigon for a few years now, they also accept the later works based on it by Nagarjuna, Asvaghosa, Vasubandhu and others, as well as Amidism or the Pure Land School, which they know to be the form of meditation most easily accessible to the majority.

PRESENT POSITION OF BUDDHISM

Here it is dealt with the actual situation of Buddhism in Vietnam seen from the standpoint of the General Buddhist Association of Vietnam. This Association, as compared with other coexisting groups, is by far the most important, the best organized, the only dynamic and also the only one that is officially recognized as being fully qualified to represent the millenary Buddhism of the country. For these purposes, it would not be necessary to mention further, still it is the only organization that reflects faithfully the genuine picture of the Vietnamese Buddhism.

Moreover, it should be noted that the General Buddhist Association of Vietnam (G.B.A) is a menber of the World Fellowship of Buddhists since the foundation of this latter in 1950 at Colombo. It has thus attended several international Buddhist conferences and is in good relation with numerous Buddhist countries in the world.

Organization - Under the GBA's authority and general direction, are grouped, on the one hand, 3 Sanghas numbering well over 3.000 monks and about 600 nuns, on the other hand, three communities of disciples which branch out their ramification as far as to remote hamlets. The figures of adherents to these three legally constituted about 1,000,000, to which it shoud be added an important number of no-associate disciples by as much as three-fold.

The responsibility is assigned as follows: the Sanghas are responsible for all spiritual tasks and to the lay communities comes the duty of relieving the religious from all material preoccupations.

Propagation of the Dharma - For the spiritual training of both associates and non associates, the propagation of the *Dharma* is organized on a large scale: weekly lectures in Saigon, periodical conferences in the provinces with movies utilization of radio – cars equipped with movies projectors, wide dissemination of magazines and vernacular pamphlets coming out of the GBA's press with a monthly rhythm of 30,000 copies. In addition, special courses are open, in Saigon and in its vicinities for commencing, to the intention of people who need a higher knowledge of the Doctrine. Activity of this kind is also assisted by the presence of numerous libraries provided with or without reading rooms.

Formation of cadres - The foregoing activities raised the problem of cadres resulting from the increasing of cadres resulting from the increasing number of monastic schools (4 in 1956, 10 in 1962) and the creation of a Preaching Corps without mentioning the sending of young monks abroad to attend perfection courses (3 at Nava Nalanda Mahavihara, 4 in Japan).

In monastic schools, the educational program is mixed, there the students learn canonical texts and the official curriculum as well. Many of them are attending or already terminated their high study at the Saigon and Hue Universities.

Buddhist Youth - Lay youths, aged from 8 to 20 years, are incorporated in a Youth Movement, known under the name of *Gia dinh Phat tu* (Buddhist Family).

Etablished in 1940, this widespreading Movement aims to give these youths a religious education, susceptible to make them, later on, fervent buddhists, practitioners, capable of sacrifices for the maintenance and expansion of their parents' religion, to become honest citizens and useful to the society.

After 23 years of existence, this Movement, benevolently conducted by a 3,000 trainer Corps, numbers about 70,000 youngsters and unequally dividing into 1,000 groups from the city to the country. One-fouth of these youngsters attend private, primary and secondary schools established by lay associations, and their brilliant success at different examinations began to attract the attention of the public.

Social welfare - Other efforts have been realized in the social welfare sphere, for instance the installation of sanitary units (clinics, dispensaries, maternities). Among these, the clinic at the Xa loi Pagoda, GBA's head-office, is most important, where free medical cares are distributed to over 200 poor patients daily. It is conducted by a Doctor, member of the Association of Saigon, assisted by two young monks working as nurses and five specialists physicians for particular cases.

Two day-nurseries are functioning in Saigon and Dalat, where nuns gratuitously take care of the children from workers' families, without discrimination of race nor distinction of religion.

Every week on Thursday, a Committee of Dames visit either a hospital or a maternity in Saigon to bring comfort and material aid to needy patients.

To these social works, which are created, conducted and financed by members of lay communities, it should be added the special relief works contributed by both rich and poor to the benefit of victims of public disasters, more particularly fires which are frequent.

This brief statement on modern Buddhism in Vietnam shows the enormous efforts performed by both religious and laities of a country which is practically in war since 1940, to maintain not only their faith but also to develop and give it a vitality conformable to the fundamentals of Buddhism: the Compassion. This effort is more meritorious especially as it is fulfilled with their own means only without any external aid.

The social reformative tendency inspired by all activities of the General Buddhist Association is a hilarious initiative. It is quite sure that with the return of peace, more encouraging results will be obtained to the mightiest glory of Buddha.

BUDDHISM'S CONTRIBUTION TO ART, LETTERS AND PHILOSOPHY IN VIETNAM

Buddhism appears to have been introduced in Vietnam towards the end of the second century by way of China, having been preceded by Confucianism and Taoism. Four hundred years later, when Vietnam succeeded in freeing itself from Chinese domination, it progressed by leaps and bounds under the patronage of the ruling families. Since then, in spite of the antagonism of other rival religions, it continued to expand almost uniterruptedly both in extent as well as by conviction. During a particular epoch of history, from 968 to 1414 it was given the status of a State religion. Several emperors of the Ly and Tran dynasties even went so far as to practise what they preached: some as faithful followers, some as monks proper, having abdicated and chosen the monastic way of life. A curious fact, this, and it would indeed be interesting to study it without necessarily digressing from the subject of the present paper.

Vietnamese Buddhism continues to hold this supremacy in our own times, not in public life it is true, but in the hearts of a good majority of the people. It is therefore easy to understand how great an influence the Dharma of Buddha has had on the Vietnamese mind, and the generous contribution it has made to the moral and spiritual training of a people whose gentleness and simple outlook on life predisposed them to accept the "Religion of Compassion."

The dominant trait in the person of the Great Teacher made his teaching known and felt throught the country. The artist, the philosopher and the poet of those days imbibed it and many of those of modern times still continue to draw their inspiration from it.

An European author, tracing back the history of Chinese philosophy wrote: "Buddhism was the first foreign influence which had a powerful bearing on the evolution of Chinese thought; and the effect of such an influence was to rekindle, stimulate and develop to the highest pitch not only the religion but also all the other spheres of its civilisation. A casual glance, even by one who is almost completely unaware of the spiritual world of China, at the plastic arts of China shows how completely they stem from the spirit of Buddhism and how wonderfully they blossomed forth during the Buddhist period". Without going too deeply into the matter, it can be said that this remark can apply word for word to the Vietnamese scheme of things as regards Buddhist influence in Vietnam on architecture, sculpture and painting. Those examples which have withstood the ravager of time and the havoc of war testify to what a degree art developed under this benign influence, as also the interesting and profitable research work done by archoeologists prior to 1945.

But if in some countries and in cetain respects the artist rather than the monks is closer to the community of the faithful in interpreting their interests and daily pursuits, a view which is held by Professor Paul Mus, in Vietnam it is actually the literateurs on whom this task devolves, especially on the poets who are also philosophers of note. That – for reasons which are difficult to explain – is because if the Vietnamese is capable of expressing his wonder at the form and colour of things, cannot really be deeply stirred except by vibrations of sounds. This tendency makes him an ardent lover of the theatre, of music which is not only instrumental or vocal, but of words whose music is magic to his ears; in other words, Poetry. Hence we seem to have been guided not towards Art but towards Letters which are the true repositories of thoughts – and Letters, only, assuming the rarity of literary works which are either lacking in philosophical reflections or which contribute nothing to the development of moral themes – if one is to know what good Vietnam has derived from her seventeen centuries of conversion to Buddhism.

In order to do that it is necessary to go back to the sixth century when the monastries both centres for the spread of Buddhism as well as schools for training men of letters. There were no public schools and besides there were few young men who were keen to study the Chinese characters apart from the Buddhist monks who were prompted by a desire to delve deep into Chinese translations for the essence of a doctrine which they found wonderful but which failed to satisfy them because they were conveyed orally up to then. The tradition was passed on from one epoch to another so that between 1010 and 1225 during the Ly dynasty it was almost impossible to find a poet with more than average talent outside the religious circle, all the Masters of Dhyana from the famous School of Meditation stemming from the themes developed by these poet-monks were generally beyond the comprehension of the general public, the work of these monks nevertheless contributed not a little towards raising the prestige of Buddhism which had already gained considerable popularity.

The position was reversed at the beginning of the fifteeth century. The literary figures who were supporters of Confucianism profited by the existing rivalry and supplanted the Buddhists by winning imperial trust and favours. This defeat however was but temporaty. The hold of Buddhism remaied firmly anchored in the minds and hearts of the people and soon became as strong as it had been in earlier times from the birth in China of syncretism whose source also gave rise to Confucianism, Taoism and Buddhism. The literary luminaries of Vietnam had perforce to submit to it without unduly protesting since after some initial hesitation they firmly admitted, like their Chinese predecessors, that the value of a true culture was based on the possession of the (three teachings.) The result of this for literature and philosophy was to enlarge their sphere of action to say the least.

However, great though the progress was which Buddhism had made during the period under review, as regards literature, it fell far short of that which was made later in the seventeeth and eighteeth centuries following the advent of (Chu-nom) a national calligraphic system which was invented to replace the Chinese characters. This was the golden age: authors and speakers spoke the same language; the obstacles provided formerly by syntax and foreign phonetics having been removed, the translation of thought into speech and writing became direct and rapid. This event provided an enormous stimulus to the spread of syncretism already referred to which it would be good to study.

It must first of all be remembered that even if there had been belief bases on prejudice no religious fanaticism existed either in China or in Vietnam to the point of provoking bloodshed as has happened in some countries. Furthuer, by seeking to know the adversary better in order the better to fight it, the adherents of each camp would have ended by noting existing lacunae in their doctrine and at the same time the identity of certain apparently contradictory declarations. For example, the Confucianist system while stating its belief in an all-powerful heaven, recogises man's personal responsibitity. Weak indeed are the nuances between its tenets and the Buddhist *Karma* that they cannot be reconciled or brought nearer to each other. Besides, Confucianist positivism, whatever one may say, is far too materialistic to satisfy the aspirations common to all men, who in the world is there who does not want to study the beyond, to lift the veil of "after-death" to question the future, and so many other questions to which the Sage's Teachings provide no answer. The poets of the old Vietnam were undoubtedly not indifferent to their metaphysical preoccupations. That is the explanation which appears most plausible to account for the fusion of thoughts of such different origins and which from the point of view of application is proof of the widest rationalism and very straitlaced logic by attributing to each of these religions, a sphere of influence which normally belongs to each. As a general rule, the doctrine of Confucius is responsible for governing earthly affairs (organisation and administration of the family, society, etc.) and for Buddhism and Taoism together to settle problems of a much higher order.

True it is that from the point of view of orthodoxy, such a mixture is hardly desirable but viewed from another angle it must be realised that it has produced – apart from appeasing the restless spirit – beneficial effects on minds and hearts, to say nothing of the fact that it has made it possible for the masses to understand the elementary ideas which each of the systems in combination needed to spread on their individual behalf.

A detailed study of the poems of the period written in "Chu-nom" – prose works were still very rare – will not fail to reveal the brighter side of that which unsuspecting persons would be tempted to refer to disdainfully as a doctrinal tangle or an unpardonable heresy. A good example of this is KIM VAN KIEU, a masterpiece which enjoys unrivalled popularity because of its lively musical quality, the beauty of its verse which is incomparable, and above all because of its rich treasure-house of thoughts from noble Buddhist inspiration. It would be no exaggeration to state that this poem which elaborates a theme which is akin to the life of the country, has of itself achieved much more than thousands of treatises on morals or philosophy as regards the good fight it led for the triumph of goodness, forgiveness, purity of thoughts, and loftiness of ideals. Even now a hundred years later and in spite of the attractions of modern culture, it still is for some a sort of encyclopoedia of the Vietnamese language or a sort of literary Bible, and for others a civic and moral code, and finally for the whole world a manual of elementary and practical Buddhism. Accepted by all social circles, loved by men and women equally, KIM VAN KIEU brought and still brings the light of Salvation to all by drawing attention to the inexorable Karma-ist reactions, by extolling interior peace promised to "those who root out passion from their lives, by putting men on their guard against evil reincarnations if they do evil." All this may seem very commonplace; but what it asks and no more is simple minds for whom all religions appear to have been founded.

In Vietnam, Buddhist influence is not limited to the realm of Art, Letters and Philosophy. It inspires the theatre, serves as a basis for certain good, customs, inspires stories and legends, provides suggestions for popular songs and proverbs. If Buddhism is the source at which intellectuals quench their thirst it is also the breast which suckles spirits enamoured of spirituality; it is in its school of wisdom that passion-troubled spirits awaken; it is the Enlightenment of its illustrious founder that Vietnam is learning to find herself, to know herself; finally it is under the roofs of her monasteries that her devotees meditate devoutly and her unfortunates seek consolation. Because Buddhism is so intimately bound up with the Vietnamese citizens, existence and daily life it has become a vital necessity.

Chapter - 7

Buddhism in Laos

Laos is a landlocked nation squeezed between Thailand to the west and Vietnam to the east, and sharing shorter borders with Burma in the northwest and Cambodia in the south. As its position on the map of southeast Asia might suggest, Laos is the product of early contacts between the Khmers of Cambodia and the Thais who eventually established Thailand. As Thai tribes migrated into the southwest Asian peninsula during the latter half of the first millennium, they came first down the Mekong river until they encountered the rear guard of the Khmer tribes who had followed that route before them. Some settled along the upper reaches of the Mekong, while others resorted to the relatively uninhabited Chao Phraya, which flows through the heart of present day Thailand, reaching the sea at Bangkok. The Thai-related people who settled in the upper Mekong region became the ancestors of the modern day Laos. Landlocked and surrounded by more powerful cultures, Laos remains the poorest country in southeast Asia in every way except for the renowned Lao sense of humour and fun.

Lao history in fact begins in the 14th century with a risqué event, the seduction of one of the king's wives by his son Phi Fa, heir apparent to the throne. For his indiscretion, Phi Fa was banished. He and his son Fa Ngum journeyed south and took up residence in the Khmer royal court at Angkor. There, Fa Ngum studied under a Theravadin monk, gained favour of the Khmer king, and eventually married one of his daughters. In about 1350, the king of Angkor provided Fa Ngum with an army so that he could reassert control over his father's lost inheritance.

By this time, Angkor was in a state of decline, and the political centre of gravity in Thailand had shifted southward from Sukkhothai to Ayutthaya. Angkor's weakness and this shift in power in Thailand left the way open for Fa Ngum to establish an independent kingdom, with ties to Angkor, along the upper reaches of the Mekong river. Fa Ngum's coronation at Luang Phrabang in 1353 marked the beginning of the historical Laos state. It also established the farthest northern extent of Khmer civilization, since Fa Ngum's kingdom was modeled on Angkoran precedents even though the Laos are racially related to the Thais. Furthermore, Fa Ngum invited his Buddhist teacher at the Khmer court to act as his advisor and chief priest. Under his influence the new kingdom of Laos became firmly Theravadin, as it has remained to the present day. This Buddhist master brought with him from Angkor a Buddha image known as the "Phra Bang". This image accounts for the capital's name and like the tooth relic of the Buddha in Sri Lanka, became the palladium of the kingdom.

From the very beginning, Laos seems to have been just barely strong enough to maintain a separate identity in the midst of its more powerful neighbours. This it was able to do only by means of a series of alliances, concessions and submissions to the Thais, Burmese and finally the Vietnamese. As the Khmers too were finding out about this time, it was a question of being dominated by the related, Indianized cultures of Burma and Thailand or by the Vietnamese, who were especially hated because of their sacking of the Lao capital in 1479. Subservient alliances with Burma and Thailand were undesirable for Laos, but they had the effect of reinforcing Theravada Buddhism, which became the country's primary symbol of continuity and identity in the face of its shifting political fortunes.

Because of the relatively weak central government of Laos, Theravada Buddhism became the primary cement holding together the numerous ethnic groups and inaccessible villages scattered through the mountainous countryside. According to the Lao model of kingship, the king sat upon the throne not so much because of divine right as because of his obviously good karma in his previous lives. He was expected to continue that good karma in this life by supporting the Sangha and promoting Buddhism through royal construction projects. Pursuing this role, King Visun (r. 1501-20) is remembered as the prime mover behind the splendour of Luang Phrabang, the first capital of Laos. Actually, Visun brought to fruition an ambitious Buddhist construction program which had been begun by his two older brothers in order to repair damage done by the Vietnamese in the previous century. Since they were made of wood, few examples of these early architectural works survive, but Luang Phrabang remains the site of some of the most attractive Buddhist monuments and ruins in southeast Asia.

Visun's grandson Setthathirat (r. 1548-71) occupied the throne in 1548. Soon, Burmese expansionism forced Setthathriat to form an alliance with the Thais in 1560. The resulting treaty entailed shifting the capital from Luang Phrabang to Vien Chan, a site closer to the Thai capital at Ayutthaya and more conducive to trade with and supervision by the Thais. Setthathriat did for Vien Chan what King Visun had done for Luang Phrabang, carrying out a large-scale Buddhist construction program.

Remnants of Sutthathriat's works still stand, the most notable being the hundred-yard square That Luang or "Great Shrine", a temple mountain built in the Khmer style. Setthathriat also built a second grand temple to house a precious jade Buddha known as the Phra Keo. This image was the second palladium of Laos until it was removed to Bangkok by a Thai invading force in 1778. It has remained in Bangkok ever since in the Wat Phra Keo as Thailand's most sacred image. This same image is also the primary symbol of Lao resentment against Thailand.

In 1778, Thailand conquered the southern kingdom of Vien Chan, asserted control over the northern kingdom of Luang Phrabang, and removed both the Phra Bang and Phra Keo Buddha images to Thailand. In 1782, the Thais restored the Vietnamese dynasty as a puppet regime in Vien Chan and returned the Phra Bang Buddha image. Despite continuing Thai domination of the entirety of Laos, the country remained divided into a northern and southern kingdom until 1893, when the French blockaded Bangkok and forced Thailand to cede to France the upper reaches of the Mekong river. The French protectorate thus established over Laos had little to do with the distribution of the Lao people, many of whom still resided in Thai territory. The Thais, on the other hand, resented having been deprived of the most valuable portion of their Laotian holdings. Again, no one was happy with European map-making when Laos eventually became independent.

Briefly during World War II, Laos was nominally independent under Japanese control. After World War II, in 1946, reassertion of French control in southeast Asia led directly to the formation of a communist independence movement under Ho Chi Minh. The French collapse in southeast Asia in 1954 led to a coalition government in which both Lao royalists and Lao communists were represented. This coalition quickly collapsed, and Laos, like Vietnam, entered the 1960's in the throes of a full-scale civil war between communist and pro-western factions, which were now aided primarily by the United States. After the defeat of American forces in Vietnam in 1975, the communists quickly gained control in Laos, at about the same time as Pol Pot's Khumer Rouge gained control in Cambodia. In Laos, however, the transition to communism was not the nightmare that the Cambodians faced.

In the course of this much more benign transition to communism in Laos, there is little evidence of significant suppression of Buddhism. Even during the revolution, one of the main propaganda tactics of the Pathet Lao was to promulgate the compatibility of Buddhism and communism and to enlist the support of monks for their revolution. While many monks worked against the communists, it is clear also that many worked actively for them. When the communists came to power, they forbade the giving of alms to monks, but announced provision of a state-controlled ration of rice for monks. This ration was to be supplemented by food produced or earned by the monks themselves. Since then, monks have been required to perform productive roles in the community, primarily their traditional roles as teachers and healers.

What they teach and the medicine they practice, however, are controlled by a Department of Religious Affairs, administered by the Ministry of Education. The Department of Religious Affairs has overseen a program designed to expunge "counter-revoulutionary" and "exploitative" material from the traditional Buddhism of Laos. Under this program, in addition to teaching Buddhism, monks have a significant responsibility for teaching literacy and a patriotic, communist version of Lao history. Monks were traditionally consulted for the relief of illness, but prior to the communist takeover they administered primarily blessings and magical amulets. Now they administer traditional herbal medicine and where possible, western medicine.

The communist reformation of Buddhism, implemented by a panel of respected Lao monks, has been criticized as repressive by some Thai and expatriate Lao Buddhists. Alternatively, it has been praised by Lao and Thai reformists as representing a return to a purer Buddhism unencumbered by superstitious accretions. There can be little doubt, from the standpoint of Theravada doctrine, that traditional herbal and western medicine are an improvement over the previous practices of performing exorcisms and selling blessings and magical amulets. It is also evident that the previous catering to traditional Lao spirit cults and ancestor worship had nothing to do with scriptural Buddhism.

It is not yet clear how extensive revisions of the Buddhist texts themselves may be, or how such revisions will effect Buddhism in Laos. On the surface, there does not appear to be much material in the Theravada texts that conflicts with the moderate communism of the Lao regime. Some of the restrictions upon monks set forth in the Vinaya Pitaka have been abandoned - most notably the prohibition upon working the soil - but Vinaya rules are not strictly observed by all monks in any Buddhist country in the world. On the whole, most reports from Laos indicate that Buddhism there thrives in harmony with the communist regime. Clearly, there is much scope for a revival of the crippled Buddhism of Cambodia with recourse to the closely related and still healthy Buddhism of Laos. Laos and Cambodia have diplomatic relations going back to the 14th century, both espouse Theravada Buddhism, and both have lived under communist regimes.

BUDDHISM AND THE PATHET LAO

In contrast with the brutal repression of the *sangha* undertaken in Cambodia, the communist government of Laos has not sought to oppose or suppress Buddhism in Laos to any great degree. Rather, since the early days of the Pathet Lao, communist officials have sought to use the influence and respect afforded to Buddhist clergy to achieve political goals, while discouraging religious practices seen as detrimental to Marxist aims.

Starting as early as the late 1950s, members of the Pathet Lao sought to encourage support for the Communist cause by aligning members of the Lao *sangha* with the Communist opposition. Though resisted by the Royal Lao Government, these efforts were fairly successful, and resulted in increased support for the Pathet Lao, particularly in rural communities.

Following the Pathet Lao's ascension to control of the government in 1975, efforts to link Buddhism and Communism in the popular imagination continued, with the government stressing the fundamental similarities of Buddhist and Communist views with regard to equality and material possessions, while simultaneously discouraging religious practices seen as wasteful or otherwise at odds with Communist doctrine-such as the donation of large sums to monastic institutions. Traditional donations of food to monks were curtailed, and replaced with a government rice ration. In response to this and other government policies limiting the traditional role of Buddhist monks in village life, the number of monks in Laos declined during the late 1970s as new ordinations declined, combined by an exodus of monks either fleeing to neighboring Thailand or leaving the *sangha* and returning to lay life.

Senior clergy, such as the sangharaja, were forbidden by the government to preach. Lower clergy were allowed to preach to the public, but their sermons were often taped or otherwise monitored by government officials to ensure that they didn't use their position as a platform for agitating against the government. As a result, in 1979, the Sangharaja of Laos, Venerable Thammayano, fled to Thailand by floating across the Mekong on a raft of inflated car inner tubes.

After 1979, government policy regarding Buddhism began to liberalize, resulting in a gradual resurgence of Buddhist institutions and practices. Party officials are no longer barred from participation in religious services, and may even undergo temporary ordination. Buddhist schools in urban areas continued to teach Buddhist doctrine to monks and laity, albeit with a political bent to their doctrine. Ordinations- both temporary and permanent- have increased, primarily in Vientiene and the Mekong River region. Lao monks are required to do productive work, with most working as teachers and physicians. The curriculum they teach- which includes basic literacy and Lao history- as well as the medicine they practice (Western medicine and traditional herbal remedies have replaced the sale of blessed amulets and other spiritualist cures) are controlled by the government.

Communist reform of the Lao *sangha* has been variously praised and criticized by outside observers, with supporters seeing it as a significant achievement in modernizing and reforming a traditional institution, and opponents criticizing the co-opting of Buddhist clergy to serve political ends.

BUDDHISM IN LAOTIAN CULTURE

Lao Buddhist are very devout and almost every Lao man joins a monastery, or temple, for at least a short period of time. Many men also become monks for the rest of their lives. Most people donate food to the monks to gain merit and improve their karma. The temples of Laos were once seen as "Universities" for monks. Lao monks are highly respected and revered in Lao communities.

ART AND ARCHITECTURE

The Pha That Luang, Wat Sisakhet, Wat Xieng Thong, and That Dam are all Buddhist structures in Laos. Lao Buddhism is also famous for images of the Buddha performing uniquely Lao mudras, or gestures, such as calling for rain, and striking uniquely Lao poses such as showing the Buddha lying down and welcoming death, after which he would achieve Nirvana.

In the Pra Lak Pra Lam, the Lao Ramayana, instead of having Rama portrayed as an incarnation of Vishnu, Rama is an incarnation of the Buddha. Lao people have also written many versions of the Jataka Tales.

Chapter - 8

Buddhism in Malaysia

The sphere of influence of the early Indian civilisations extended well beyond the sub-continent to include most of what is now called South East Asia. That trade was the motivating force in this is clear from the Sanskrit names given to South East Asian ports such as Takkolo (market of cardamom), Karpuradvipa (island of camphor) and Suvarnabhumi (land of gold).

Colonists from India established a number of independent States in the Malay Peninsula during the first five centuries CE. Buddhism (along with Hinduism) may therefore have entered the Malay Peninsula at a very early period, in association with Indian trading and colonising activities in the region. There is evidence for this early contact in the mention of several place names from the peninsula in Pali canonical works such as the Niddesa and the Milindapanha.

Buddhist missionary activities in Malaysia might have occurred as early as the 3rd century CE. A Buddhist text describes how two Indian Buddhist monks, Sona and Uttara, came to South East Asia after the Third Buddhist Council in India. A Tibetan text also mentions that Dharmapala visited the Malay Peninsula, followed by Dipankara Atisa around the same period. The journals of Fa-Hsien, a Chinese monk, record that he stopped over Java and Malaysia on his voyage back from Sri Lanka to China in 413 CE.

From the 8th to the 13th centuries CE, the entire region was under the influence of the powerful Sailendra dynasty from central Java and the maritime empire of Sri Vijaya that they founded. The rulers of this dynasty built many Buddhist monuments, including the famous temple of Borobodur in central Java. The Chinese Buddhist pilgrim I-Tsing in 671 CE described the Sri Vijayan capital at Bukit Seguntang as an important centre of Buddhist learning, with more than a thousand monks devoting their days to study and good works. I-Tsing used Chien-Ch'a (Kedah) and Lang-Chia-Shu (Langkasuka) as stopping points on his pilgrimage to India. It is generally believed that the earliest form of Buddhism practised in South East Asia was the so-called Hinayana (present-day Theravada) but with the rise of Sri Vijaya, Mahayana Buddhism became more important.

Even after the kingdom of Sri Vijaya fell, Buddhist ideas and practice could have continued to enter the Malay Peninsula as the northern Malayan States fell under the influence of the Thais, and the southern Malayan States fell under the control of the Javanese empire of Majapahit.

THE ARCHAEOLOGICAL AND HISTORICAL EVIDENCE

Archaeologists have found evidence of this early Buddhist influence in finds of Buddhist sculptures from the Amaravati school (2nd to 4th century CE) in the present day Malaysian State of Kedah, in the north west of the peninsula. Unfortunately, these finds have not so far included any written evidence, such as inscriptions on stone, from this very early period.

Written evidence is however available from Chinese sources that Buddhism was well established in the Malayan States by the 6th century CE. The Chinese Annals record, for instance, that the ruler of a Malayan State described as P'an P'an sent envoys to the Chinese court in 527, 530 and 536 CE with gifts including Buddhist relics, miniature painted stupas and leaves of the Bodhi Tree. Other Malayan States recorded in the Annals as having despatched envoys and gifts at this time were described as Tan-Tan, Ch'ip-tu and Fo-Lo-An. It was recorded that the Buddha's birthday was celebrated every year on the full moon of the sixth month with processions and music, and that foreign merchants participated in the celebrations. The Buddhist priests were named in the Chinese records as Pi-ch'iu (bhikkhu).

Chinese trading contact with South East Asia can be traced to as early as the 3rd century CE, when the Southern kingdom of Wu sent a mission to South East Asia to report on the political situation there. They wrote of more than a hundred kingdoms in what they referred to as the 'Southern Seas'. The mission had important consequences. It encouraged many more South East Asian states to open official relations with China. The rich markets of China became even more important to South East Asian states as the Chinese became more ardent in their new Buddhist faith. Because of Buddhism, the Chinese began to use incense, and the best incense was made from the aromatic woods found in South East Asia. The Chinese also valued some of the objects of worship to be found in the Buddhist centres of the region, both in India and Sri Vijaya.

Excavations of sites in Kedah and in the neighbouring State of Penang have brought to light a large number of buildings which appear to have been temples, sanctuaries or other kinds of Buddhist settlements and in which were found stupas and mutilated sculptures. These sites have been dated to as early as the 4th or 5th century CE from inscriptions in Sanskrit inscribed on stone or slate slabs. One of these inscriptions, found on a stone slab under a ruined house in Kedah near Bukit Merian, contained the Buddhist formula "Ye dharma hetuprabhava...." as well as verses which have been translated as "Karma is accumulated through Ajnana, Karma is the cause of birth. Jnana leads to desistance from Karma, and in the absence of Karma, there is no rebirth".

Another important find is a clay tablet found in Kedah on which is inscribed three Sanskrit verses in a 6th century South Indian script. The verses may be the earliest Mahayana inscriptions yet found in South East Asia. Further evidence of the prevalence of Mahayana Buddhism can also be seen in the large number of clay tablets of somewhat later date (around 10th century CE) also found in Kedah that bear Mahayana texts. Also of interest are two miniature paintings of Avalokitesvara described as "Avalokitesvara of the Valavati Hill in Kataha-dvipa" (this being the ancient name for Kedah).

Buddhist inscriptions dating back to the 4th century CE have been found in other parts of Peninsular Malaysia, especially in Cheruk Tekun opposite Penang and other parts of Province Wellesley. Buddha images and other articles were found at Kuala Selinsing, Kinta Valley, Tanjung Rambutan, Bidor and Sungei Siput, all in Perak State. Buddhist images were also discovered as far into the interior as in the State of Pahang, located in the central region of the country.

There is also historical evidence that in 1006 CE, Chulamanivarmadeva, described in inscriptions as "the king of Kataha (Kedah) and Srivishaya (Sri Vijaya)", built a Buddhist temple at Negapatam. The Chola King Rajaraja I (present day Coromandel in India) gave the revenue of a large village to support the temple.

Ruins of ancient Buddhist temples have also been excavated on the eastern coast of the Malay Peninsula, although some of these sites are in what is now Thailand. Stone and bronze images of the Buddha and of the Buddha in his aspect as Lokesvara (Lord of the World) have been found at these sites. These have been dated to as late as the 13th century CE. As some of these sites were located in the State known as P'an P'an, which as already mentioned was known to the authors of the Chinese Annals from as early as the 6th century CE, it appears that Buddhist influence in the area spread over 700 years.

Much of the archaeological work referred to above was carried out in the early 1900s, during the British colonial period in Malaya. More recent work has been done from the 1970s in Kedah as part of the Bujang Valley archaeological project. This has established that the Bujang Valley was once a prosperous centre for settlement and trade, situated as it was on one of the main transit routes connecting the east and west coasts of the Peninsula.

Numerous temple sites have been found in the Bujang Valley and Merbok Estuary in Kedah, providing further proof of the existence of a Hindu-Buddhist period in Malaysian history from the 4th to the 14th century CE. The site museum is situated at the foot of Bukit Batu Pahat. Visitors can view some of the Bujang Valley excavation area finds, and can inspect some of the excavated ruins in the vicinity.

THE COMING OF ISLAM TO MALAYSIA

With the conversion of the Melaka Sultanate (the Malay kingdom which ruled both side of the Straits of Melaka for over a hundred years), Islam was established as the religion of the Malays, and had profound effect on Malay society.

The early period of Buddhist influence in the peninsula had begun to wane due to the revival of Hinduism, and then was brought to a close by the growing prevalence of Islam as a commercial and political force in the region. The spread of Islam, introduced by Arab and Indian traders, brought the Hindu-Buddhist era in the Malay Peninsula to an end by the turn of the 14th century. Around the beginning of the 15th century CE, the Malay-Hindu rulers of the kingdom of Malacca were converted to Islam and Malacca became a centre for the further spread of Islam throughout the Malay Peninsula.

Though Buddhism largely disappeared from the Malay Peninsula at this time, traces of its influence remained in the cultures of the local people. The performing arts in the States of Kedah, Perlis and Kelantan have been strongly influenced by Buddhist legends and stories. The shadow play or wayang kulit and dance forms such as menora and makyung are all testimonies that Buddhism was once a powerful religious and cultural influence in Malaysia.

CONTACT WITH CHINA

We know from the accounts of Fa-Hsien and I-Tsing that Chinese pilgrims used various points on the Malay Peninsula as stopovers on their way to and from India. We also know from Chinese records that there was diplomatic contact between China and the Malay States from very early times. Perhaps the most significant official contacts between China took place during the period of the burgeoning influence of Islam in the region. It was during this time that the Chinese admiral, explorer, and diplomat Zheng He (Cheng Ho) made his seven voyages to South East Asia and beyond to India, the Persian Gulf, East Africa, and Egypt. His seven voyages between 1405 and 1431 CE opened trade and diplomatic ties for China with at least 35 countries, and encouraged the emigration that was the basis of Chinese colonisation in South East Asia. The scale of these expeditions can be gauged from the Chinese records, which show that Zheng's first expedition alone comprised 62 large ships and 27,800 crew.

Zheng's journeys, including the very first, usually included Malacca. As Buddhism by that time was well established in China, it is interesting to speculate whether this contact provided any opportunity for the locals to be exposed to Chinese Buddhist philosophy and practice. In the Sejarah Melayu or Malay Annals, a very early history of the Malay kingdoms, it is recorded that a princess from the Chinese imperial court named Hang Liu (Hang Li Po) was given in marriage to Mansur, the Sultan of Malacca from 1456 to 1477. The princess was said to be the daughter of the Chinese Emperor.

The Sejarah Melayu also records that the princess was accompanied by five hundred young men of high rank (sons of Chinese ministers) and a number of maidservants. The Chinese who accompanied the princess settled in Malacca on and around the hill known even to this day as Bukit Cina (Chinese Hill). It can be assumed that many of the Chinese men took local wives and that many of the maidservants became wives or consorts to local men. Such domestic alliances would have provided other channels through which

Chinese influence could be transmitted to supplement the mercantile, military and colonial channels that are usually the focus of our history books.

THE CONTEMPORARY PERIOD

The arrival of significant numbers of Chinese immigrants in the Malay Peninsula after the 17th century marked the beginning of a new wave of Buddhist influence in Malaysia. This grew stronger in the 19th century during the British colonial period in Malaya, when a much larger influx of Chinese immigrants came to work in the tin mines and in other occupations. This was a time favourable to the growth of Buddhism, as well as other religions, because the official British policy was one of non-interference in the religions of the local people.

The Chinese were strongly influenced by Confucianism and Taoism but they also believed in Buddhism. Therefore, the Buddhism practised by the Chinese in Malaysia was a combination of Confucian values, Taoist beliefs, indigenous Chinese folk practices and mainly Mahayana (predominantly Pure Land) Buddhism.

The population census conducted by the Malaysian Government in 1991 listed 3.2 million Malaysians as Buddhists and 0.9 million as Confucianists/Taoists out of a total population of 17.6 million. On these figures, it would appear that Buddhists accounted for 18 percent of the total population in 1991, but since many of those categorised as 'Confucianists/Taoists' in the Census also followed Buddhist practices, the total number of Malaysians following Buddhism would be closer to 24 percent. Most of the Chinese in Malaysia are Mahayana Buddhists, though a smaller number, especially among the English-educated, follow the Theravada tradition.

MAHAYANA BUDDHISM IN MALAYSIA

Some of the earliest Mahayana Buddhist temples were set up in Penang. The Kuan Imm Teng Temple in Pitt Street traces its origin to the early 1800s. The Cheng Hoon Teng Temple built even earlier in Malacca is also dedicated to Avalokitesvara Bodhisattva. These two temples are reputedly the oldest Buddhist temples in the country. However, both temples today are perhaps better known as tourist spots rather than as dhamma centres, though it is common to see thousands of devotees during various Mahayana Buddhist festivals.

In 1887, Venerable Miao Lian from Fuchow in China came to Penang and started the construction of the Kek Lok Si Monastery, which was officially opened in 1905. The architecture reflects the influence of Thai, Burmese and Chinese Buddhism as can be seen in its multi-tiered pagoda. The words "Kek Lok" in the temple's name are the Chinese equivalent of the Sanskrit term "Sukhavati", meaning `pure land'. In the 1980s the monastery was also used as a retreat centre and for the ordination of monks and nuns following the Mahayana tradition. The temple was for a time considered to be the largest Buddhist temple in South East Asia. It has continued to expand and refurbish its buildings, and is still today a very popular tourist destination.

The Penang Buddhist Association was founded in 1925 and its temple in Anson Road was completed in 1931. It is clear from the stated aim of the Association, which was to propagate the correct teachings of Buddhism, that many considered that Buddhism was not being properly disseminated in the country at that time. The Penang Buddhist Association became one of the earliest Buddhist temples to realise that much of the Buddhism that was practised in the country had become a distorted version of the true teaching under the influence of local superstitions and non-Buddhist traditional practices.

A Youth Circle of the Penang Buddhist Association to cater to both the Chinese and English speaking membership was set up in 1955 by the American Buddhist monk, Venerable Sumangalo, who was a resident monk at the temple from 1955 until his death in 1963. Some of the innovations introduced by Venerable Sumangalo were the singing of Buddhist hymns, and a Dharma Sunday School. The youth organisation he established became the forerunner of many similar Buddhist youth groups throughout the country such as the Malayan Buddhist Youth Fellowship and the Federation of Malayan Buddhist Youth Fellowships. Venerable Sumangalo visited Australia for a few weeks in 1956, attracting large audiences to the series of Dharma talks he gave in Melbourne and Sydney, and giving a considerable impetus to the fledgling Buddhist movement in Australia at that time.

Although the Penang Buddhist Association was a Mahayana temple, it adopted a non-sectarian approach by inviting Theravada monks such as the late Venerable K. Gunaratana Maha Nayaka Thera and Venerable P. Pemaratana Maha Nayaka Thera from the nearby Sinhalese Mahindarama Temple to give religious talks. Venerable Sumangalo himself has been quoted as saying, "I do not call myself a Theravadin or a Mahayanist. I am simply a follower of Lord Buddha".

A Buddhist nun of the Mahayana tradition, Venerable Fang Lian (or Hong Lien) established the Phor Thay Institute (or Nunnery) in 1936. Within a few years, this institution also set up an orphanage and a school, the Phor Thay Chinese Primary School, to cater for the needs of Chinese Buddhist children by teaching the Buddha Dhamma as well as the usual subjects. Later, the Phor Thay (National Type) Chinese High School and the Phor Thay (Private) Chinese High School were added to cater for the secondary education of Buddhist students. These three schools now cater for over 3,000 students from Penang and the northern states of Malaysia.

In 1950, a group of 14 Buddhists from Malaya, which at that time included Singapore, went to Colombo, Sri Lanka to attend the Inaugural General Conference of The World Fellowship of Buddhists (WFB). On their return, the Buddhists in Penang formed The World Fellowship of Buddhists Penang Regional Centre in 1951. Later, WFB Regional Centres were also established in Selangor and Singapore.

The Malaysian Buddhist Association was formed on April 19, 1959. Its first President was Venerable Chuk Mor. The Association is the umbrella body for Chinese Mahayana monks and numerous temples in Malaysia. Its building at 182 Burmah Road in Penang also houses the independently managed Buddhist Free School and the Malaysian Buddhist Institute. The Buddhist Free School has for many years been providing adult education for Chinese Buddhists, giving them an opportunity to learn languages such as Chinese, English and Bahasa Malaysia, as well as other useful subjects. The Malaysian Buddhist Institute is an organisation that trains Chinese Buddhist monks and nuns, while giving other Buddhists an opportunity for more in-depth study of Buddhism.

Venerable Chuk Mor, a well-known scholar monk of the Mahayana tradition, was born on August 13, 1913 in China. He was ordained a monk at age 12 in 1924 and came to Penang on May 4, 1954. In July 1962, Venerable Chuk Mor founded the Triple Wisdom Hall to teach Ch'an (Chinese Zen) meditation to devotees. This became the first Chinese Buddhist temple in Malaysia where systematic Ch'an meditation was taught. He was a prime mover in establishing the Malaysian Buddhist Institute in 1969 to provide a more comprehensive training to Chinese Mahayana monks and nuns.

One of his many disciples, Venerable Sik Chi Chern, became the president of the Young Buddhist Association of Malaysia (YBAM) for three terms, from 1990-1996, becoming the first monk to head a major lay Buddhist organisation with over 200 affiliate members throughout the country.

For his contribution to Buddhism, Venerable Chuk Mor was conferred one of the highest awards of the State of Penang, the Darjah Setia Pangkuan Negeri (DSPN). The award carries the title of Datuk, the nearest English equivalent to which might be the title of Sir. He is the first Buddhist monk to be conferred this prestigious award.

The second president of YBAM was Venerable Kim Beng, who was also the Chief Abbot of Cheng Hoon Teng Temple in Malacca. He headed the organisation for many years, before he gave up the post due to his advanced age. He played an active role in the propagation of Buddhism in Malaysia and was also a prolific writer. The Malaysian Government honoured him with the Jasa Setia Mahkota (JSM) award for his contributions to Buddhism.

Venerable Chip Hong, the current President of the Malaysian Buddhist Association is also the Chief Abbot of a Buddhist temple in Seremban, Negri Sembilan. He is a well-known Chinese physician.

The Than Hsiang Temple in Bayan Lepas, Penang, should also be mentioned for its contribution to Buddhism in Malaysia. Established by Venerable Wei Wu, a Malaysian Chinese who had formerly been an engineer, the temple has become well known for its charitable and welfare activities, including counselling. In the field of education, it runs a kindergarten school and has also started a Diploma in Buddhist Studies course in association with the Pali and Buddhist University of Sri Lanka. Though Venerable Wei

Wu was ordained in the Chinese Mahayana tradition, he is very open to Theravada teachings, as can be seen in the Sri Lanka-based diploma program he initiated.

Other major Chinese Mahayana temples are found in the Kuala Lumpur area. They include the Kuan Imm Teng in Petaling Jaya established by Venerable Keng Aun, Hoeh Beng Temple, Tham Wah Wan and Wisma Buddhist. There are also large Chinese Buddhist temples and monasteries in all the state capitals of the country.

Buddhism from China has traditionally influenced Chinese Buddhism in Malaysia. For instance, most of the senior Chinese Buddhist monks in Malaysia were born in China and migrated to the country during the British period or after mainland China became a Communist country in 1949.

More recently, Buddhist teachers from Taiwan have started centres in Malaysia. The most significant is the Fo Kuang Shan group under Venerable Hsing Yun. They started the Buddha's Light Vihara in Kuala Lumpur, which was headed by a local monk, Venerable Hui Hai, until recently. The temple conducts dhamma classes and other religious activities and has a growing number of well-educated supporters. In 1998 Venerable Hsing Yun was invited to Malaysia to give a series of Buddhist talks to the public, in a joint effort between the Buddha's Light Vihara and the Malaysian Chinese Association, the Chinese political party in the ruling coalition under Prime Minister Dr Mahathir Mohamed. This is the first time in Malaysia that a political party has jointly organised a series of public lectures on Buddhism with a Buddhist organisation.

The other influence from Taiwan is the Buddhist Tzu Chi Merit Society started by Venerable Zheng Yen in Hualien in 1966. In Malaysia, Tzu Chi activities in charity and welfare started in 1990. In 1993 the first official Tzu Chi centre was established in Kuala Lumpur, and was soon followed by similar centres in Penang, Melaka and Ipoh.

The late Venerable Hsuan Hua with many of his Chinese and American disciples visited Malaysia during the 1980s and 1990s to give dhamma teachings. The local disciples of Venerable Hsuan Hua have since started a monastery in Kuala Lumpur where visiting monks from the City of Ten Thousand Buddhas in California, USA, can reside during their dhamma visits to Malaysia.

THERAVADA BUDDHISM IN MALAYSIA

While those of Chinese descent form the majority of the Buddhist population in Malaysia, a smaller number of Thais, Burmese and Sinhalese in the country also practise Buddhism. The Chinese tend to follow the Mahayana tradition, whereas the Thai, Burmese and Sinhalese communities generally follow the Theravada tradition.

The Thai community is found mainly in the northern states of Perlis, Kedah and Kelantan, which were once Thai territory until it was ceded to the British in 1909 to become part of the Unfederated Malay States of British Malaya. Some Thais have also moved to Penang and Kuala Lumpur. It is estimated that there are about 200 Thai temples, including small village wats, in the country. Most are located in the northern part of Malaysia.

The Thai temples also attract many local Chinese devotees. Although some of the monks at these temples are Malaysian born, there are few of them who are fluent enough in the national language, Malay, or in the other widely spoken languages of Chinese or English, to give teachings on Buddhism. Therefore, the activities at these temples are mostly limited to Pali chanting, blessing services, and offering of food (sanghika dana) to the monks.

An exception is the Malaysian Buddhist Meditation Centre in Green Lane, Penang. It is a Thai temple established in 1918 and historically known as Wat Candaram. As the name by which it is now known implies, it is a meditation temple. During the 1970s the abbot of the temple was Phra Khru Dhammabanchanvud (or Abhidhammapalanana Maha Thero), a learned Thai monk trained in the Mahasi Sayadaw form of vipassana meditation at Wat Mahathat in Bangkok. When he was the abbot, he gave teachings on Buddhism, including the abhidhamma, and perhaps for the first time in Malaysia, introduced vipassana meditation to the devotees. His dhamma activities attracted many young Malaysians, including high school students and undergraduates from the nearby Universiti Sains Malaysia. This was quite a contrast to other Thai temples that attracted the less educated and generally older Chinese devotees who came mainly for the ceremonies and rituals.

However, Phra Khru Dhammabanchanvud's religious ministry had to be cut short and he had to return to Thailand because his visa to Malaysia could not be renewed. Nevertheless, his efforts had borne fruits. Some of his students, including Venerable Sujivo, a Malaysian Chinese monk, followed up his noble work by continuing to teach vipassana meditation at the Centre and later in other parts of the country. Lately, Burmese monks of the Mahasi tradition have been visiting the Centre and also other parts of Malaysia to teach vipassana meditation to Malaysians.

The other Thai monk who has contributed to spreading Buddhism in Malaysia is Venerable Phra Silananda, during the time he was residing at Wat Pin Bang Onn (founded in 1889) in Penang. The temple is situated next to the Malaysian Buddhist Meditation Centre in Green Lane and had an active Sunday School when the venerable monk was its teacher. However, when he left the country for England, its Sunday School and many other religious activities ceased. Today Venerable Phra (now Chao Khun) Silananda continues his dhamma work at the Buddhapadipa Temple in London.

The Burmese and Sinhalese communities are much smaller than the Thai community. The Burmese are mainly concentrated in Penang, and their Dhammikarama Temple in Burmah Lane (popularly regarded as having been founded in 1803 but perhaps more accurately dating to around 1828) is the only Burmese temple in Malaysia. The Dhammikarama Burmese Temple in Burmah Lane was active with religious activities when Venerable U Pannavamsa was residing there. A learned scholar, he taught abhidhamma and meditation to the devotees. He also supported the Sunday School at the temple. However, religious talks and meditation classes are now organised on a less regular basis due to lack of monks with the necessary experience and skills.

However, it is interesting to note that the Burmese contribution to Malaysian Buddhism has extended well beyond their only temple in Penang. Thanks to the connection Venerable Phra Khru Dhammabanchanvud has made with the Mahasi Sayadaw tradition, many Burmese monks are now teaching vipassana meditation in Malaysia. Venerable Mahasi Sayadaw himself visited Malaysia in 1980 to give teachings and introduce vipassana meditation classes. Regular vipassana meditation retreats are now held at the Malaysian Buddhist Meditation Centre, Santisukarama Buddhist Centre in Kota Tinggi (Johor), Taiping Buddhist Society (Perak), Buddhaganu Sasana Centre (Malacca), Selangor Vipassana Centre (Petaling Jaya), Subang Jaya Buddhist Association (Selangor) and also in East Malaysia. Some of the Burmese monks who have been regularly teaching vipassana meditation to Malaysians include Venerable Sayadaw U Pandita, Venerable Sayadaw U Pannathami and Venerable Sayadaw U Rewatta. Another Burmese teacher, Venerable Sayadaw U Janaka, though from a different Burmese meditation tradition, has also taught meditation in Malaysia.

The other major contribution to Theravada Buddhism in Malaysia comes from the Sinhalese monks. They are generally English-speaking and have been formally trained in Buddhism. The Sinhalese have a temple in each of Penang and Taiping and two in Kuala Lumpur, and these temples attract a largely English-educated group of devotees.

A leading Theravada Buddhist centre in Penang is the Mahindarama Temple in Kampar Road, Penang. Founded in 1918 by Venerable A. Pemaratana, the Mahindarama Temple was very active in dhamma propagation activities under Venerable K. Gunaratana Maha Nayaka Thera (1933-1964). An eloquent preacher, Venerable Gunaratana was able to attract a large number of young and educated Buddhists to the temple. He also gave dhamma talks in other parts of the country. He organised regular dhamma activities and a Sunday School for children. After his death, Venerable P. Pemaratana Maha Nayaka Thera continued with many religious activities at the temple.

Compared to Thai monks in Malaysia, the Sinhalese monks are generally more missionary minded. This could be because they had received a more formal training in Buddhism at the monastic colleges in Sri Lanka, and are able to communicate in English, the language of the educated during that time. Also, there was an on-going Buddhist revival in Sri Lanka following the conversion of Col. H.S. Olcott and the missionary zeal of Buddhist reformers such as Venerable Anagarika Dharmapala (1864-1933).

The other major Sinhalese Buddhist centre is at the Buddhist Maha Vihara in Brickfields, Kuala Lumpur. The temple was founded by the Sasana Abhiwurdhi Wardhana Society in 1895. Originally set up to cater to the religious needs of the Sinhalese community in the Kuala Lumpur area, the temple today caters to Buddhists of all ethnic groups, including the Chinese who undoubtedly form the largest group of devotees. It has a very well organised Sunday School that has an enrolment of over 200 students from pre-school to junior high school. There are also regular religious talks on Sunday mornings and Friday evenings, counselling sessions and meditation classes on other days. The temple also houses an active Youth Section and a Ladies Section.

Much of the success of the Buddhist Maha Vihara must be attributed to the Venerable Dr K. Sri Dhammananda Maha Nayaka Thera. Born on March 18,1919, he first arrived in Malaysia on January 2, 1952 and has since then embarked on a comprehensive missionary program for the Malaysian Buddhist community. He started the Buddhist Missionary Society in 1963 to propagate Buddhism to the masses. Through the Society, he gave public talks and organised seminars on Buddhism throughout the country. He also wrote and published numerous books on Buddhism, especially with the objective of clearing misconceptions about Buddhism in Malaysia. Many of these books, including "What Buddhists Believe" and "Treasures of the Dhamma" are classic texts for any class on Buddhist studies. Buddhist groups in other countries have also translated a number of his books into foreign languages.

One of Venerable Dhammananda's disciples is Venerable Mahinda from Malacca. Venerable Mahinda was influenced by Buddhism during his younger days at the Malacca Buddhist Association (Seck Kia Eenh) and his interest in the Buddha's teachings deepened when he was studying at university in New Zealand. He later became a monk under Venerable Dhammananda and since then has assisted in numerous missionary activities in both Malaysia and Singapore. He now heads the Australian Buddhist Mission in Sydney but returns regularly to Malaysia to assist in dhamma activities, especially during the annual Novitiate Program held at the Buddhist Maha Vihara.

JAPANESE BUDDHISM IN MALAYSIA

Japanese Buddhism, including Zen, has not made a significant impact on Malaysian Buddhism so far. The only form of Japanese Buddhism that has spread to Malaysia is Nichiren Shoshu, sometime during the early 1960s. It was brought to Malaysia by Japanese businessmen working in Malaysia as well as by Malaysians who had studied in Japan.

During the 1980s, when the Malaysian Government was emphasising the "Look East Policy" of emulating Japan in industrialisation, management styles and work ethics, other things "Japanese" also became in vogue. Japanese Buddhism was one of them. Today there are Nichiren Shoshu centres in most major towns in the country, including Kuala Lumpur, Penang, Ipoh, Malacca and Kuantan. The fellowship among the followers is strong but they seldom have contacts with other Buddhist groups within Malaysia.

TIBETAN BUDDHISM IN MALAYSIA

Tibetan Buddhism is the latest to enter Malaysia but is perhaps the most widely known form of Buddhism in some circles because of the considerable publicity it attracts. The publicity over His Holiness the Dalai Lama winning the Nobel Peace Prize in 1995, the publication of Sogyal Rinpoche's Tibetan Book of Living and Dying, the Free Tibet Movement led by movie stars and rock singers and the Hollywood portrayal of Tibet in "Seven Years in Tibet" and "Kundun", have aroused the interest and imagination of many in Malaysia, Buddhists and non-Buddhists alike, in Tibetan Buddhism.

Historically, the visit of the Venerable Gwalya Karmapa of the Kagyu school in December 1980 marked the first official introduction of Tibetan Buddhism to Malaysia. Subsequently, other Tibetan lamas, including Venerable Tai Situpa Rinpoche, have visited Malaysia for both teachings and initiations. Today, the Karma Kagyu school has numerous centres in the country but they work closely with Buddhist organisations of both the Theravada and Mahayana traditions.

His Holiness The Dalai Lama also visited Malaysia in 1981 and was accorded a warm welcome by Buddhists of both the Theravada and Chinese Mahayana traditions. Other Tibetan teachers have continued to visit Malaysia, usually at the request of their devotees in the country. The most celebrated teachers have included Lama Yeshe's incarnation Osel Tenzin and Lama Yeshe's successor Lama Zopa Rinpoche. In 1996 Lama Zopa's followers started the Losang Drapga Centre in Ampang, Kuala Lumpur, where regular teachings on Tibetan Buddhism are provided. Many of Lama Zopa's Western disciples, including Venerable Sangye Khadro, Venerable Thubten Chodron and Venerable Thubten Tsultrim have given talks and conducted seminars in Malaysia.

Associations of Buddhist lay people have played a vital role in sustaining and developing Buddhism in Malaysia, not only in the traditional area of support for temples and for the Sangha, but also in the fields of education and publishing.

THE YOUNG BUDDHIST ASSOCIATION OF MALAYSIA

The Young Buddhist Association of Malaysia (YBAM) was established in 1970. It is a federation of 243 Buddhist youth organisations throughout the country, with a total membership of over 100,000. The YBAM also has an associate membership of over 3,000 members. The YBAM was established to unite Buddhist groups throughout the country, especially the youth, under one umbrella organisation. It runs a range of activities, from religious talks and meditation camps to social welfare activities for its members. Together with the Malaysian Buddhist Association, it conducts the annual Malaysian Buddhist Examinations for students at various levels. The YBAM has also received recognition from the Government and is represented at the Malaysian Youth Council.

Closely associated with the YBAM is the Young Buddhist Foundation that was established in 1976 to provide funding support to the YBAM for its activities. Through the Foundation, the YBAM has taken up a significant stake in a Vegetarian Restaurant and also started a typesetting business, both in Penang. The Foundation is involved in various religious as well as welfare activities, including awarding scholarships to needy but bright students, and supporting a Sangha Fund for monks and nuns.

THE BUDDHIST GEM FELLOWSHIP

Originally started as the Buddhist Graduates Fellowship (BGF) in 1980 by a group of local university graduates, the BGF has grown to become a prominent group of Buddhist leaders providing training and leadership support to college students in local universities. Through the Inter-College and Varsity (INCOVAR) Camps, the BGF has been successful in providing support and training to the students in managing the Buddhist societies at the various universities in Malaysia. Many of these students subsequently become members of the BGF when they graduate, and then in turn help their juniors back on campus.

MEDITATION GROUPS

During the past 20 years, meditation has become an increasing part of Buddhist practice among devotees in Malaysia. In the Chinese Mahayana tradition, temples that teach meditation include Hoe Beng Si in Kuala Lumpur, Taiping Buddhist Society (Perak) and Triple Wisdom Hall and Malaysian Buddhist Institute in Penang.

In the Theravada tradition, many meditation centres were established recently. Those in the Kuala Lumpur area include the Selangor Vipassana Centre, Wisdom Centre and the Subang Jaya Buddhist Association. Their teacher is Venerable Sujivo, who teaches meditation based on the Mahasi Sayadaw tradition. There are also other smaller meditation groups in Johor Bahru (Metta Lodge) and in Kota Tinggi (Santisukarama Buddhist Centre), both in the southern state of Johor.

In the northern region, there are meditation centres in Lunas and Bukit Perak in Kedah and at the Taiping Insight Meditation Centre in Taiping, Perak. All these centres follow the Burmese method of meditation as taught by the late Venerable Mahasi Sayadaw. In addition to Venerable Sujivo, two other well-known local Theravada meditation monks, Venerable Suvanno and Venerable Visuddhacara, are teaching vipassana meditation. Venerable Suvanno, who is now in his 70s, has a meditation hermitage in Lunas (Kedah) and another centre in Penang Hill. Venerable Vissudhacara, a prolific writer, used to reside at the Malaysian Buddhist Meditation Centre but now has no specific place of residence.

Other Malaysian Theravada monks who teach meditation include Venerable Chamriang in Kedah, Venerable Javanna in Kota Bahru, Kelantan, and Venerable Dhammavuddho who used to be based in Penang but has recently moved to Perak where he is setting up a Centre.

DHARMA PUBLICATIONS

A number of Malaysian Buddhist organisations are prominent in the publication of

Dharma books in English and Chinese, such as the Buddhist Missionary Society and the Wisdom Audio Visual Exchange in Kuala Lumpur, and Sukhi Hotu and the Malaysian Buddhist Meditation Centre, both in Penang. These publications, many of which are for free distribution, are of great value in providing wider access to the Buddha's teachings. As these books are often available outside Malaysia, the influence of Malaysian Buddhism is being felt throughout the region. This influence is also evident in the high esteem in which prominent Malaysian monks such as Venerable Dhammananda and Venerable Mahinda are held in other countries, including Australia.

CONCLUSION

Indications are that Buddhism is again on the rise in Malaysia. Although Islam is the State religion of Malaysia and the religion of the Malay people who constitute the majority of the population, Malaysian Buddhists have enjoyed the freedom to practise their religion. The majority of Malaysian Buddhists are of Chinese ethnic origin, with smaller numbers from other ethnic backgrounds such as Thai, Burmese and Sinhalese. Unlike most other Asian countries, where the form of Buddhism practised is predominantly either Mahayana or Theravada, all the major traditions of Buddhism are thriving in happy coexistence in Malaysia.

The many Buddhist temples and organisations which have been established over the past 20 years bear testimony to the fact that the Buddha's teaching is alive and well. Many Malaysians have also become monks, and a number of them have been in the monkhood for more than 10 years. Many young and educated Malaysian Chinese are also rediscovering Buddhism, as can be seen in the increasing enrolment in Buddhist classes at the major Buddhist centres in Kuala Lumpur and other cities. They are interested in exploring the Buddha's teaching rather than relying on traditional customs and beliefs practiced by the older generation of their parents and grandparents.

The future of Buddhism in Malaysia is bright but, as is the case throughout the world, much depends on the continuation and extension of the good work that is being done in the area of Buddhist education. Much also depends on the continued willingness of the major Buddhist organisations, whether Theravada, Mahayana or Vajrayana, to work together with a common vision. May the Triple Gem guide Malaysian Buddhists in the next millennium with the energy, resourcefulness and innovation they have applied so successfully to their efforts in the last years of the present millennium.

Chapter - 9

Buddhism in Indonesia

Buddhism is the second oldest religion in Indonesia, just after Hinduism. Before the arrival of these two religions, people believed that nature had supernormal power. Trees and stones were worshipped as sacred object, where beings with supernormal power reside.

Hinduism came to Indonesia at around the second century. The first two major kingdoms (Tarumanegara in Western Java and Kutai in Western Borneo) were based on Hinduism. Buddhism came to Indonesia a few hundred years after Hinduism. It reached its peak at the time of the Sriwijaya's dynasty rule, which was once the largest Buddhist kingdom in South East Asia, from around the 7th century until the 14th century. During that time, many Buddhist colleges and monasteries were built, and famous Buddhist scholars, such as Dharmapala and Sakyakirti, were teaching there. Another major Buddhist kingdom was the Mataram kingdom, which was ruled by the Sailendra clan during the eight and ninth century in Central Java. Many Buddhist temples were built and Buddhist texts were inscribed on the stones tablets (called prasasti) during this time.

HISTORY OF INDONESIAN BUDDHISM

Before Hinduism or Buddhism staged an entry into Indonesia, the people of the country were the worshippers of nature and its components. Trees, stones and many other such things were believed to have supernatural power. Then, in the 2nd century, Hinduism became the first religion to make inroads into Indonesia. The first two major kingdom of Indonesia - Tarumanegara in Western Java and Kutai in Western Borneo - were Hindu.

A few centuries later, Buddhism emerged on the religious scene of Indonesia and became the second religion of the country. Buddhism reached its zenith during the reign of Sriwijaya's dynasty which at that point of time was the largest Buddhist Kingdom in the South East Asia. This period saw the construction of number of Buddhist colleges and monasteries. Also, renowned Buddhist scholars Dharmapala and Sakyakirti taught in these colleges and monasteries.

In the 8th and the 9th century, another important Buddhist Kingdom, Mataram kingdom ruled by the Sailendra clan, had its influence in Indonesia. Hence, many Buddhist Temples were constructed and Buddhist texts inscribed on the stone tablets at this point of time. The world famous Borobudur Temple was one of the most important temples built during this time.

Buddhism and Hinduism continued to exist peacefully together till the time Islam was introduced by the people of Gujarat, India in the 15th century. Buddhism began to loose its significance and became confined in the areas of Java and Bali.

The year 1934 saw the arrival of the revered missionary monk from Sri Lanka, Narada Thera. Narada Thera was on his mission to propagate Dhamma in Southeast Asia and the local Buddhist monk found in this an opportunity to revive Buddhism in Indonesia. A Bodhi Tree planting ceremony was organised and few upasakas were ordained as monks. The attempt to bring back Buddhism was further accelerated when a monk called Ashin Jinarakkhita commenced a tour across different regions in Indonesia to spread the Dhamma. This was in the year 1955 and since then Theravada Buddhism began to stage a comeback on the religious scene of Indonesia spearheaded by local monks trained in Thailand.

As of today, Buddhism is amongst the five religion recognised by the Indonesian Government, the other four being Islam (87%), Christianity (Catholic and Protestant 10%) and Hinduism (2%). Buddhists comprise around 1% of the total population as per the official records, however, the actual figure could be much less owing to the fact that the followers of Confucianism and Taoism also recognise themselves as Buddhist. This is so because neither Confucianism nor Taoism are recognised religion in the Constitution.

BUDDHIST TEMPLES IN INDONESIA

Many Buddhist temples were built and Buddhist texts were inscribed on the stones tablets (called prasasti) in Indonesia. The best known of these temples is Borobudur one of the Seven Wonders of the World. Borobudur represents three views of the universe according to the Indian Vajrayana tradition. The apex of the structure is a stupa, which represents the concept of Emptiness or Sunnata. Every year on the full moon in May, the Vesak celebration (called Tri Suci Waisak in Bahasa Indonesian), commemorating the birth, enlightenment, and passing away of the Buddha is held at Borobudur.

TEMPLE OF BOROBUDUR

Borobudur is a ninth-century Mahayana Buddhist monument in Magelang, Central Java, Indonesia. The monument comprises six square platforms topped by three circular platforms, and is decorated with 2,672 relief panels and 504 Buddha statues. A main dome, located at the center of the top platform, is surrounded by 72 Buddha statues seated inside perforated stupa.

The monument is both a shrine to the Lord Buddha and a place for Buddhist pilgrimage. The journey for pilgrims begins at the base of the monument and follows a path circumambulating the monument while ascending to the top through the three levels of Buddhist cosmology, namely *Kamadhatu* (the world of desire), *Rupadhatu* (the world of forms) and *Arupadhatu* (the world of formlessness). During the journey the monument guides the pilgrims through a system of stairways and corridors with 1,460 narrative relief panels on the wall and the balustrades.

Evidence suggests Borobudur was abandoned following the fourteenth century decline of Buddhist and Hindu kingdoms in Java, and the Javanese conversion to Islam. Worldwide knowledge of its existence was sparked in 1814 by Sir Thomas Raffles, the then British ruler of Java, who was advised of its location by native Indonesians. Borobudur has since been preserved through several restorations. The largest restoration project was undertaken between 1975 and 1982 by the Indonesian government and UNESCO, following which the monument was listed as a UNESCO World Heritage Site. Borobudur is still used for pilgrimage; once a year Buddhists in Indonesia celebrate Vesak at the monument, and Borobudur is Indonesia's single most visited tourist attraction.

In Indonesian, ancient temples are known as *candi*; thus "Borobudur Temple" is locally known as *Candi Borobudur*. The term *candi* is also used more loosely to describe any ancient structure, for example gates and bathing structures. The origins of the name *Borobudur* however are unclear, although the original names of most ancient Indonesian temples are no longer known. The name Borobudur was first written in Sir Thomas Raffles' book on Javan history. Raffles wrote about a monument called *borobudur*, but there are no older documents suggesting the same name. The only old Javanese manuscript that hints at the monument as a holy Buddhist sanctuary is Nagarakertagama, written by Mpu Prapanca in 1365.

The name 'Bore-Budur', and thus 'BoroBudur', is thought to have been written by Raffles in English grammar to mean the nearby village of Bore; most *candi* are named after a nearby village. If it followed Javanese language, the monument should have been named 'BudurBoro'. Raffles also suggested that 'Budur' might correspond to the modern Javanese word *Buda* ('ancient') – i.e., 'ancient Boro'. However, another archaeologist suggests the second component of the name ('Budur') comes from Javanese term *bhudhara* (or mountain).

LOCATION

Approximately 40 kilometers (25 mi) northwest of Yogyakarta, Borobudur is located in an elevated area between two twin volcanoes, Sundoro-Sumbing and Merbabu-Merapi, and two rivers, the Progo and the Elo. According to local myth, the area known as Kedu Plain is a Javanese 'sacred' place and has been dubbed 'the garden of Java' due to its high agricultural fertility. Besides Borobudur, there are other Buddhist and Hindu temples in the area, including the Prambanan temples compound. During the restoration in the early 1900s, it was discovered that three Buddhist temples in the region,

Borobudur, Pawon and Mendut, are lined in one straight line position. It might be accidental, but the temples' alignment is in conjunction with a native folk tale that a long time ago, there was a brick-paved road from Borobudur to Mendut with walls on both sides. The three temples (Borobudur–Pawon–Mendut) have similar architecture and ornamentation derived from the same time period, which suggests that ritual relationship between the three temples, in order to have formed a sacred unity, must have existed, although exact ritual process is yet unknown.

Unlike other temples, which were built on a flat surface, Borobudur was built on a bedrock hill, 265 m (869 ft) above sea level and 15 m (49 ft) above the floor of the dried-out paleolake. The lake's existence was the subject of intense discussion among archaeologists in the twentieth century; Borobudur was thought to have been built on a lake shore or even floated on a lake. In 1931, a Dutch artist and a scholar of Hindu and Buddhist architecture, W.O.J. Nieuwenkamp, developed a theory that Kedu Plain was once a lake and Borobudur initially represented a lotus flower floating on the lake. Lotus flowers are found in almost every Buddhist work of art, often serving as a throne for buddhas and base for stupas. The architecture of Borobudur itself suggests a lotus depiction, in which Buddha postures in Borobudur symbolize the Lotus Sutra, mostly found in many Mahayana Buddhism (a school of Buddhism widely spread in the east Asia region) texts. Three circular platforms on the top are also thought to represent a lotus leaf. Nieuwenkamp's theory, however, was contested by many archaeologists because the natural environment surrounding the monument is a dry land.

Geologists, on the other hand, support Nieuwenkamp's view, pointing out clay sediments found near the site. A study of stratigraphy, sediment and pollen samples conducted in 2000 supports the existence of a paleolake environment near Borobudur, which tends to confirm Nieuwenkamp's theory. The lake area fluctuated with time and the study also proves that Borobudur was near the lake shore circa thirteenth and fourteenth century. River flows and volcanic activities shape the surrounding landscape, including the lake. One of the most active volcanoes in Indonesia, Mount Merapi, is in the direct vicinity of Borobudur and has been very active since the Pleistocene.

HISTORY

Construction

There is no written record of who built Borobudur or of its intended purpose. The construction time has been estimated by comparison between carved reliefs on the temple's hidden foot and the inscriptions commonly used in royal charters during the eight and ninth centuries. Borobudur was likely founded around 800 AD. This corresponds to the period between 760–830 AD, the peak of the Sailendra dynasty in central Java, when it was under the influence of the Srivijayan Empire. The construction has been estimated to have taken 75 years and been completed during the reign of Samaratungga in 825.

There is confusion between Hindu and Buddhist rulers in Java around that time. The Sailendras were known as ardent followers of Lord Buddha, though stone inscriptions found at Sojomerto suggest they may have been Hindus. It was during this time that many Hindu and Buddhist monuments were built on the plains and mountain around the Kedu Plain. The Buddhist monuments, including Borobudur, were erected around the same time as the Hindu Shiva Prambanan temple compound. In 732 AD, the Shivaite King Sanjaya commissioned a Shivalinga sanctuary to be built on the Ukir hill, only 10 km (6.2 miles) east of Borobudur.

Construction of Buddhist temples, including Borobudur, at that time was possible because Sanjaya's immediate successor, Rakai Panangkaran, granted his permission to the Buddhist followers to build such temples. In fact, to show his respect, Panangkaran gave the village of Kalasan to the Buddhist community, as is written in the Kalasan Charter dated 778 AD. This has led some archaeologists to believe that there was never serious conflict concerning religion in Java as it was possible for a Hindu king to patronize the establishment of a Buddhist monument; or for a Buddhist king to act likewise. However, it is likely that there were two rival royal dynasties in Java at the time—the Buddhist Sailendra and the Saivite Sanjaya—in which the latter triumphed over their rival in the 856 battle on the Ratubaka plateau. This confusion also exists regarding the Lara Jonggrang temple at the Prambanan complex, which was believed that it was erected by the victor Rakai Pikatan as the Sanjaya dynasty's reply to Borobudur, but others suggest that there was a climate of peaceful coexistence where Sailendra involvement exists in Lara Jonggrang.

Abandonment

Borobudur lay hidden for centuries under layers of volcanic ash and jungle growth. The facts behind its abandonment remain a mystery. It is not known when active use of the monument and Buddhist pilgrimage to it ceased. Somewhere between 928 and 1006, the center of power moved to East Java region and a series of volcanic eruptions took place; it is not certain whether the latter influenced the former but several sources mention this as the most likely period of abandonment. Soekmono (1976) also mentions the popular belief that the temples were disbanded when the population converted to Islam in the fifteenth century.

The monument was not forgotten completely, though folk stories gradually shifted from its past glory into more superstitious beliefs associated with bad luck and misery. Two old Javanese chronicles (*babad*) from the eighteenth century mention cases of bad luck associated with the monument. According to the *Babad Tanah Jawi* (or the History of Java), the monument was a fatal factor for a rebel who revolted against the king of Mataram in 1709. The hill was besieged and the insurgents were defeated and sentenced to death by the king. In the *Babad Mataram* (or the History of the Mataram Kingdom), the monument was associated with the misfortune of the crown prince of the Yogyakarta Sultanate in 1757. In spite of a taboo against visiting the monument, "he took what is written as *the knight who was captured in a cage* (a statue in one of the perforated stupas)". Upon returning to his palace, he fell ill and died one day later.

Rediscovery

Following the Anglo-Dutch Java War, Java was under British administration from 1811 to 1816. The appointed governor was Lieutenant Governor-General Thomas Stamford Raffles, who took great interest in the history of Java. He collected Javanese antiques and made notes through contacts with local inhabitants during his tour throughout the island. On an inspection tour to Semarang in 1814, he was informed about a big monument deep in a jungle near the village of Bumisegoro. He was not able to make the discovery himself and sent H.C. Cornelius, a Dutch engineer, to investigate.

In two months, Cornelius and his 200 men cut down trees, burned down vegetation and dug away the earth to reveal the monument. Due to the danger of collapse, he could not unearth all galleries. He reported his findings to Raffles including various drawings. Although the discovery is only mentioned by a few sentences, Raffles has been credited with the monument's recovery, as one who had brought it to the world's attention.

Hartmann, a Dutch administrator of the Kedu region, continued Cornelius' work and in 1835 the whole complex was finally unearthed. His interest in Borobudur was more personal than official. Hartmann did not write any reports of his activities; in particular, the alleged story that he discovered the large statue of Buddha in the main stupa. In 1842, Hartmann investigated the main dome although what he discovered remains unknown as the main stupa remains empty.

The Dutch East Indies government then commissioned F.C. Wilsen, a Dutch engineering official, who studied the monument and drew hundreds of relief sketches. J.F.G. Brumund was also appointed to make a detailed study of the monument, which was completed in 1859. The government intended to publish an article based on Brumund study supplemented by Wilsen's drawings, but Brumund refused to cooperate. The government then commissioned another scholar, C. Leemans, who compiled a monograph based on Brumund's and Wilsen's sources. In 1873, the first monograph of the detailed study of Borobudur was published, followed by its French translation a year later. The first photograph of the monument was taken in 1873 by a Dutch-Flemish engraver, Isidore van Kinsbergen.

Appreciation of the site developed slowly, and it served for some time largely as a source of souvenirs and income for "souvenir hunters" and thieves. In 1882, the chief inspector of cultural artifacts recommended that Borobudur be entirely disassembled with the relocation of reliefs into museums due to the unstable condition of the monument. As a result, the government appointed Groenveldt, an archeologist, to undertake a thorough investigation of the site and to assess the actual condition of the complex; his report found that these fears were unjustified and recommended it be left intact.

Contemporary Events

Following the major 1973 renovation funded by UNESCO, Borobudur is once again used as a place of worship and pilgrimage. Once a year, during the full moon in May or June, Buddhists in Indonesia observe Vesak (Indonesian: *Waisak*) day commemorating the birth, death, and the time when Siddhârtha Gautama attained the highest wisdom to become the Buddha Shakyamuni. Vesak is an official national holiday in Indonesia and the ceremony is centered at the three Buddhist temples by walking from Mendut to Pawon and ending at Borobudur.

The monument is the single most visited tourist attraction in Indonesia. In 1974, 260,000 tourists of whom 36,000 were foreigners visited the monument. The figure hiked into 2.5 million visitors annually (80% were domestic tourists) in the mid 1990s, before the country's economy crisis. Tourism development, however, has been criticized for not including the local community on which occasional local conflict has arisen. In 2003, residents and small businesses around Borobudur organized several meetings and poetry protests, objecting to a provincial government plan to build a three-story mall complex, dubbed the 'Java World'.

On 21 January 1985, nine stupas were badly damaged by nine bombs. In 1991, a blind Muslim evangelist, Husein Ali Al Habsyie, was sentenced to life imprisonment for masterminding a series of bombings in the mid 1980s including the temple attack. Two other members of a right-wing extremist group that carried out the bombings were each sentenced to 20 years in 1986 and another man received a 13-year prison term. On 27 May 2006, an earthquake of 6.2 magnitude on the Richter scale struck the south coast of Central Java. The event had caused severe damage around the region and casualties to the nearby city of Yogyakarta, but Borobudur remained intact.

ARCHITECTURE

Borobudur is built as a single large stupa, and when viewed from above takes the form of a giant tantric Buddhist *mandala*, simultaneously representing the Buddhist cosmology and the nature of mind. The foundation is a square, approximately 118 meters (387 ft) on each side. It has nine platforms, of which the lower six are square and the upper three are circular. The upper platform features seventy-two small stupas surrounding one large central stupa. Each stupa is bell-shaped and pierced by numerous decorative openings. Statues of the Buddha sit inside the pierced enclosures.

Approximately 55,000 cubic metres (72,000 cu yd) of stones were taken from neighbouring rivers to build the monument. The stone was cut to size, transported to the site and laid without mortar. Knobs, indentations and dovetails were used to form joints between stones. Reliefs were created *in-situ* after the building had been completed. The monument is equipped with a good drainage system to cater for the area's high stormwater run-off. To avoid inundation, 100 spouts are provided at each corner with a unique carved gargoyles in the shape of giants or makaras.

Borobudur differs markedly with the general design of other structures built for this purpose. Instead of building on a flat surface, Borobudur is built on a natural hill. The building technique is, however, similar to other temples in Java. With no inner space as in other temples and its general design similar to the shape of pyramid, Borobudur was first thought more likely to have served as a *stupa,* instead of a temple. A *stupa* is intended as a shrine for the Lord Buddha. Sometimes stupas were built only as devotional symbols of Buddhism. A temple, on the other hand, is used as a house of deity and has inner spaces for worship. The complexity of the monument's meticulous design suggests Borobudur is in fact a temple. Congregational worship in Borobudur is performed by means of pilgrimage. Pilgrims were guided by the system of staircases and corridors ascending to the top platform. Each platform represents one stage of enlightenment. The path that guides pilgrims was designed with the symbolism of sacred knowledge according to the Buddhist cosmology.

Little is known about the architect Gunadharma. His name is actually recounted from Javanese legendary folk tales rather than written in old inscriptions. He was said to be one who "... bears the measuring rod, knows division and thinks himself composed of parts." The basic unit measurement he used during the construction was called *tala,* defined as the length of a human face from the forehead's hairline to the tip of the chin or the distance from the tip of the thumb to the tip of the middle finger when both fingers are stretched at their maximum distance. The unit metrics is then obviously relative between persons, but the monument has exact measurements. A survey conducted in 1977 revealed frequent findings of a ratio of 4:6:9 around the monument. The architect had used the formula to lay out the precise dimensions of Borobudur. The identical ratio formula was further found in the nearby Buddhist temples of Pawon and Mendhut. Archeologists conjectured the purpose of the ratio formula and the *tala* dimension has calendrical, astronomical and cosmological themes, as of the case in other Hindu and Buddhist temple of Angkor Wat in Cambodia.

The main vertical structure can be divided into three groups: base (or foot), body, and top, which resembles the three major division of a human body. The base is a 123x123 m (403.5x403.5 ft) square in size and 4 meters (13 ft) high of walls. The body is composed of five square platforms each with diminishing heights. The first terrace is set back 7 meters (23 ft) from the edge of the base. The other terraces are set back by 2 meters (7 ft), leaving a narrow corridor at each stage. The top consists of 3 circular platforms, with each stage supporting a row of perforated *stupas,* arranged in concentric circles. There is one main dome at the center; the top of which is the highest point of the monument (35 meters (115 ft) above ground level). Access to the upper part is through stairways at the centre of each side with a number of gates, watched by a total of 32 lion statues. The main entrance is at the eastern side, the location of the first narrative reliefs. On the slopes of the hill, there are also stairways linking the monument to the low-lying plain.

The monument's three divisions symbolize three stages of mental preparation towards the ultimate goal according to the Buddhist cosmology, namely *Kamadhatu* (the world of desires), *Rupadhatu* (the world of forms), and finally *Arupadhatu* (the formless world). *Kamadhatu* is represented by the base, *Rupadhatu* by the five square platforms (the body), and *Arupadhatu* by the three circular platforms and the large topmost stupa. The architectural features between three stages have metaphorical differences. For instance, square and detailed decorations in the *Rupadhatu* disappear into plain circular platforms in the *Arupadhatu* to represent how the world of forms – where men are still attached with forms and names – changes into the world of the formless.

In 1885, a hidden structure under the base was accidentally discovered. The "hidden foot" contains reliefs, 160 of which are narrative describing the real *Kamadhatu*. The remaining reliefs are panels with short inscriptions that apparently describe instruction for the sculptors, illustrating the scene to be carved. The real base is hidden by an encasement base, the purpose of which remains a mystery. It was first thought that the real base had to be covered to prevent a disastrous subsidence of the monument through the hill. There is another theory that the encasement base was added because the original hidden foot was incorrectly designed, according to Vastu Shastra, the Indian ancient book about architecture and town planning. Regardless of its intention, the encasement base was built with detailed and meticulous design with aesthetics and religious compensation.

RELIEFS

Borobudur contains approximately 2,670 individual bas reliefs (1,460 narrative and 1,212 decorative panels), which cover the façades and balustrades. The total relief surface is 2,500 square meters (26,909.8 sq ft) and they are distributed at the hidden foot (*Kamadhatu*) and the five square platforms (*Rupadhatu*).

The narrative panels, which tell the story of Sudhana and Manohara, are grouped into 11 series encircled the monument with the total length of 3,000 meters (9,843 ft). The hidden foot contains the first series with 160 narrative panels and the remaining 10 series are distributed throughout walls and balustrades in four galleries starting from the eastern entrance stairway to the left. Narrative panels on the wall read from right to left, while on the balustrade read from left to right. This conforms with *pradaksina,* the ritual of circumambulation performed by pilgrims who move in a clockwise direction while keeping the sanctuary to their right.

The hidden foot depicts the workings of karmic law. The walls of the first gallery have two superimposed series of reliefs; each consists of 120 panels. The upper part depicts the biography of the Buddha, while the lower part of the wall and also balustrades in the first and the second galleries tell the story of the Buddha's former lives. The remaining panels are devoted to Sudhana's further wandering about his search, terminated by his attainment of the Perfect Wisdom.

The law of karma (Karmavibhangga)

The 160 hidden panels do not form a continuous story, but each panel provides one complete illustration of cause and effect. There are depictions of blameworthy activities, from gossip to murder, with their corresponding punishments. There are also praiseworthy activities, that include charity and pilgrimage to sanctuaries, and their subsequent rewards. The pains of hell and the pleasure of heaven are also illustrated. There are scenes of daily life, complete with the full panorama of *samsara* (the endless cycle of birth and death).

The birth of Buddha (Lalitavistara)

The story starts from the glorious descent of the Lord Buddha from the Tushita heaven, and ends with his first sermon in the Deer Park near Benares. The relief shows the birth of the Buddha as Prince Siddhartha, son of King Suddhodana and Queen Maya of Kapilavastu (in present-day Nepal).

The story is preceded by 27 panels showing various preparations, in heavens and on earth, to welcome the final incarnation of the Bodhisattva. Before descending from Tushita heaven, the Bodhisattva entrusted his crown to his successor, the future Buddha Maitreya. He descended on earth in the shape of white elephants with six tusks, penetrated to Queen Maya's right womb. Queen Maya had a dream of this event, which was interpreted that his son would become either a sovereign or a Buddha.

While Queen Maya felt that it was the time to give birth, she went to the Lumbini park outside the Kapilavastu city. She stood under a plaksa tree, holding one branch with her right hand and she gave birth to a son, Prince Siddhartha. The story on the panels continues until the prince becomes the Buddha.

Prince Siddhartha story (Jataka) and other legendary persons (Avadana)

Jatakas are stories about the Buddha before he was born as Prince Siddhartha. Avadanas are similar to jatakas, but the main figure is not the Bodhisattva himself. The saintly deeds in avadanas are attributed to other legendary persons. Jatakas and avadanas are treated in one and the same series in the reliefs of Borobudur.

The first 20 lower panels in the first gallery on the wall depict the *Sudhanakumaravadana* or the saintly deeds of Sudhana. The first 135 upper panels in the same gallery on the balustrades are devoted to the 34 legends of the *Jatakamala*. The remaining 237 panels depict stories from other sources, as do for the lower series and panels in the second gallery. Some jatakas stories are depicted twice, for example the story of King Sibhi (Rama's forefather).

Sudhana's search for the Ultimate Truth (Gandavyuha)

Gandavyuha is the story told in the final chapter of the Avatamsaka Sutra about Sudhana's tireless wandering in search of the Highest Perfect Wisdom. It covers two galleries (third and fourth) and also half of the second gallery; comprising in total of 460 panels. The principal figure of the story, the youth Sudhana, son of an extremely rich merchant, appears on the 16th panel. The preceding 15 panels form a prologue to the story of the miracles during Buddha's *samadhi* in the Garden of Jeta at Sravasti.

During his search, Sudhana visited no less than 30 teachers but none of them had satisfied him completely. He was then instructed by Manjusri to meet the monk Megasri, where he was given the first doctrine. As his journey continues, Sudhana meets (in the following order) Supratisthita, the physician Megha (Spirit of Knowledge), the banker Muktaka, the monk Saradhvaja, the upasika Asa (Spirit of Supreme Enlightenment), Bhismottaranirghosa, the Brahmin Jayosmayatna, Princess Maitrayani, the monk Sudarsana, a boy called Indriyesvara, the upasika Prabhuta, the banker Ratnachuda, King Anala, the god Siva Mahadeva, Queen Maya, Bodhisattva Maitreya and then back to Manjusri. Each meeting has given Sudhana a specific doctrine, knowledge and wisdom. These meetings are shown in the third gallery.

After the last meeting with Manjusri, Sudhana went to the residence of Bodhisattva Samantabhadra; depicted in the fourth gallery. The entire series of the fourth gallery is devoted to the teaching of Samantabhadra. The narrative panels finally end with Sudhana's achievement of the Supreme Knowledge and the Ultimate Truth.

BUDDHA STATUES

Apart from the story of Buddhist cosmology carved in stone, Borobudur has many statues of various Buddhas. The cross-legged statues are seated in a lotus position and distributed on the five square platforms (the *Rupadhatu* level) as well as on the top platform (the *Arupadhatu* level).

The Buddha statues are in niches at the *Rupadhatu* level, arranged in rows on the outer sides of the balustrades, the number of statues decreasing as platforms progressively diminish to the upper level. The first balustrades have 104 niches, the second 104, the third 88, the fourth 72 and the fifth 64. In total, there are 432 Buddha statues at the *Rupadhatu* level. At the *Arupadhatu* level (or the three circular platforms), Buddha statues are placed inside perforated stupas. The first circular platform has 32 stupas, the second 24 and the third 16, that add up to 72 stupas. Of the original 504 Buddha statues, over 300 are damaged (mostly headless) and 43 are missing (since the monument's discovery, heads have been stolen as collector's items, mostly by Western museums).

At glance, all the Buddha statues appear similar, but there is a subtle difference between them in the *mudras* or the position of the hands. There are five groups of *mudra*: North, East, South, West and Zenith, which represent the five cardinal compass points according to Mahayana. The first four balustrades have the first four *mudras*: North, East, South and West, of which the Buddha statues that face one compass direction have the corresponding *mudra*. Buddha statues at the fifth balustrades and inside the 72 stupas on the top platform have the same *mudra*: Zenith. Each *mudra* represents one of the Five Dhyani Buddhas; each has its own symbolism. They are *Abhaya mudra* for Amoghasiddhi (north), *Vara mudra* for Ratnasambhava (south), *Dhyana mudra* for Amitabha (west), *Bhumisparsa mudra* for Aksobhya (east) and *Dharmachakra mudra* for Vairochana (zenith).

RESTORATION

Borobudur attracted attention in 1885, when Yzerman, the Chairman of the Archaeological Society in Yogyakarta, made a discovery about the *hidden foot*. Photographs that reveal reliefs on the hidden foot were made in 1890–1891. The discovery led the Dutch East Indies government to take steps to safeguard the monument. In 1900, the government set up a commission consisting of three officials to assess the monument: Brandes, an art historian, Theodoor van Erp, a Dutch army engineer officer, and Van de Kamer, a construction engineer from the Department of Public Works.

In 1902, the commission submitted a threefold plan of proposal to the government. First, the immediate dangers should be avoided by resetting the corners, removing stones that endangered the adjacent parts, strengthening the first balustrades and restoring several niches, archways, stupas and the main dome. Second, fencing off the courtyards, providing proper maintenance and improving drainage by restoring floors and spouts. Third, all loose stones should be removed, the monument cleared up to the first balustrades, disfigured stones removed and the main dome restored. The total cost was estimated at that time around 48,800 Dutch guilders.

The restoration then was carried out between 1907 and 1911, using the principles of anastylosis and led by Theodor van Erp. The first seven months of his restoration was occupied with excavating the grounds around the monument to find missing Buddha heads and panel stones. Van Erp dismantled and rebuilt the upper three circular platforms and stupas. Along the way, Van Erp discovered more things he could do to improve the monument; he submitted another proposal that was approved with the additional cost of 34,600 guilders. At first glance Borobudur had been restored to its old glory.

Due to the limited budget, the restoration had been primarily focused on cleaning the sculptures, and Van Erp did not solve the drainage problem. Within fifteen years, the gallery walls were sagging and the reliefs showed signs of new cracks and deterioration. Van Erp used concrete from which alkali salts and calcium hydroxide leached and were transported into the rest of the construction. This caused some problems, so that a further thorough renovation was urgently needed.

Small restorations have been performed since then, but not sufficient for complete protection. In the late 1960s, the Indonesian government had requested from the international community a major renovation to protect the monument. In 1973, a master plan to restore Borobudur was created. The Indonesian government and UNESCO then undertook the complete overhaul of the monument in a big restoration project between 1975–1982. The foundation was stabilized and all 1,460 panels were cleaned. The restoration involved the dismantling of the five square platforms and improved the drainage by embedding water channels into the monument. Both impermeable and filter layers were added. This colossal project involved around 600 people to restore the monument and cost a total of US$ 6,901,243. After the renovation was finished, UNESCO listed Borobudur as a World Heritage Site in 1991.

THE REVIVAL OF BUDDHISM IN INDONESIA

In 1934, Venerable Narada Thera, a famous missionary monk from Sri Lanka, visited Indonesia for the first time as part of his journey to spread the Dhamma in Southeast Asia. This opportunity was used by a few local Buddhists to revive Buddhism in Indonesia. A Bodhi tree planting ceremony was held in front of Borobudur on 10th March 1934 under the blessing of Narada Thera, and some Upasakas were ordained as monks.

In about 1955, Buddhism started to make a comeback in Indonesia when a monk called Ashin Jinarakkhita started a tour across various regions in Indonesia to spread the Dharma. Since that time there has been a revival of Theravada Buddhism in Indonesia led by indigenous monks trained in Thailand, although the Mahayana tradition is still well represented.

Buddhism is one of five religions recognized by the Indonesian government, besides Islam, Catholic, Protestant, and Hinduism. According to a census conducted in 1990, the majority of the population is Moslem (around 87%). About 1.8 million people (which was slightly more than 1% of the population) are Buddhism. Provinces with relatively high percentage of Buddhists are Jakarta, Riau, North Sumatra, and West Borneo. The majority of Buddhists now practice in the Theravadin tradition. Two of the large Buddhist monasteries are located in North Jakarta (Sunter) and West Java (Pacet). Unfortunately, because Confucianism and Taoism are not recognized in the Constitution, followers from these two religions also call themselves "Buddhist" (therefore, the actual numbers of Buddhists are believed to be less than the official figure).

Chapter - 10

Buddhism in the Philippines and Singapore

BUDDHISM IN SINGAPORE

One will be able to find monasteries and Dharma centres from all three major traditions of Buddhism in Singapore: Theravada, Mahayana and Vajrayana. Most Buddhists in Singapore are Chinese. Chinese Mahayana is the most predominant form of Buddhism in Singapore with missionaries from Taiwan and China for several decades. However, Thailand's Theravada Buddhism has seen growing popularity amongst the people (not confining to the Chinese) in the past decade. Tibet Buddhism is also making a slow inroad into the country in recent years.

The presence of Buddhism in Singapore was evident during the Srivijayan times. However, as Islam spread to the local Orang Laut population in the 14th and 15th century, the influence of Buddhism and Hinduism were severely hampered, but through the influxes of Chinese immigrants from southern China, mostly from the Fujian Province, Buddhism was revived and managed to survive and grow. With the passage of time, Buddhism in Singapore develops its own unique culture and rituals. Practices and rituals of Taoisim, Confucianism, and even Hinduism are absorbed and assimilated into a single faculty. This development may seem odd to some people but it is definitely a concrete reflection of a multi-racial and multi-culture society, which in turn depicts the grace of Buddhism.

As of 2000, 42.5% of the Singaporeans register themselves as Buddhist by religion. Adherents of Buddhism are mostly by the Chinese majority ethnic group, although small minorities of Sinhalese and Thai Buddhists do exist as well.

Chinese Mahayana Buddhism is the most prevalent form of Buddhism in Singapore. Sizeable communities following other traditions include Theravada and Tibetan Buddhism. The representative organization of Buddhism in Singapore is the Singapore Buddhist Federation.

The presence of Buddhism in Singapore was evident during the Srivijayan times. Buddhism remains the main religion in Singapore with more than three-fifth of its population declared to be adherents of the faith. In line with ancestorial practices, many of the Chinese inhabitants also mix in Taoism and Confucianism to Buddhism. By virtue thereof, there is a strong trend blending towards Thai Buddhism, especially amongst the younger generation Singaporeans, which is seen to bear cultural similarities for its ability in encompassing Chinese culture and practices as represented in Taoism. Buddhism as represented by Theravada Buddhism, the oldest Buddhist school of thought, is seeing a potent growth in Singapore in the past decade.

The Singapore census includes detailed data on religion and ethnicity. Figures on Buddhism in 1980 shown that 27% of Singaporeans are Buddhists, up to 31.2% in 1990 and 42.5% in 2000. It is also noted that there is a significant increase of interest in the Buddhist teachings (Dharma), practices, and customs(i.e chanting, meditation, and offering formality). With a younger and more informed population, Buddhism is seen as the most viable religion in Singapore.

Buddhsim in Singapore is gaining popularity day by day. The Deputy Prime Minister, Lee Hsien Loong delivered this speech at the Opening Ceremony of the 7th World Buddhist Sangha Council Extraordinary General Meeting held on 24 Nov at Swissotel The Stamford. Here is given the text of this speech and how he emphasized the growing popularity of Buddhism in Singapore.

The following is the text of the speech delivered by the Deputy Prime Minister, Lee Hsien Loong at the Opening Ceremony of the 7th World Buddhist Sangha Council Extraordinary General Meeting held on 24 Nov at Swissotel The Stamford.

TRADITIONS AND CEREMONIES

There has been an effort to distinguish certain customs and practices in both Buddhism and Taoism as folks traditions and practices by a minority group of people. The sentiment of the majority of adherents of these faiths, however, outrightly rejected any such interference. This is to be seen in the vagueness of identification distinction amongst the followers of the faiths. Buddhism in Singapore takes on a far wider meaning than in its country of origin. It encompasses the various Buddhist thoughts and practices as well as Chinese customs, traditions, and practices that are in the past represented by the Chinese indigenous religion, Taoism. Such developments are a positive reflection of religious and cultural harmony in a nation made up from diverse enthnicity. Similar trends are also witnessed in countries such as Taiwan, Hong Kong, Malaysia, and Thailand.

Singapore Buddhism is inherent of Chinese Buddhism, which comprises a strong flavor of the Chinese indigenous religion, Taoism as early as in the 11th century. Such Buddhist-Taoist syncretism has provided China with religious harmony and prosperity of which the Chinese emigrants brought with them to Singapore. It has since gain roots and became a unique culture for the Singapore Chinese. Buddhist monks, nuns, and devotees are able to understand and respect the wider societal needs, which in turn created Buddhist joy and peace in line with Buddhist mission.

TRADITIONS

The Mahayana school, Theravada school, and Tibetan Buddhism have acquired sizable followings. Monks from Sri Lanka, Thailand and other South-eastern countries have come to teach their form of the Dharma to the Chinese in Singapore. As a result, a number of Theravada and other Buddhist temples like the Sakya Muni Buddha Gaya Temple have sprung up in recent years.

BUDDHISM IN MODERN SINGAPORE

In recent years, due to the increasing publication of Buddhist books, the appearance of internet sites in English, the availability of modern Buddhist music as well as courses conducted in English, more and more English-speaking Chinese, especially the younger Singaporeans, are joining Buddhist circles. As a nation of immigrants, majority from mainland China, Buddhism in Singapore inevitably took the form of Chinese Mahayana perspection. Therefore practitioners of Chinese Mahayana remain the majority of the Buddhist populations in Singapore. However, the rise of Thai Buddhism in Asia, which denomination rests on the oldest school of thought of Theravada Buddhism, there is a strong proliferating trend of averting to this intrinsic form of Buddhism. Another sect of Buddhism that is seen making slow inroad into Singapore is Tibetan Buddhism that seems to benefit from the writings of western monks and writers (e.g., the Dalai Lama, Thubten Chodron, Tenzin Palmo).

Singapore's Buddhist temples and religious circles are highly organized and very often have a connection with foreign religious organizations, especially in China, Taiwan, Thailand, the USA, the UK, Sri Lanka, etc. Many foreign Buddhist associations and temples have also established branches in Singapore to propagate Buddhist teachings and activities. Buddhist temples and associations are spread all over Singapore, ranging from small to large.

The largest Chinese Mahayana Buddhist temple in Singapore is Kong Meng San Phor Kark See Monastery, whilst Thai Theravada Buddhism is represented by an equally prominent temple, the Wat Ananda Metyarama Temple. These temples hold many Buddhist activities such as chanting, meditation, retreats, and dharma talks, as well as offering Buddhist courses on dharma and meditation, very often attended by thousands of devotees and adherents of the respective lineage.

Religious liberty in Singapore has also provided a conducive environment for the development of varying Buddhist practices. Furthermore, as with Taoism, Buddhism is taking a turn into a new vista with the elevation of educational levels amongst followers and devotees, where more are seen to indulge in spiritual practices and self-enhancement such as meditation, practicing mindfulness, studies and understanding of religious history and etc. with proper altar set up at home for paying homage to Lord Buddha.

BUDDHISM IN PHILIPPINES

Buddhism, specifically Vajrayana, gained a foothold in the Philippines with the rise of the Indianized Buddhist Srivijaya Empire centered in Sumatra in the 7th century. Archaeological finds in the Philippines include a number of Buddhist images common to Vajrayana iconography that dates back to this period. These include a number of Padmapani images and the Golden Tara found in 1917 at Esperanza, Agusan.

LAGUNA COPPERPLATE

Evidence of the extent of cultural influence from the Srivijaya empire can be seen in the so-called "Laguna Copper Plate", which is written in the Kavi (old Javanese) alphabet in a mixed vocabulary of Tagalog, Old Malay, and Sanskrit in the year 900AD.

The transliteration is as follows:

Swasti Shaka warsatita 822 Waisaka masa di(ng) Jyotisa. Caturthi Krisnapaksa somawara sana tatkala Dayang Angkatan lawan dengan nya sanak barngaran si Bukah anak da dang Hwan Namwaran dibari waradana wi shuddhapattra ulih sang pamegat senapati di Tundun barja(di) dang Hwan Nayaka tuhan Pailah Jayadewa. Di krama dang Hwan Namwaran dengan dang kayastha shuddha nu diparlappas hutang da walenda Kati 1 Suwarna 8 dihadapan dang Huwan Nayaka tuhan Puliran Kasumuran. dang Hwan Nayaka tuhan Pailah barjadi ganashakti. Dang Hwan Nayaka tuhan Binwangan barjadi bishruta tathapi sadana sanak kapawaris ulih sang pamegat dewata [ba]rjadi sang pamegat Medang dari bhaktinda diparhulun sang pamegat. Ya makanya sadanya anak cucu dang Hwan Namwaran shuddha ya kapawaris dihutang da dang Hwan Namwaran di sang pamegat Dewata. Ini grang syat syapanta ha pashkat ding ari kamudyan ada grang urang barujara welung lappas hutang da dang Hwa

English Translation:

"Long Live! Year of Saka 822, month of Vesak, according to Jyotisha. The fourth day of the waning moon, Monday. On this occasion, Lady Angkatan, and her brother whose name is Bukah, the children of the Honourable Namwaran, were awarded a document of complete pardon from the Commander in Chief of Tundun [modern day Tondo in Manila], represented by the Lord Minister of Pailah [Paila, Bulacan], Jayadewa. By this order, through the scribe, the Honourable Namwaran has been forgiven of all and is released from his debts and arrears of 1 Katî and 8 Suwarna before the Honourable Lord Minister of Puliran [Pulilan, Pampanga or Pulilan, Angat, Bulacan], Kasumuran, by the authority of the Lord Minister of Pailah. Because of his faithful service as a subject of the Chief, the Honourable and widely renowned Lord Minister of Binwangan [Binwagan, Pampanga] recognized all the living relatives of Namwaran who were claimed by the Chief of Dewata, represented by the Chief of Medang. Yes, therefore the living descendants of the Honourable

Namwaran are forgiven, indeed, of any and all debts of the Honourable Namwaran to the Chief of Dewata. This, in any case, shall declare to whomever henceforth that on some future day should there be a man who claims that no release from the debt of the Honourable..."

Vesak is the Buddhist name of the month—though now it's shortened to a single day—which celebrates Buddha's birthday and enlightenment. Vesak or Vesakha (in Pali) is the holiest month in the Buddhist calendar and is usually the time when debts are forgiven and festivals held. *Swasti* is also a very traditional Sanskrit-Buddhist greeting (similar to the modern Thai, *sawatdee*). The Laguna copper plate therefore indicates that the areas mentioned — Pampanga, Tondo, and Bulacan — had already adopted Buddhism.

HISTORY

Pre-Colonial Period

In the 9th century, Butuan (in Mindanao, southern Philippines) and Ma-i (Mindoro, central Philippines) began extensive trading with the Buddhist Kingdom of Champa (South Vietnam).

In 1001 AD, the Buddhist ruler of Butuan (P'u-tuan in the Sung Dynasty records), Sari Bata Shaja, made the first tributary mission to China and this was followed by the rulers of Basilan (in southern Philippines) and the Luzon Empire more than two hundred years later, and by Mindoro, Sulu and Pangasinan (northern Philippines) four hundred years later. However, according to the *Sung Shih*, the official History of the Sung Dynasty, Butuan made regular tributary missions to China since 1001 AD, and that it rulers usually arrived at the same time as the rulers of Tibet, Champa (Southern Vietnam), and the Mongols.

In 1279 AD, some Chinese historians now speculate that the last Song Emperor, Bing Di, may managed to escape across the sea with Grand Admiral Zhang Shijie to Taiwan or to Luzon (traditional Chinese: BT‹[W; pinyin: LÚsòng Guó) because of the similarity of a few Chinese and Tagalog place names. However, official Chinese sources state that Emperor Bing died during the Mongol Conquest of southern China and most Chinese-sounding place names can be traced to Malaysia and Indonesia.

Spanish Colonial Period

With the advent of Spanish colonialism in the 16th century, the Philippines became a closed colony and cultural contacts with other Southeast Asian countries were closed. In 1481, the Spanish Inquisition commenced with the permission of Pope Sixtus IV and all non-Catholics within the Spanish empire were to be expelled or to be "put to the question" (tortured until they renounced their previous faith). With the refounding of Manila in 1571, the Philippines became subject to Spanish law and the Archbishop of New Galicia (Mexico) became the Grand Inquisitor of the Faithful in Mexico and the

Philippines. In 1595, the newly appointed Archbishop of Manila became the Inquisitor-General of the Spanish East Indies (the Philippines, Guam, and Micronesia) and until 1898, the Spanish Inquisition was active against Protestants, Buddhists, Hindus and Muslims. As was the case in Latin America and Africa, forced conversions were not uncommon and any attempt not to submit to the authority of the Roman Catholic Church was seen as both rebellion against the Pope and sedition against the Spanish King, which was punishable by death.

Buddhist practices, festivals and iconography had to be converted and adopted to Catholicism if they were to survive Spanish persecution. A good example of this was is the *saniculas* biscuit of Pampanga that has its roots in Buddhism. Syncretism (the blending indigenous religions such as Hinduism, Buddhism, Catholicism and indigenous folk religions) became necessary. This can be seen instantly with statues of the Virgin Mary, including the depiction of the halo, hand poses, and rainbow-arches, look almost identical to statues of Tara especially in Binondo and other areas. In time, Buddhism seemed to have virtually disappeared during the 400 years of Spanish rule.

American Colonial Period

With Revolution of 1896 against Spain and later with the coming of the American colonial regime in 1898, religious freedom was instituted. Mahayana and Zen Buddhist temples began to be built in the 1920s and 30s. Davao, due to the large number of Japanese residents, and Cebu, due to the large number of Chinese settlers had the largest Buddhist populations in the Philippines. After World War II, most Japanese were expatriated to Japan and the Chinese and Chinese-Filipinos became the predominant Buddhist ethnic group. In the 1960s, Vietnamese refugees arrived and established a temple in Palawan. At the same time, Japanese Buddhist temples and organizations began to re-emerge such as Sokka Gakkai International.

Buddhism Today

Today, Buddhists account for about 1-3% of the Philippine population. Currently, only the Mahayana and Zen are present in the Philippines. Theravada Buddhism is now confined with nationals from Sri Lanka, Thailand and Myanmar, as well as Cambodia and Laos.

Language

However, the linguistic influence left its most lasting marks on every Philippine language throughout the archipelago with the following Buddhist and Hindu concepts directly from the original Sanskrit. About 25% of the words in many Philippine languages are Sanskrit terms:

From Tagalog:

- *budhi* "conscience" from Sanskrit *bodhi*

- *dukha* "one who suffers" from Sanskrit *dukkha*
- *guro* "teacher" from Sanskrit *guru*
- *sampalataya* "faith" from Sanskrit *sampratyaya*
- *mukha* "face" from Sanskrit *mukha*
- *laho* "eclipse" from Sanskrit *rahu*

From Kapampangan:

- *kalma* "fate" from Sanskrit *karma*
- *damla* "divine law" from Sanskrit *dharma*
- *mantala* "magic formulas" from Sanskrit *mantra*
- *upaya* "power" from Sanskrit *upaya*
- *lupa* "face" from Sanskrit *rupa*
- *sabla* "every" from Sanskrit *sarva*
- *lawu* "eclipse" from Sanskrit *rahu*
- *galura* "giant eagle (a surname)" from Sanskrit *garuda*
- *laksina* "south (a surname)" from Sanskrit *dakshin*
- *laksamana* "admiral (a surname)" from Sanskrit *lakshmana*

From Tausug:

- *suarga* "heaven"
- *neraka* "hell"
- *agama* "religion"

Sanskrit and Sanskrit-derived words common to most Philippine languages:

- *sutla* "silk" from Sanskrit *sutra*
- *kapas* "cotton" from Sanskrit *kerpas*
- *naga* "dragon or serpent" from Sanskrit *naga*

Chapter - 11

Buddhism in the West

Buddhism has spread and developed not only in the land of its birth, but in many other lands as well. Why does Buddhism present such an attractive religious option to so many different cultures? Buddhism is no different from other religions in claiming to possess the means by which to attain that most cherished of human goals—eternal peace. Where Buddhism differs is in its acceptance of a number of alternate methods by which to attain this goal, each suited to different temperaments and conditions. Buddhism developed a sophisticated worldview very early. At the core of this worldview is what later Western philosophers would define as *angst,* that vague feeling of uneasiness and separateness from the world that often tinges life. This inherent element of human existence, say the Buddhists, is an inevitable part of life that is caused by life's intrinsic instability.

This concept that the universe is unstable is reminiscent of modern physics. The ancient Buddhist philosophers saw the world not as a stable, material, entity, but rather as a constantly changing cloud of interactive forces. The Buddhist analysis of the unsatisfactory and unstable nature of existence is the foundation of a whole way of life. That way of life is based not only on the Buddhist understanding of the nature of reality, but also on their understanding of human fate and the factors that affect it. For the Buddhist, human existence is not a brief excursion between birth and death. It extends endlessly through time and space (for the Buddhists believe that there are an almost limitless number of alternate worlds to this one), and the human being can look forward only to an infinite series of rebirths either in this world or elsewhere.

BUDDHISM AND THE CHALLENGE OF THE MODERN WORLD

Buddhism has had a long and interesting history but it would be unwise to assume that its glories are all in the past or that it is no longer a dynamic religion. Buddhism has been forced to adapt itself to the swiftly changing conditions of the modern world. In some cases, the transition has gone smoothly. In others, however, the tensions between Buddhism and modern ideologies have not been resolved without severe difficulties.

PLANTING NEW FLOWERS: BUDDHISM IN EUROPE AND THE UNITED STATES

Buddhism is so much a part of modern culture, at least on a superficial level, that it is hard to imagine that as little as 200 years ago people in the West had almost no idea of the nature of this religion. It was not until the European powers began to carve out their colonial empires in South and Southeast Asia, and meddle in the affairs of the East Asian nations, that they began to pay attention to the indigenous belief systems of the conquered peoples. But generally this attention had little or nothing to do with the intrinsic worth of these systems. Rather, these early administrators saw religion as a means of social control. As time progressed, however, some Europeans came to appreciate Buddhism and the other Asian religions in their own right. As they began to master the classical languages of Asia, such as Sanskrit, Chinese, Japanese, and Pali, European scholars began to piece together what was to them a new and fascinating universe of thought.

This group of scholars tended to emerge from the lower ranks of the colonial administrators who spent most of their days dealing with the administrative problems of the common people over whom they ruled. Since there were very few other Europeans to socialize with, these officers often took up study of the local culture. A good example of this was the case of T.W. Rhys-Davids (1843-1922). An administrator in Sri Lanka, he spent his leisure hours learning Pali, the sacred language of Theravada Buddhism. What he found astonished him. The Buddhism that began to emerge from the texts was not the (seemingly) superstitious religion that surrounded him, but rather an elegant, subtle philosophy that resonated with the logical, scientific thought that was coming to dominate European thinking. He became so enthusiastic about his studies that he founded the Pali Text Society with the intention of editing the entire Pali canon and translating it into English. This is a goal that the Society (which still exists) has very nearly achieved.

The next major change in Buddhist-European relations came in 1879, when Sir Edwin Arnold published his famous epic poem, *The Light of Asia*. This was a retelling in English verse of the life of the Buddha, not from an academic standpoint but from that of someone who appreciated Buddhist teaching as religious expression. Soon after this, Helen P. Blavatsky, a Russian, and Henry Steele Olcott, an American, two founders of the religious movement known as Theosophy, traveled to India and Sri Lanka to study Eastern thought. In Sri Lanka, they participated in a ceremony that formally accepted them into the Buddhist faith. Although their understanding of Buddhism was somewhat peculiar, these new converts were enthusiastic.

But these early enthusiasts in Europe and America tended to misunderstand Buddhism. As we have seen, Buddhism does not suggest that more powerful beings than humans do not exist. Rather, it simply asserts that their influence is limited and that *ultimate* salvation lies elsewhere. Early European and American adherents to

Buddhism tended to interpret Buddhism as being completely atheistic and self-oriented. This was certainly not the case for many, if not most, Buddhists. It is not surprising, therefore, that early converts to Buddhism tended toward Theravada Buddhism where "supernatural" elements seem to be the least pronounced. When Europeans began to investigate Buddhism seriously in the middle of the last century, they were very attracted to the Pali scriptures of this school of Buddhism. This was because they saw modern European thinking embodied in these ancient works.

BUDDHISM IN THE TWENTY-FIRST CENTURY

Buddhism is no different from other world religions in that it faces challenges in the modern world as well as opportunities. The twentieth century has not been kind to Buddhism. Large areas of the Buddhist world have disappeared due to political and social changes. A good example of this is China, where Buddhism had once been widespread. After the Communists took power, Buddhism (and all other religions) was systematically suppressed so that it is difficult today to discern how many Buddhists still remain in that huge country. As we have seen, the Communists carried their dislike of Buddhism to Tibet in 1951 where they attempted to stamp out Buddhism entirely, often by extraordinarily violent means. Likewise during the hideous excesses of the Khmer Rouge in Cambodia between 1975 and 1979, virtually the entire Buddhist monastic Order was murdered along with perhaps as much as half of the entire population of this Theravadin Buddhist country Many estimate that at the end of this period, out of an initial 80,000 monks, only a few hundred managed to survive. In China, Cambodia, and Tibet, temples were destroyed, scriptures burned, and valuable pieces of Buddhist art sold to the highest bidder.

Terrible as this overt attempt to destroy Buddhism has been, it is eclipsed by a more concerted and subtler assault on the *Cultural Synthesis in Western Buddhism*

One of the notable features of the developing Buddhism in the West is the degree to which women teachers have taken a leading role in transmitting the teachings. While women have never been excluded from Buddhism, the male-oriented nature of most Asian societies has assigned them a subordinate role in religious matters. In the West, this is not the case. Indeed, many of the pioneers of Buddhist scholarship, such as Mrs. Caroline Rhys-Davids (1858-1942) and I.B. Horner (1896-1981), are still remembered as notable scholars. However, it is as religious teachers that Western women have come into their own.

THE TIMELESS MESSAGE OF THE BUDDHA

What are the factors which contribute to this continuing appeal of Buddhism, and more particularly its growing appeal to Europeans and Americans? The simplest answer lies in the fact that the problems which Buddhism first addressed some 2500 years ago are still with us today more or less unchanged. People still question the nature of life and its ultimate meaning. People still wonder why the good suffer and the evil go unpunished. People still ponder the unstoppable forces of nature and their relationship to human existence. For many of these searchers, the Buddhist analysis of reality and its practical program for achieving transcendence from the pains of human life are very appealing. But other religions, such as Islam, Christianity, and Hinduism, offer answers to these questions as well. What is unique in Buddhism?

One of the features of Buddhism which is attractive to many people, especially people raised in the scientific milieu of Western society, is that Buddhism does away with the idea of the "supernatural," a split between this world and some unseen, totally other, reality. The universe, says the Buddhist, is a vast system of processes, not things.

Another reason that Buddhism maintains its popularity is that it tends toward individual rather than corporate expressions of religiosity. Among the Western religions, the core religious actions are defined as taking place in community. The believing Christian or Jew is enjoined to attend weekly services in association with his or her fellow believers. Buddhism, on the other hand, sees religious activity to consist of personal actions. The individual has, of course, opportunities to associate with and take comfort from the community of believers, but he or she can be just as good a Buddhist without ever encountering another coreligionist. It is the interior work of the individual that matters.

Although Buddhism spread throughout Asia it remained virtually unknown in the West until modern times. The early missions sent by the emperor Ashoka to the West did not bear fruit. Knowledge of Buddhism has come through three main channels: Western scholars; the work of philosophers, writers and artists; and the arrival of Asian immigrants who have brought various forms of Buddhism with them to Europe, North America and Australia.

The 'come and see for yourself' attitude of Buddhism attracts many Westerners. They are not asked to believe in anything, but to follow the Buddha's advice of testing ideas first. With the growth of easy travel and communications, the West has been able to find out more about Buddhism in this century than in all the time before. The informality and emphasis on practice of Buddhism appeals to many Westerners.

THE INFLUENCE OF BUDDHISM

Buddhist attitudes of peace, mindfulness and care for all living creatures have come to be the concern of many groups in the West. Buddhist believe that all things should be looked after: the earth, plants, birds, insects and animals. This is close to the feeling among many people in recent years that the human race should stop polluting the atmosphere and destroying the surface of the earth by cutting down forests.

BUDDHISM TRAVELS WEST

Although the Buddha's teachings have been known in countries throughout Asia for over 2,500 years, very few people in Europe or America would have known what the word 'Buddhist' meant unless they had been born in the last 50 years.

Over a century ago people from France, the Netherlands, Great Britain, and other European countries began to travel in the Far East. Many of them returned with Eastern ideas, and so Europeans began to hear about Buddhism.

More recently, Buddhist people have moved to the West. Many of them have been refugees from conflict. Many Tibetans, for example, fled from their country after the Chinese takeover in 1959. The wars in Indochina in the 1950s and 1960s led many Vietnamese people to move to and settle in Europe, Australia and America. Other Buddhists from countries such as Thailand have established businesses in the larger Western cities. They have all brought their Buddhist beliefs to their new homes, and helped to set up Buddhist centres.

Occasional intersections between Western civilization and the Buddhist world have been occurring for thousands of years. Alexander the Great's conquest of much of Central Asia set the stage for contacts between the civilizations of Greece and India.

In the latter half of the 19th century, Buddhism (along with many other religions and philosophies) came to the attention of Western intellectuals. The first English translation of the *Tibetan Book of the Dead* was published in 1927 and the reprint of 1935 carried a commentary from C.G. Jung. The book is said to have attracted many westerners to Tibetan Buddhism.

The first Buddhists to arrive in the United States were Chinese and Japanese immigrants who established many temples mainly for their own purposes of worship. In 1959 Suzuki Roshi (a Japanese teacher) arrived in San Francisco. At the time of Suzuki's arrival, Zen had become a hot topic amongst some groups in the United States, especially beatniks. In 1965, monks from Sri Lanka established the Washington Buddhist Vihara in Washington, D.C., the first Theravada monastic community in the United States. In the 1970s, interest in Tibetan Buddhism grew dramatically.

Today, Buddhism is practiced by large numbers of people in the Americas, Europe and Oceania. Buddhism has become the fastest-growing religion in Australia and some other Western nations. Many Hollywood movies with Buddhist themes, such as *Kundun*, *Little Buddha* and *Seven Years in Tibet*, have had considerable commercial success.

Buddhism and Western Intellectuals

In the latter half of the 19th century, Buddhism (along with many other religions and philosophies) came to the attention of Western intellectuals. These included the pessimistic German philosopher Schopenhauer, who encountered Buddhism, and Eastern thought in general, after having devised a philosophical system of considerable compatibility. The American philosopher Henry David Thoreau translated a Buddhist sutra from French into English.

There are frequent comparisons between Buddhism and the German philosopher Friedrich Nietzsche, who praised Buddhism in his 1895 work *The Anti-Christ*, calling it "a hundred times more realistic than Christianity". Theologist David Loy argues that there is "a deep resonance between them" as "both emphasise the centrality of humans in a godless cosmos and neither looks to any external being or power for their respective solutions to the problem of existence".

The first English translation of the *Tibetan Book of the Dead* was published in 1927 and the reprint of 1935 carried a commentary from none other than C.G. Jung. The book is said to have attracted many westerners to Tibetan Buddhism. Jung also provided the forward for the 1935 publication of D.T. Suzuki's Introduction to Zen Buddhism.

Western spiritual seekers were attracted to what they saw as the exotic and mystical tone of the Asian traditions, and created esoteric societies such as the Theosophical Society of H.P. Blavatsky. The Buddhist Society, London was founded by Theosophist Christmas Humphreys in 1924. At first Western Buddhology was hampered by poor translations (often translations of translations), but soon Western scholars such as Max Müller began to learn Asian languages and translate Asian texts. During the 20th century the German writer Hermann Hesse showed great interest in Eastern religions, writing a book entitled *Siddhartha*. It must also be noted that there are significant differences between the finer points of Theosophical and Buddhist Philosophy, in particular regarding the common doctorine of reincarnation, which on the surface might at first be overlooked by the interested westener.

American beat generation poet Jack Kerouac became a well-known literary Buddhist, for his roman-a-clef *The Dharma Bums* and other works. Also influential was Alan Watts, who wrote several books on Zen and Buddhism. The cultural re-evaluations of the hippie generation in the late 1960s and early 1970s led to a re-discovery of Buddhism, which seemed to promise a more methodical path to happiness than Christianity and a way out of the perceived spiritual bankruptcy and complexity of Western life.

Buddhists Arrive in the West

The first Buddhists to arrive in the United States were Chinese. Hired as cheap labor for the railroads and other expanding industries, they established temples in their settlements along the rail lines. At about the same time, immigrants from Japan began to arrive as laborers on Hawaiian plantations and central-California farms. In 1899, they established the Buddhist Missions of North America, later renamed the Buddhist Churches of America.

In 1959, Suzuki Roshi (a Japanese teacher) arrived in San Francisco. At the time of Suzuki's arrival, Zen had become a hot topic amongst some groups in the United States, especially beatniks. Suzuki Roshi's classes were filled with those wanting to learn more about Buddhism, and the presence of a Zen master inspired the students.

In 1965 Philip Kapleau traveled to Rochester, NY with the permission of his teacher, Haku'un Yasutani to form the Rochester Zen Center. At this time there were few if any American citizens that had trained in Japan with ordained Buddhist teachers. Kapleau had spent 13 years (1952-1965) and over 20 sesshin before being allowed to come back and open his own center. During his time in Japan after World War II, Kapleau wrote his seminal work; The Three Pillars of Zen.

In 1965, monks from Sri Lanka established the Washington Buddhist Vihara in Washington, D.C., the first Theravada monastic community in the United States. The Vihara was quite accessible to English-speakers, and Vipassana meditation was part of it activities. However, the direct influence of the Vipassana movement would not reach the U.S. until a group of Americans returned there in the early 1970s after studying with Vipassana masters in Asia.

In the 1970s, interest in Tibetan Buddhism grew dramatically. This was fuelled in part by the 'shangri-la' view of this country and also because Western media agencies are largely sympathetic with the 'Tibetan Cause'. All four of the main Tibetan Buddhist schools became well known.

Tibetan lamas such as the Karmapa (Rangjung Rigpe Dorje), Chögyam Trungpa Rinpoche, Geshe Wangyal, Geshe Lhundub Sopa, Dezhung Rinpoche, Sermey Khensur Lobsang Tharchin, Tarthang Tulku, Lama Yeshe and Thubten Zopa Rinpoche all established teaching centers in the West from the 1970s.

Perhaps the most widely visible Buddhist teacher in the west is the much-travelled Tenzin Gyatso, the current Dalai Lama, who first visited the United States in 1979. As the exiled political leader of Tibet, he is now a popular cause célèbre in the west. His early life was depicted in glowing terms in Hollywood films such as *Kundun* and *Seven Years in Tibet*. He has attracted celebrity religious followers such as Richard Gere and Adam Yauch.

In addition to this a number of Americans who had served in the Korean or Vietnam Wars stayed out in Asia for a period, seeking to understand both the horror they had witnessed and its context. A few of these were eventually ordained as monks in the Theravadan tradition, and upon returning home became influential meditation teachers establishing such centres as the Insight Meditation Society in America. Another contributing factor in the flowering of Buddhist thought in the West was the popularity of Zen amongst the counter-culture poets and activists of the 60's, due to the writings of Alan Watts, D.T. Suzuki and Philip Kapleau.

Historically, Buddhism has absorbed elements of the culture of the countries in which it is practiced. This can be seen in the artistic style of Buddha statues; a Chinese statue looks different to a Thai, which differs from a Sri Lankan, and similarly across most Asian countries. Different local customs are included also, and may influence the form of rituals and ceremonies.

There is a general distinction between Buddhism brought to the West by Asian immigrants, which may be Mahayana or a traditional East Asian mix, and Buddhism as practiced by converts, which is often Zen, Pure Land, Indian Vipassana or Tibetan Buddhism. Some Western Buddhists are actually non-denominational and accept teachings from a variety of different sects, which is far less frequent in Asia.

The largest Buddhist temple in the Southern Hemisphere is Nan Tien Ssu (translated as "Southern Paradise Temple"), situated at Wollongong, Australia. It is operated by the Fo Guang Shan Order, founded in Taiwan, and around 2003 the Grand Master, Venerable Hsing Yun, asked for that temple and Buddhist practice there to be operated by Australians within about thirty years.

Western Buddhism Today

Today, Buddhism is practiced by large numbers of people in the Americas, Europe and Oceania. Buddhism has become a growing religion in Australia and some other Western nations.

For the most part, Western Buddhism is identical to Buddhism in East Asia, borrowing Asian practices such as the sangha and meditation (although most Asian Buddhist rituals are not borrowed). Western Buddhism, however, also has its roots in the Western concepts of freethought and secular humanism. The Foundation for the Preservation of the Mahayana Tradition (FPMT) is a network of Buddhist centers focusing on traditional Tibetan Buddhism. Founded in 1975 by Lamas Thubten Yeshe and Thubten Zopa Rinpoche, who began teaching Buddhism to Western students in Nepal, the FPMT has grown to encompass more than 142 teaching centers in 32 countries.

A feature of Buddhism in the West today is the emergence of other groups which, even though they draw on traditional Buddhism, are in fact an attempt at creating a new style of Buddhist practice. Controversial lama Chögyam Trungpa, the founder of the Shambhala meditation movement, claimed in his teachings that his intention was to strip the ethnic baggage away from traditional methods of working with the mind and to deliver the essence of those teachings to his western students. Chögyam Trungpa also founded Naropa University in Boulder, Colorado in 1974.

Another example of a school evolving new idioms for the transmission of the dharma is the Friends of the Western Buddhist Order (FWBO), founded by Sangharakshita in 1967.

Commercialization of Buddhism

Buddhist practitioners in the West are catered for by a minor industry that has grown up around them, providing such items as charm boxes, meditation cushions, and ritual implements. Shakya has criticized this industry as the publication of Buddhist books has uprooted small forests and consequently killed thousands of insects. And many Hollywood movies such as *Kundun, Little Buddha* and *Seven Years in Tibet* have had considerable commercial success.

BUDDHISM IN THE NEW WORLD

Because the above examples produced very little real religious interaction, the European settlers who would come to colonize the Americas had virtually no exposure to Buddhism. This almost complete isolation would last largely undisturbed until the 19th century, when significant numbers of immigrants from East Asia began to arrive in the New World. In the United States, the first immigrants from China entered around 1820, but they began to arrive in large numbers following the California Gold Rush of 1849. The first Buddhist temple in America was built in 1853 in San Francisco by the Sze Yap Company, a Chinese American fraternal society. Another society, the Ning Yeong Company, built a second in 1854; by 1875, there were eight such temples, and by 1900 there were approximately 400 Chinese temples on the west coast of the United States, most of them containing at least some Buddhist elements. These temples were often the subject of suspicion and ignorance by the rest of the population, and were dismissively referred to as *joss houses*.

THE CONDITIONS FOR POPULARIZATION

For the transition to Phase III to take place, that is, for Buddhism to spread more widely through the general population, certain additional conditions were necessary, and these only became sufficiently widespread in the second half of the twentieth century. One was the triumph of liberal democracy over autocratic political systems. Under the heading of democracy we must include not only political democracy, but also the democracy of the mind, an openness to new ways of thought and tolerance for viewpoints that differ radically from those of one's own intellectual heritage. This openness was encouraged by a partial change in the attitude of the Christian churches towards other faiths, which in the West after the Second Vatican Council (1963–65) swung towards greater respect and tolerance for non-Christian religions.

A second preparatory factor was a fair degree of economic affluence, which freed Europeans from excessive concern with material security and gave them the leisure to explore new avenues of thought. The rise of the consumerist society also helped them see the limitations to material development as a final solution to our quest for happiness.

A third factor was the relatively high standard of liberal education established in the 1960s, enabling a large proportion of young people to attend the university. Higher education exposed them to multiple viewpoints in all the domains of human knowledge, and also trained them to think critically and deeply about new ideas.

A fourth preparatory factor was improved means of transportation and communication, which facilitated contacts between East and West. Now curious

Westerners could easily travel to the East to experience Buddhism first hand in its own native setting, while Buddhist teachers from Asia could move West to propagate the Dhamma.

The fifth factor, following naturally from the fourth, was the actual arrival in the West of Buddhist teachers, both Asians and Westerners trained in Asia. These teachers brought Buddhism as a dynamic faith that they embodied in their lives through years of serious training.

THE GREAT TRANSITION

While the five factors constituted the necessary conditions for Buddhism to become accessible to a sizable number of Europeans, they are not a sufficient explanation for the rapid escalation of Western interest in Buddhism. To pinpoint the decisive cause for this phenomenon, I must refer back to the vacuum or void that had opened up right beneath the feet of European civilization, that is, the absence of a solid, authoritative spiritual tradition that could give guidance in the mastery of life. In the late nineteenth and early twentieth centuries this void was acutely felt only by the more discerning Western minds, disenchanted with both doctrinaire Christianity and economic materialism. Ordinary people were somehow able to balance their ancestral Christian faith with a bright optimism about the coming Golden Age, to be achieved through science and technology.

By the late 1950s, however, the picture had drastically changed. After two world wars and a prolonged cold war that threatened the whole world with thermonuclear destruction, countless people found their trust in the intrinsic goodness of human nature crumble into dust. Such horrors as the Nazi Holocaust and the Hiroshima atom bomb not only undermined faith in a benevolent God guiding the whole creation, but also brought to light the dangers in mere rationality not illuminated by a higher wisdom and staunch commitment to ethics. The most brilliant minds of the West, relying on the rational intellect, had twice plunged the whole world into barbaric irrationality, with death tolls numbering in the tens of millions. Now, with even more lethal weapons of destruction at hand, they threatened to do so again. Thus the void that sensitive nineteenth century thinkers had seen on the horizon had expanded until it had swallowed up almost everyone. And not only had it expanded, but for many it had acquired a sharp and compelling urgency that could not be quenched by any system of ideas, however noble. What they needed was a programme of action, which in many cases meant a deep personal engagement in the spiritual quest.

At the same time that the fear of nuclear war cast long shadows over the entire globe, unprecedented material affluence in the West brought into easy reach the comforts, conveniences, and sensory delights that earlier generations had only dreamt about. Yet while this consumerist paradise mesmerized many (and still continues to do so), at least a few people "with little dust in their eyes" realized that such mundane pleasures could bring no lasting peace to the heart. At this point, for such spiritually sensitive Westerners, the message embedded in the Four Noble Truths was no longer a splendid system of ideas, to be admired in the comfort of an armchair. The message had become, rather, a medicine for curing a terrible disease, the disease of suffering, and the one sensible thing to be done with it, as with any medicine, was to take it. Hence for the Buddhists in Phase III of Western Buddhism, the Dhamma presented itself as a path of practice pivoting on the training and mastery of the mind. As teachers and centres became available, growing numbers of Westerners took up the practice eagerly, ready to follow it wherever it might lead.

AN INCONCLUSIVE CONCLUSION

At the present stage in its evolution, Buddhism in the West is taking on a form that focuses on the Dhamma as a path of inner transformation through meditation and contemplation, with other aspects of Buddhist practice subordinated to this concern. We should not immediately conclude that Western Buddhism is therefore an ideal model for Asians to emulate. Western Buddhists often lack a solid knowledge of the texts, and thus are prone to bend the teachings to fit their own agendas and expectations. It is here, I think, that Asian monks with a sound scholarly knowledge of the Dhamma can make a valuable contribution. But while corrective measures are needed in Western Buddhism to ensure right understanding, it is clear that the central focus of Western Buddhists will be on personal meditative experience as the way to inner peace and wisdom.

If Sri Lankan Buddhists are to make a significant contribution to the healthy growth of Buddhism in the West, we will need representatives of the Dhamma who are also living embodiments of the Dhamma. That is, we need monks — and nuns as well — who express in their lives and characters the potentials of the Dhamma as a way of life that brings real wisdom, purity, and peace within, and overflows in expressions of kindness and compassion for others. This is a difficult challenge, but it is an indispensable requirement if Sri Lanka is to contribute to the development of Buddhism in the West. Since the main responsibility for transmitting the Dhamma rests with the monastic order, the Sangha in this country must set its own house in order if it is to be qualified to perform this task. This will require some intense internal criticism and attempts at genuine reform, especially in the system of monastic training. If such changes do not take place, it is unlikely that Sri Lanka will be able to contribute much more to the growth of Buddhism in Europe than to maintain viharas that serve Sri Lankan expatriates.

BIBLIOGRAPHY

Adikaram, E.W. (1953) *Early History of Buddhism in Ceylon,* (2nd ed.) Colombo: Gunasena.

Anisaki Masaharu (1916) *Nichiren: The Buddhist Prophet,* reprint Gloucester, Massachussets (1966).

Aris, Michael (1978) *Bhutan, the Early History of a Himalayan Kingdom,* Warminster, UK: Aris & Phillips.

________________ (1994) Raven *Crown: The Origins of Buddhist Monarchy in Bhutan,* London: Serindia.

Banerjee, A.C. (1957) *Sarvastivada Literature,* Calcutta.

Basham, A. L. (1954) *The Wonder That Was India,* London.

Beyer, Stephan V. (1973) *The Cult of Tara: Magic and Ritual in Tibet,* Berkeley: University of California Press.

Chakravarti, Uma (1987) *The Social Dimensions of Early Buddhism,* New Delhi: Oxford University Press.

Ch'en Kenneth (1964) *Buddhism in China: A Historical Survey,* Princeton.

Cozort, Daniel (1986) Highest *Yoga Tantra: An Introduction to Esoteric Buddhism of Tibet,* Ithaca, NY: Snow Lion.

Dasgupta, Shashi Bhusan (1974) An *Introduction to Tantric Buddhism.* 3rd ed. Calcutta: University of Calcutta.

Dutt, Nalinaksha (1970) *Buddhist Sects in India,* Calcutta.

Dutt, Sukumar (1957) *The Buddha and Five After-Centuries,* London.

________________ (1962) *Buddhist Monks and Monasteries of India,* London: G. Allen and Unwin.

Gombrich, Richard F. (1996) *How Buddhism Began: The Conditioned Genesis of the Early Teachings,* London: Athlone.

________________ (1988) *Theravada Buddhism: A Social History from Ancient Benares to Modern Colombo,* London: Routledge and Kegan Paul.

Grousset, Rene (1931) *The Civilizations of the East, vol. 2,* India, London.

Hanayama Shinsho (1960) *A History of Japanese Buddhism,* Tokyo.

Hazra, Kanai Lal (1982) *History of Theravada Buddhism in South-East Asia: With Special Reference to India and Ceylon,* New Delhi: Munshiram Manoharlal.

Hirakawa, Akira (1974-1979) Indo bukkyoshi, 2 vols., Tokyo.

Hirakawa, Akira (1990) A *History of Indian Buddhism: From Sakyamuni to Early Mahayana,* Honolulu: University of Hawaii Press.

Holt, John Clifford (1996) *The Religious World of Kirti Sri: Buddhism, Art, and Politics in Late Medieval Sri Lanka,* New York: Oxford University Press.

Hopkins, Jeffrey (1985) *The Kalacakara Tantra,* trans. London.

Horner, I.B. (1936) *Early Buddhist Theory of Man Perfected,* London.

Jayatilleke, K.N. (1963) *Early Buddhist Theory of Knowledge,* London.

Joshi, Lal Mani (1967) *Studies in the Buddhistic Culture of India, During the 7th and 8th Centuries A.D.* Delhi: Motilal Banarsidass.

———————— (1967) *Studies in the Buddhistic Culture of India,* Delhi.

King, Winston Lee (1980) *Theravada Meditation: The Buddhist Transformation of Yoga,* University Park: Pennsylvania State University Press.

Kitagawa, Joseph M. (1966) *Religion in Japanese History,* New York.

Law, B.C. (ed.) (1931) *Buddhistic Studies,* Calcutta.

Legge, James (1886) *A Record of Buddhist Kingdoms,* Oxford.

Lester Robert C (1973) *Theravada Buddhism in Southeast Asia,* Ann Arbor.

Malalgoda, K. (1976) *Buddhism in Sinhalese Society, 1750-1900.* Berkeley: University of California Press.

Masuda Jiryo, (1925) 'Origins and Doctrines of Early Indian Buddhist Schools', *Asia Major, vol. 2, pp.1-78.*

Matsunaga, Alicia (1969) The *Buddhist Philosophy of Assimilation,* Tokyo.

McGovern W.M. (1922) *An Introduction to Mahayana Buddhism,* New York.

Miler, Robert J. (1959) *Monasteries and Culture Change in Mongolia,* Wiesbaden.

Mitra, Rajendaralala (1971) *The Sanskrit Buddhist Literature of Nepal,* Calcutta.

Mullin, Glenn H. (1986) *Death and Dying: The Tibetan Tradition,* East Grinstead, W. Sussex: New Knowledge Books.

Nakamura Hajime (1980) *Indian Buddhism: A Survey with Bibliographical Notes,* Tokyo.

Narain, A.K. (1980) *Studies in History of Buddhism,* Delhi: B.R. Pub. Corp.

Radhakrishnan, Sarvepalli (1927) Indian Philosophy, vol.1 (2nd ed.), London.

Rahula, Walpola (1956) *History of Buddhism in Ceylon,* Colombo: Gunasena.

________________ (1974) *What the Buddha Taught* (Rev. ed.) New York: Grove.

Rao, S. K. Ramachandra (1979) *Tibetan Meditation: Theory and Practice*, New Delhi: Arnold-Heinemann.

Ray, Reginald A. (1994) *Buddhist Saints in India: A Study in Buddhist Values and Orientations*, New York: Oxford University Press.

Reynolds, Frank E (1981) *Guide to Buddhist Religion*, Boston.

Rhys Davids, T.W. (1903) *Buddhist India*, London.

Robinson, Richard H., and Willard Johnson (1982) *The Buddhist Religion: A Historical Introduction* (3rd ed.) Belmont, CA: Wadsworth.

Ruegg, David S. (1967) *The Study of Indian and Tibetan Thought*, Leiden.

________________ (1981) *The Literature of the Madhyamaka School of Philosophy in India*, Wiesbaden.

Sarao, K.T.S., (ed.) (1995) A *Textbook of the History of Theravada Buddhism*, Delhi: University of Delhi.

Saunders, E. Dale (1964) *Buddhism in Japan*, Philadelphia.

Seneviratne, H. L. (1978) *Rituals of the Kandyan State*, Cambridge: Cambridge University Press.

Skilton, Andrew (1994) *A Concise History of Buddhism*. Birmingham: Windhorse.

Snellgrove, David L. (ed.) (1957) *Buddhist Himalaya*, Oxford.

________________ (1984) Indo-*Tibetan Buddhism: Indian Buddhists and their Tibetan Successors*, Boston: Shambhala.

Snellgrove, David, and Hugh Richardson (1968) *A Cultural History of Tibet*, New York: F.A. Praeger.

Streng, Frederick J. (1967) *Emptiness: A Study in Religious Meaning*, Nashville.

Suzuki, B.L. (1938) *Mahayana Buddhism* (3rd ed.), NewYork.

Thomsen Harry (1963) *The New Religions of Japan: Rutland*, Vt.

Tucci, Giuseppe (1949) *Tibetan Painted Scrolls, 2 vols*. translated by Virginia Vacca, Rome.

Varma, V.P. (1973) *Early Buddhism and Its Origins*, New Delhi.

Warder, Anthony Kennedy (1980) *Indian Buddhism* (2nd ed.) Delhi: Motilal Banarsidass.

Watters, Thomas (1904-1905) *On Yuan Chwang's Travel in India, 2 vols*. London.

Wayman, Alex (1973) *The Buddhist Tantras: Light on Indo-Tibetan Esotericism*, New York.

INDEX

W

Y